PROVIDING PROMISE

A Navy Widow's Journey to Hope

KRIS RYSTROM EMMERT
with JULIE VOUDRIE

PROVIDING
PROMISE

PROVIDING PROMISE

For information visit:
www.providingpromise.com

Book and Cover design by Tyton Rock

ISBN-13: 978-1721735181
ISBN-10: 1721735186

First Edition: July 2018

10 9 8 7 6 5 4 3 2 1

TABLE OF CONTENTS

In loving memory of my beloved husband,

Commander Jon Alvin Rystrom,

And the crew of

VAW-124 Bear Ace 603.

Lost but never forgotten.

Dedication

To my girls, Jordyn and Taylor,
Your light and laughter have made my life full of joy.
You have loved me through the storms, and I am forever grateful
to have you as my daughters.
May you continue to hold onto God's promises
throughout your lives, and always
remember that your father deeply loved you.

Love, Mom

Acknowledgements

Here is a grateful salute to family and some special friends who made this book possible.

OUR FAMILIES

The Emmerts

To my loving husband Joe who is my "kinsman redeemer." You took a widow and her little girls and made us your family. You have always encouraged me to tell my story all these years and words cannot express how grateful I am. Jon was the love of my youth, and you are the love of my life. 5-11-95.

To my daughter Jordyn for insisting that I finally write this book. I owe this project to your persistent but loving push. To my daughter Taylor for helping keep my focus on the prize—to God be the glory. To my other children, Cole and Makenzie, for being patient as I spent hours in solitude writing and for putting up with all of Daddy Jon's unpacked boxes scattered all over the house. To my precious Isabella, this story is written so that you will always know your other grandpa.

To my mom Doris Windham: Dad would be so proud.

To my other mom Faye Emmert: Richard would love this story.

To my Nebraska family: Barb and Gary Dean, Mike and Matt; Pat and Ken Everingham, Eric, Sara, and Joey; Jim and Laurie Parsley. Jon was proud to be a Rystrom and he loved his hometown of Stromsburg.

To my Boston family: Martin and Maria Rystrom, Dan, Adam, and Nick. Jon loved playing with you boys in your pool and showing off his one-armed push-ups!

In memory of my other parents: Mervin and Josephine Rystrom— Jon loved them dearly.

The Voudries

To my beloved husband Jeff who has patiently endured loss of use of his pool table for months while it was used for the spreading out of boxes of research material. Thank you for being patient with me as I disappeared into another world and spent countless hours holed up at my desk day and night, for believing in me when I doubted myself, being an objective sounding board, assisting in any way you could, and reassuring me as I pressed on to the finish line. You are the wind in my sails. And you're still the song in me.

To my children: Jonathan, Danielle (and Bryan and Davona), Hannah, Josh, Aaron, Grace, and Leah. Thanks for your understanding as Mom was preoccupied for a season and for your encouragement as I labored away.

To my friend Kris: Your little acorn of an idea quickly grew into a massive project that has transcended anything either of us ever expected. Thank you for trusting me with your precious story. Thank you for being brave, opening your box, and sharing your scars and your treasures with the rest of us. I will be forever changed because of meeting you. And I have gained a faithful friend. This is only the beginning.

To my Abba: Your timing is perfect. You are the God of the open door. Your grace is sufficient. Thank You for choosing me for this project, but most of all for loving me above and beyond what I deserve or comprehend. Through my life, may the Lamb receive the reward for His suffering.

My Military Family

Without your help this book would have been impossible to write. Thank you for giving us your expertise in writing the military scenes and making sure we were "Navy ready."

U.S. Navy retired Chief of Chaplains Lt. Cmdr. Dave E. Mullis, U.S. Marine Corp retired Maj. Ed Van Haute, U.S. Navy retired Capt. Randy "Bubba" Bannister, U.S. Navy retired Cmdr. John "Waffle" Eggert, U.S. Navy retired Cmdr. Scott "Lenny" Bruce, U.S. Navy retired Lt. Cmdr. Mike Purcell, U.S. Navy retired Chief of Chaplains Capt. Timothy R. Eichler, and U.S. Navy retired Capt. Steve Squires.

Julie would like to especially give out a Bravo Zulu to Dave Mullis who so graciously opened his home and gave her a solid indoctrination into all things Navy, and to Randy Bannister who so willingly shared his immense knowledge and expertise, taking the time to patiently answer so many questions in great detail without making her feel foolish in the least.

To Capt. Richard McCormack, commanding officer, and Capt. Brent Gaut, executive officer, USS Gerald R. Ford, and the crew for welcoming the families and squadron mates of Bear Ace 603 onto her deck for our 25th commemorative reunion tour.

To Capt. Nicholas Dienna, commanding officer, and Capt. Cassidy Norman, executive officer, USS Harry S. Truman, and the crew for welcoming the Rystrom family onto her deck on the 25th anniversary of Jon's mishap. A special thank you to Lt. Cmdr. Laura Stegherr, public affairs officer, for making our visit personal and memorable.

To Chaplain Lt. Cmdr. Kimberly Cain for ministering to our families at David Adams Memorial Chapel at Naval Station Norfolk for the 25th anniversary commemorative service. Your words and prayers inspired by God uplifted our spirits, and we were all blessed to be a part of your worship service. It was also a special honor to have Vice Adm. Herman A. Shelanski, Naval Inspector General; and Rear Adm. Jesse A. Wilson, Jr., Cmdr., Naval Surface Force Atlantic, give their words of support and encouragement to the Bear Ace 603 family. We are eternally grateful.

To Cmdr. Christian Goodman, commanding officer, and Cmdr. Gregory Machi, executive officer of VAW-124 Bear Aces, and the rest of the squadron for making our 25th commemorative visit to the hangar very special. An added thank you to Lt. Cmdr. Blake "Sharpie" Baccigalopi for going the "extra mile" to help make our visit memorable. Thank you to U.S. Navy retired Capt. Chris "Bolter" Bolt and his precious wife Shelley for organizing our 25th anniversary reunion in Norfolk, Virginia. Thank you also to Rear Adm. John Lemmon and his wife Julie for your kind words and warm welcome.

A special thank you to my CACO officer, U.S. Navy retired Capt. Rick Vanden Heuvel, who was my gentle companion through the darkest days of my life.

My Supportive Friends

Dr. Bob Reccord, my pastor, for graciously writing my foreword. You and your sweet wife Cheryl have made an impact on my life like no other. Your ministering words each week helped awaken, for the first time, a faith in Christ for me. Thank you for following your personal call to help the widows and orphans. I will always call you "my pastor."

Teresa Stanley, my editor and "Seester." You have wanted me to write this book for years, and you believed in my "calling" before anyone else. Your brilliant mind and attention to detail have kept me out of the "grammar doghouse." I truly appreciate your talent and most of all our friendship.

Christy and Randy Horn, Kim and Rick Peters, Dennis Stanley, Cathy Huntley, and Vicki Hicks for your support and being my second pair of eyes on the final edit.

The Thrive marketing team in Morristown, Tennessee: Leigh Sempkowski, Bobbi Odom, and Brittany Cross. You all caught my vision from the very start and encouraged me to be confident in my calling.

Becca Perry. This dream became true because of you. Our trip to Arlington National Cemetery in April 2017 sparked the flame for this book. I am blessed to call you my friend.

Premier Designs, Inc., and the Horner family. My jewelry company that gave me the opportunity to tell my story to thousands of women across the country. I am thankful that you are a company that stands on biblical principles.

My photographers: Casey Lauren Townsend, Ashley Lodge, Leah Belcher, Ben Gibson, Scotty Bruce, Craig Moran, and Harry Gerwien. Each one of you has an amazing craft, and I am so thankful that God brought you into my life to capture the images to help tell my story.

My creative team: Robert and Amber Till, Tyton Rock. Your creative vision is a gift from God! Thank you for creating my website and using your artistic talents to design my life story for others to experience my story in print.

Jamie Lewis. You are my friend whom I love like a sister. Praying for open doors for us to walk through as I tell my story and give hope.

Rebecca Statzer. We will continue to look for our "glimmers of hope" every day.

Finally, to my coauthor and friend, Julie Voudrie. Little did I know what God was going to do when He joined our lives together. You willingly took a vision and made it a dream come true. I cannot thank you enough for the hours, weeks, months and now a year that you poured your life into this project. My prayer is that you will be rewarded and blessed beyond measure. I have found a true sister in you, my friend. May you rest in our Provider as He blesses you with His promises in your future.

To God be the glory.

Foreword

"**S**ince you've never served in the military, what makes you think that you could minister to those of us who are serving when we suffer tragedy?" The attractive young woman who had voiced the penetrating question was the wife of a Navy lieutenant commander soon to be deployed. I knew she hadn't meant it harshly but simply out of honest concern and uncertainty.

I was being interviewed by the historic First Baptist Church of Norfolk, Virginia, as the potential new senior pastor. Norfolk is home to arguably the largest concentration of military in the world. While both my biological father and my adoptive father had served in the military, I had not. At that moment, I searched for some amazingly wise and profound answer that would satisfactorily answer this piercing question. But nothing brilliant came to mind.

Instead, I simply knew through experience that when people walk through tragedy, whether they are privileged to be in the military or not, they must transition through the same stages of grief. Tragedy—regardless of the context—shatters life, never allowing it to be quite the same again. And when tragedy is experienced by people anywhere—and under any condition—they cry for understanding, empathy, compassion, love, and support. That is all I could offer.

Who but God could have known, or foreseen, that only a few short months later I would stand before this Navy wife to officiate the funeral for her husband.

It is said that heartache and tragedy often can make a person. While this is somewhat true, I have discovered that far more often, it reveals the person.

For Kris, tragedy ushered in a crisis of belief that continually bombarded her with soul-searching questions:

Where was God in this?

Why did God let this happen?

Why us? Jon and I were working hard to live like we should!

Why now? We have two little girls!

What now?

As my wife and I came to know Kris in the wake of the disaster, we saw a woman with two young daughters slugging through the slough of despond which tragedy brings. Although drowning in grief, she grasped for answers to her questions, began to take increasingly significant steps in her faith, deepened her dependence upon Him, and started the long and often lonely journey toward healing. After all, God is not threatened by our questions.

After a long journey resulting in no great answers to life's Why questions, Kris began to refocus on two important What questions:

- What is it that God is teaching me in the wake of this tragedy?
- What does God desire to change in me through this tragedy?

I have found it true that God shapes us far more in the valleys of heartache and loss than on the mountaintops of success and victory. It is not that he causes them—He redeems them. Recovery is so often dependent upon the choices we make when moving through what feels like the impossible. But the ultimate outcome is often found in 2 Corinthians 1:3-4 where we are told that God "comforts us in all our troubles, so that we can comfort those in any trouble with the comfort we ourselves receive from God."

And now, 25 years later, this truth has been fleshed out repeatedly in Kris' life. Remarried and the proud mom of four, she is constantly giving herself away to others, sharing with them the support, care, love, and understanding she received from so many. Having found hope in the midst of heartbreak, she now works tirelessly at giving it away to those who need it most.

So, grab a cup of coffee or a hot tea, find a comfortable and quiet place to relax, and walk through this remarkable journey with Kris. It just may reshape your focus on what's really important, offer hope to you amid the challenges through which you may be walking, and show you that God is NEVER finished with us, regardless of the heartache which may be suffocating us. And don't ever forget the promise He holds out to you in the midst of every struggle:

"Do not fear, for I have redeemed you; I have summoned you by name; you are mine.

"When you pass through the waters, I will be with you; and when you pass through the rivers, they will not sweep over you. When you walk through the fire, you will not be burned; the flames will not set you ablaze.

"For I am the Lord your God, ..." (Isaiah 43:1-3 NIV)

Dr. Robert E. (Bob) Reccord
Author and Founder
of Total Impact Ministries

March 15, 2018

Canton, Georgia

Introduction

Behind the scenes ...
A Coauthor's View, Before We Begin

I remember the moment when Kris handed me the pieces of wreckage that she had from Jon's plane. We were well into the interview process, and she kept bringing in items dating from the tragic mishap. That day, she brought in some special framed letters, various photographs, newspaper clippings, and the like, but the pieces of wreckage were what impacted me most.

Small, white, ragged pieces of honeycomb metal with sharp edges—no more than 3 inches wide—one stamped with letters, the other with rivet holes ripped open by the plane's violent impact with the Ionian Sea. I cried as I held them, their weight far exceeding their few grams of mass. I shouldn't be holding these—two pieces from the fractured fuselage of an E-2C Hawkeye that once housed $60 million of technology and the souls of five airmen. I looked up and met Kris' gaze as she witnessed my initial reaction.

"I'm so sorry," I whispered. I didn't know what else to say. For her, the wound was old, well-healed, softened with grace and time. For me, I was experiencing the tragedy little by little, as Kris unfolded her story for me. But that day, the actuality of her loss, the loss of the other families, and the tragedy of five precious lives cut painfully short became extremely real to me, as I held that wreckage in the palm of my hand.

> *... FOR TRULY, I SAY TO YOU IF YOU HAVE FAITH LIKE A GRAIN OF MUSTARD SEED, YOU WILL SAY TO THIS MOUNTAIN, "MOVE FROM HERE TO THERE," AND IT WILL MOVE, AND NOTHING WILL BE IMPOSSIBLE FOR YOU. (MATTHEW 17:20 ESV)*

Wreckage. We all have it—perhaps not pieces of a plane, but the shattered pieces left behind from the losses we have suffered. Whether it's a loved one's death, a divorce, chronic disease, a failed business, broken dreams, childhood traumas, or estranged relationships, every one of us has or will suffer loss. It's simply a fact of life. We live in a fallen world where bad things happen to good people. The question is not whether we will suffer loss but, rather, what do we do with the pieces left behind. Can shattered lives truly be put together again?

That is the central question which Kris answers in this book. Kris is transparent as she shares her sorrow, struggle with faith, loneliness, and doubt in her journey through grief and into hope. As Kris so bravely shows us, yes, the shattered pieces of your life can be put together again. And though the process is not without pain, tears, and trials, there is joy, life, and peace for anyone who surrenders their broken heart to the only One who can heal it.

I challenge you to face your shattered pieces as you read this book and take courage from one who has traveled the road of loss and found life again. Like Kris, you too can find that there is joy after disaster, peace after heartache, and purpose after loss. "Weeping may endure for the night, but joy comes in the morning." My sincere prayer is that whatever your broken pieces may be, you will experience the healing that is available to every heart that releases its wreckage to the One with nail-scarred hands.

Blessings,

Julie Voudrie

Author

CHAPTER 1

Daddy Jon

"**D**o you know who this is?" I ask as I hold a framed family portrait and point to a man in his Navy dress blues, smiling broadly, standing next to his wife and their two little girls.

"That's Daddy Jon," replies Isabella cheerfully. "And this is you, and this is Taylor, and this is Mommy," she continues, her bright, hazel eyes scanning the other familiar faces. She's seen this picture many times: There's me with shoulder-length, curly, brown hair, dressed in pearls and a white blazer with a lace overlay and shoulder pads typical of early 90s fashion. On my lap is baby Taylor in her pink, ruffled dress and pink headband with a white bow on her nearly bald head, reaching to touch her older sister. Jordyn's three-year-old face is framed by curly, dark-blond hair—the same color as her father's—topped with a dark-pink bow that matches her polka-dot jumper with white, capped sleeves—her sparkling eyes a mirror-image of Isabella's. Behind us is Jon, his hair neatly trimmed and his dark-blue eyes set off with laugh lines, looking dashing in his Navy uniform with his Joint Services Medal and rows of award ribbons under his gold wings. All four of us are smiling—so happy, so close, and so content.

For as long as she can remember, my granddaughter has seen this picture on the shelf, sitting next to other family portraits taken over the years. And while she knows the names and the faces and giggles at my out-of-style hairdo and how little her aunt and mommy once were, there's so much more that she doesn't know about this photograph.

There's so much that I didn't know back in 1993 when I donned my Sunday best, dolled up my girls in their cute outfits, and primped their hair. I was elated as Jon drove our sweet family to Olan Mills Portrait Studios a few weeks before he deployed on the aircraft carrier USS Theodore Roosevelt. This was our first formal family portrait to include Taylor, who had been born six months earlier. While I was dreading the thought of Jon being at sea for the next six months and me having to hold down the fort alone, I was thankful that we could capture our growing family at this moment in time. As I posed for that picture, all I knew was that with Jon by my side, life was good and the future was bright.

What I didn't know was that my picture-perfect life was about to be shattered into a million pieces, as every wife's worst nightmare became my reality. The smiles would be erased, replaced by gut-wrenching grief; the sparkling eyes would overflow with tears; and the innocence of my daughters' childhoods would be stolen—forever lost—by a harsh and tangible loss. My optimism, contentment, and happiness would be overcome by heartache, confusion, doubt, anger, uncertainty, and loneliness in ways that I never could have imagined. Yes, there was so much I didn't know when the photographer snapped our picture that day.

But I also didn't know that out of the rubble of my shattered life, hope would return. That out of disaster, my life would reemerge, not destroyed but redeemed. That my daughters—who were too young to truly know their father—would grow into lovely young women filled with purpose and a reflection of their father's strong character. And that one day Jon's firstborn would have a precocious, lively, and radiant daughter of her own, named Isabella, who would fill our lives with love and laughter. And through Isabella, I once again would enjoy Jon's high-energy personality and his famous sense of humor.

Twenty-five years had passed since that family portrait was taken, and I decided the time was right to take the photo off the shelf and tell Isabella the story behind the picture. She knew the basics already.

"Daddy Jon was very kind, loving, and caring. He was a 'flight attendant' in the Navy and died in a plane crash," explained Isabella. I guess that in the mind of a seven-year-old, a flight attendant and a naval flight officer is pretty much the same thing. Jon would have grinned at her explanation. He would have belly-laughed when Isabella reacted to his college wrestling picture taken back in the late 1970s.

"Why did he have that poufy hair and wear those weird clothes?" She frowned, wrinkling her nose in disapproval. I showed her other pictures of Daddy Jon in his flight suit and of his plane, the E-2C Hawkeye, along with some of Jon's patches and his flight jacket. When I handed Isabella the two small pieces of wreckage, which I was given from Jon's plane, she studied them carefully, turning them over and over with her small, inquisitive fingers.

"They're very light," she stated as she poked at the mangled, honeycomb material on the back side. "It looks like they hit something hard—not the water." She continued to examine them and then moved on to one of Jon's extra dog tags stamped with his name, serial number, religious affiliation, and blood type. "Is that my blood type?" Isabella wondered.

I knew many things about my granddaughter but not her blood type. But I understood that Jon passed down not only his genetics but also his intangible traits to his daughters and granddaughter. One of those traits was an inquisitive mind. And Isabella was full of questions.

"When and where was he born? How did he become a 'flight attendant'? How was he able to get there and do good grades? Why did he go into the Navy?" Glancing back through the pictures, she asked again, "And why was he a wrestler and wear those funny clothes and have that poufy hair?" Her inherited sense of humor was on full display. Not only did she have questions for Daddy Jon but also there were things she wished he knew.

"I'd want to tell him that Mom is doing great—got straight A's and passed the bar." My oldest daughter, Jordyn, had recently become a lawyer. Isabella lowered her voice noticeably as she added, "I really miss him, and I wish he was still alive. I don't like sad endings."

No one likes sad endings or sad middles or sad beginnings. And yet life is filled with them. Some of us had picture-perfect lives, but some had childhoods loaded with burdens and traumas from the start. Others, like me, found themselves blindsided by the unthinkable and were left reeling with the heart-breaking consequences.

Whenever and however your "sad" comes, questions are certain to follow: Why? Why me? Why us? Could this have been prevented, and why wasn't it? How can I go on? How will I survive? Is it even possible to do so?

Our questions go deeper as our world is rocked to its core. Where is God? Why didn't He stop it? Why didn't He fix it? How can a loving, powerful God let something like this happen? Does He understand my pain? Does He see me at all? Does He even care? Does He even exist? Is there one good reason that I should live another day?

These are some of the questions that I asked myself and—while I struggled to find the answers—I couldn't help but remember something else: promises—promises that Jon made, promises that we made together, promises that I made of my own, and the promises that

God made. I questioned them all. But like a spinning compass whose needle eventually points back to true north, I found myself returning to what I had always known to be true and what I had, perhaps naively, promised to others before my picture-perfect life fell apart.

Isabella understood about promises and had already made several. "No matter what happens, I will always keep my promises to God. I will never, ever, ever not keep my promises to the Lord, my family, and friends." To emphasize her resolve, she became very animated. "I will keep my promises and BOOM! I will keep my promises safe!"

That's easy to say when you're 7 years old and playing with your toys. It's much harder to say when you're several decades older, and life has hit you hard in the gut. Suddenly, you find that keeping your promises is much harder and costlier than you ever imagined. And what about God's promises to us? Isabella had ideas about that as well.

"God never breaks his promise. NEVER." And what about all the evil and pain and suffering in the world? "The devil made sin," she explains. "The devil is mean, cruel, and unfair. One day the devil will be destroyed." Isabella continued dramatically, "Finally, he's gone forever!"

As simple as a second-grader's theology can be, it does raise some meaningful questions: Does God ever break His promises? Does He keep his promises safe? And when the storms of life overtake us, what do we hang on to and what do we let go of? Do we keep our own promises safe?

I've made promises that I intend to keep, as Isabella says, no matter what: promises to Jon, to myself, to my family, and to God. This book is born out of that resolve—not only to keep my promises but also to provide promise to others—to provide promise to you. By sharing my journey of grief to hope, my wish is to offer you a rope you can hang on to in the midst of your storm and healing from the pains of your past. If God can mend a shattered heart like mine, He can certainly do the same for you.

I also want to leave a legacy for my daughters who never knew their amazing father and to honor Jon's memory and sacrifice for our country. As a public speaker, I have shared my experience with thousands of people but never with this level of detail and never in writing. With the benefit of 25 years of perspective, now is the perfect time to present these precious, and sometimes painful, memories and the valuable, life-giving lessons that I learned.

How do I answer Isabella's questions about Daddy Jon? And how do I include answers to questions that in her young innocence she doesn't know to ask? And how do I do it all while providing promise to anyone who reads this book?

Everyone loves a good story, and Jon's life is filled with them. Since Jon's life would make a great novel, why not tell it as one? Jon's story is told as a narrative, based on my first-person accounts and those of his family and friends, along with lengthy research into his service records, interviews with military personnel, Jon's personal letters, photographs, newspaper articles, and other documents and memorabilia.

To honor Jon's service in the Navy, his career is told with an accuracy that former and present military will respect but in a way that civilians will understand. Be assured that as fictionalized as the story may seem, our story is true. The words quoted from our letters and correspondence are real and the scenes depicted reflect actual events. By surrounding the hard facts with an entertaining tale, I know that Jon would be pleased with how his story is told.

Jon's story and the circumstances around it touched many lives, but it is Jon's and my story alone that I am telling. I could never presume to tell the story of others, nor could I personally contact every person involved in his life and mine. As a result, every name used will be an alias, unless they are family members, well-known public figures, or they have given me permission to use their real names.

As for my story, I'm telling it to you in my own words—from my perspective. It's a story of love and loss, romance and remorse, heartbreak and healing. My journey has taken me from the highest highs to the lowest lows. We'll face some tough questions, and to be honest, I won't have all the answers. But my goal through it all is to provide promise to you.

So, my dear Isabella, the old family portrait is off the shelf, and it's time for Grandma to tell you the story—the whole story.

Jon's childhood home, the Rystrom farmhouse, near
Stromsburg, Nebraska.

CHAPTER 2

Cornhusker Swede

L ife was good that Friday morning, filled with promise and with hope. My little girls and I were up early for our normal weekday routine—making breakfast, packing lunches, getting dressed—before we hopped into our minivan to drive to preschool. The late March skies were gray and the air was cool. We were anxiously awaiting warmer days so that we could enjoy the playgrounds and walking trails throughout our beautiful neighborhood nestled in the wooded wetlands of Coastal Virginia.

My husband Jon had been at sea for two weeks at the beginning of a six-month deployment on USS Theodore Roosevelt, also known as the TR. Jon was now a Bear Ace, a member of the E-2C Hawkeye Squadron VAW-124, assigned to the TR for a cruise to the Mediterranean. After 15 years of service in the Navy, he was one of the most senior officers in the squadron and wore his Bear Ace patch proudly. He was up for promotion to the rank of commander, but all of that seems so insignificant now that I look back on the events that were to unfold that March morning.

At the age of 31, I was living the perfect life. My Jon adored me and he was a loving father to our precious girls: three-year-old Jordyn and 7-month-old-baby Taylor. We lived in a stunning Georgian-styled, brick home that we designed ourselves, built on Seagrass Reach, in one of the most prestigious areas in Chesapeake, Virginia. I was blessed during this season of our lives to be a stay-at-home mom with plans to pursue my doctorate degree in communications after Jon returned from his deployment. The rich relationships that Jon and I had built with friends and families in our neighborhood, our church, and our Bear Ace Squadron provided security for the girls and me while Jon was away.

My world on Seagrass Reach was one of contentment, peace, and predictability. I was coasting through my Navy-wife life naively unaware of much of the pain, suffering, and conflict in our fallen world. As a person of faith, I wore my relationship with God like a lucky rabbit's foot—expecting protection from "undeserved" calamity. My false sense of security created an air of arrogance that, because I had my "Christian box" checked, I was immune to life's heartaches.

Two weeks into Jon's TR deployment, I trusted in the promises that Jon had made to me. He promised, as always, to write to me every day that he was gone. While many Navy marriages fell apart when a spouse was deployed, I took great comfort knowing that Jon was committed to our family and to our marriage. We had no angst over our finances or Jon's future in the Navy. Jon and I shared a deep faith and rested in God's promise to take care of us. That morning on Seagrass Reach, I had no doubt that my perfect life would continue its predictable, peaceful course.

What I didn't know that "normal" Friday morning was that before the day's end, the gray spring skies would turn into pitch-black storm clouds that would plunge my perfect life into a dark, hopeless abyss. My peaceful world would be replaced with a frenzied chaos that catapulted my sheltered life, uninvited, onto a world-wide stage. In an instant—in one horrific, gut-wrenching second—my hopes and dreams would lie shattered and scattered at my feet.

Nothing could have prepared me as my heart, nurtured by Jon's tender love and devotion, was ripped to shreds. How I wished that he could have been by my side that fateful March morning, standing with me on the peach-colored tile that we chose together, looking out our lovely glass double doors, holding me close as I heard the news no wife ever wants to hear, and breaking my fall as I crumbled to the floor in shock.

One glance, one sound, and my perfect life was irreversibly changed. Suddenly, so unexpectedly, an eruption of shock and grief and devastation swallowed my soul and left me staggering and alone. Without my beloved Jon. Without the love of my life. Without my soul mate. Forever.

If this were the end of the story, what a sad story it would be. But it's only the beginning. Jon was the kind of man you met only once in a lifetime. He truly was. And I'm not the only one who thought so. Jon's love for life, his unselfish nature, and his strong work ethic rubbed off on those who had the privilege to know him. He almost never complained and made a point to treat everyone around him fairly. He loved kids, dogs, and underdogs. And I'll be forever blessed that Jon loved me.

When people first hear about my story, they always want to know, "How did you survive? How did you make it? What was it like to lose a husband and the father of your children? How did you find hope?" I will answer those questions and more.

But to comprehend what I lost that fateful March morning on Seagrass Reach, you need to grasp the depth of the extraordinary love we shared and the lasting impact of Jon's character, affirmation, and affection on my life. Jon and I were two lonely people, each carrying the baggage of our own past and pain, who managed to build a remarkable life together in seven short years. Once you see what I lost, you'll more fully appreciate what I suffered and what I eventually gained.

Let me start the story by introducing you to my beloved Jon. Isabella's first question about her grandfather was: "When and where was he born?" I think that is as good a place as any to start.

Cornhusker Swede

SPRINGTIME, 1965
1400 CENTRAL TIME ZONE
STROMSBURG, NEBRASKA, USA
41.11.53 N, 97.59.16 W

Midwestern towns have their own unique charm and Stromsburg was no exception. With streets laid out in perfect grids, quaint storefronts lining the old city square, and modest homes dating back to another time, "The Swedish Capital of Nebraska" created an island of trees, homes, shops, and churches in an ocean of prairie. Located in the East Central Region of the state, Stromsburg, with a population slightly north of a thousand, was the largest city for miles around.

Outside of town, the land opened to wide prairies and endless acres of cropland punctuated with the occasional farmhouse and barn and a windbreak of trees, all topped with a sky so big that you could see a thunderstorm coming from miles away. The unhindered winds created waves of swaying green in the summer and massive snowdrifts in the winter. Under the gentle flat-to-rolling land lay some of the richest and most productive soil on the planet. There's a good reason Nebraska is known as "The Cornhusker State."

A few miles outside of town was the modest farm of Mervin and Josephine Rystrom. Along with their five children, they lived in a humble, two-story, wooden-clad, white farmhouse that had seen its fair share of bitter winters and sweltering summers. Farm life was a wonderful way to raise their family. With acres of corn, milo, and wheat to raise and an aging house to care for, there was always plenty of work for Barb, Martin, Laurie, Pat, and Jon to do. But it wasn't all work and no play. The farm's outbuildings were like a child's year-round playground where, in the dead of winter, snowdrifts could reach the roof of the barn, and the old, narrow grain crib created a makeshift indoor basketball court. In those more innocent days, no one would think twice about a young boy riding five miles on his bike to go swimming with a friend.

While the Rystroms' soil was rich, their bank account was not. As part-time farmers, both Mervin and Josephine worked other manual-labor jobs to keep their family clothed and fed, but in reality money was always tight. One thing about being a child raised in poverty is that at the time you don't realize how poor you are, especially when your family is rich in love. Doing without can either make you greedy or grateful. For the Rystrom children, the latter was true.

> *... For I know the plans I have for you, declares the Lord, plans for welfare and not for evil, to give you a future and a hope ....*
> *(Jeremiah 29:11 ESV)*

With seven mouths to feed, the kitchen was the heart of the Rystrom home and a hubbub of activity, whether the kids were trying out new recipes when blizzards snowed them in, or the family was enjoying the rejected chicken pot pies Mervin brought home from his part-time winter job at the nearby Swanson's Foods factory. The Rystrom gals had a reputation for being great cooks and bakers, and their efforts fueled them all for the rigors of farm living.

One afternoon, Laurie, the second oldest of the Rystrom girls, shut the oven door with a clang, signaling that the simple farmhouse kitchen would soon be filled with the aroma of fresh-baked, chocolate-chip cookies. But even before the first batch was out of the oven, ten-year-old Jon's sweet tooth told him that something delicious was coming from the kitchen, and he positioned himself to take advantage of it. Why wait around for cookies to bake when you can grab a bite of dough right away? And there on the edge of the well-worn kitchen table, sat a large mixing bowl filled with tasty cookie dough just begging to be eaten. But there was one thing standing between Jon and cookie-dough happiness: his sister, who was working at the table placing spoonfuls of dough onto a second pan.

Peering in through the doorway, he formulated a strategy and waited for the perfect moment to put his plan into action. As soon as his sister walked over to the sink and turned her back to wash some dishes, he cautiously tiptoed into the kitchen and silently slid under the table. All he had to do was reach his hand up and around the edge of the table, find the bowl, and sneak some dough while Laurie wasn't looking. But he knew he'd have to keep his head down or he'd be caught for sure. The sound of running water was his cue that the coast was clear. Or so he thought.

What Jon hadn't counted on was that his sister, much like his mother, had eyes in the back of her head where Jon was concerned. As the youngest of the five children, Jon was the live wire of the bunch, and he was always joking with and playing games on his older siblings. Truthfully, the family relished Jon's outgoing personality, and he was his parents' pride and joy. There was never a dull moment when Jon was around, and this cookie-baking session was no exception.

His sister, glancing back at the table, had to grin when she noticed a small hand reaching ever so slowly and carefully trying to find the coveted bowl of cookie dough. Jon might be good at playing tricks, but Laurie had a few tricks up her sleeve. She calmly turned off the faucet, hummed a little to herself, and strolled over to the table pretending to put away the ingredients. Up came the little hand, searching in vain for the object of its desire. Down went the hand in defeat. She quietly scooted the bowl of dough away from the table's edge and waited. Up came the little hand again, this time more bravely than before, but not knowing where to go, stopped short of its goal. The bowl kept moving, first left and then right, and the little hand was getting impatient.

From under the table, Jon knew something was wrong, but what? A quick glance should help him figure out where to aim. When he slowly raised his buzz-cut head to peek over the table's edge, the first thing he saw wasn't the coveted bowl but Laurie staring right back at him instead. She quickly burst out laughing, and Jon had to laugh too. This wasn't the first time he'd been caught with his hand in the cookie jar or the cookie-dough bowl, and it probably wouldn't be the last.

Even from an early age, Jon showed distinctive qualities that would follow him into adulthood: a tactical, strategic mind, combined with practical problem solving; a persistent, can-do attitude; an active, high-energy personality; a contagious sense of humor; and yes, a sweet tooth. As he grew into adolescence, his family and friends quickly learned that this blond-haired, blue-eyed Swede could beat them handily at pitch and chess as easily as he could pin an opponent to the ground in wrestling. (As a high school wrestler, Jon came in second place in the state. Twice.)

But no one really minded losing to Jon. Jon was the kind of guy everyone loved being around. Due to his Midwest upbringing, Jon was galvanized in a down-to-earth nature and genuine value of relationship that would mark him for life. While those closest to him realized that the typical Nebraska farm life in which he was raised would never be able to satisfy Jon's adventurous nature, no one guessed at the time how far his unique qualities would take him.

Take Me Home Country Roads

I truly appreciated Jon's Midwest upbringing. Jon didn't get flustered or upset about anything. In our relationship, his cool composure contrasted with my more emotional one. His plainspokenness cut through my confusion and helped me maintain a positive perspective. Sometimes his work ethic pushed me out of my comfort zone, but I never questioned his dedication or desire to always put my needs and the needs of our family above his own.

My own childhood was quite different from Jon's. My older brother and I were raised in a middle-class family in Charleston, the capital of West Virginia. My parents, Chuck and Doris Windham, both worked but they didn't have high-paying jobs. My dad was a civil engineer, and my mother was a cartographer (a unique job choice for a woman back in the 1970s). Our family wasn't poor, but my parents had to be creative to provide what we needed and wanted. We always drove used cars, and vacations usually consisted of camping trips built around southern gospel sings in our region. A night out meant getting "lickers" or ice-cream cones at the local Dairy Queen.

My parents were loving and caring, happily married, and never fought with each other. They were strong Christians and very involved in our local church. While I had a genuine conversion experience with God when I was 9 years old, my own faith was more of a formality than a lifestyle. I was more interested in being popular and having all the things that I saw my wealthier classmates enjoying. While Jon came from a large family and had to work for everything, my parents sacrificed so that I didn't have to.

Neither of my parents, who were both incredibly accepting of me, knew how driven I was to feel significant. As an awkward preteen, my classmates bullied me without mercy, calling me "bushwoman" because of my curly hair and big eyes. They even howled at me in class as though I were a dog. My determination to overcome their insults led me to work extra hard to earn straight A's in all my classes. But nothing healed the sting of their rejection, and their rude remarks would haunt me for years.

Significance was important to Jon as well and was one of the main reasons he chose a career in the Navy. Jon wanted to fly and, like the career of every aviation officer in the Navy, that path always started in the same place: Pensacola, Florida. No matter what their duties or where they served, the crucible of Pensacola forged a bond that all naval aviators shared. After reading about Jon's introduction to the Navy, you'll understand why

CHAPTER 3

Silver-Dollar Salute

26 SEPT 1978
1200 CENTRAL DAYLIGHT TIME UTC-5
NAVAL AIR STATION PENSACOLA
PENSACOLA, FLORIDA, USA
30.35.57 N, 87.28.83 W

The pungent odors of Brasso and WD-40 filled the air of the barracks as the young Navy officer candidates—dressed in matching white T-shirts and blue shorts and sporting military buzz cuts—painstakingly prepared every part of their uniforms for inspection. One spot on a buckle or boot, a solitary wrinkle on a sleeve, or a single badge a fraction out of place would be sure to incur the wrath of Drill Instructor (DI) Staff Sergeant McAffee. After weeks of grueling training, that was one thing these Navy recruits had learned to avoid.

Jon Rystrom remembered the way "Dad" had greeted him and his fellow classmates on their first day of Aviation Officer Candidate School (AOCS). The school was "Navy-owned" but "Marine-Corps trained." Arriving in front of Building 626, with its iconic white columns, one of the eager recruits made the mistake of saying "hello" to the staff sergeant, who didn't waste any time introducing himself in return.

"I'm gonna tell you what there, candidate!" yelled SSGT McAffee in his unmistakable gruff voice, his words shooting out rapidly like hot lead through a machine gun. "You don't speak to me unless you're spoken to! And you don't speak to me unless you're in a position of attention! That means your heels are together, your feet are at a 45-degree angle, your thumbs are on your trouser seams, your fingers are curled, your shoulders are rolled back, and your eyeballs are straight to the front! You don't do anything around here unless, I tell you to do it! Do you understand me?"

They thought they understood the sergeant, but obviously they didn't, for soon they all found themselves on the ground doing countless pushups at every infraction of the sergeant's orders. It turned out there were many things that Jon and his classmates didn't understand. For instance, Jon thought he knew how to make a bed and how to fold his skivvies, but he obviously didn't. When he'd left his high-school teaching job to start his career as an aviation officer in the Navy, he figured he would be spending his time studying aerodynamics and aviation physiology. He didn't count on learning how to properly stand in line, endlessly practicing the detailed technique of polishing shoes, or differentiating his right foot from his left.

SSGT McAffee was like a dad to AOCS Class 15-78. He put them to bed at night and woke them up at oh dark thirty each morning. He marched them off to class, yelled them through endless hours of physical training

(PT), and made sure they ate their meals in less time than anyone thought humanly possible. He even helped them dress, berating them for every scuff mark, every piece of lint, and any button out of place. While the candidates were exhausted, SSGT McAffee never seemed to run out of energy or intensity. He was like a machine, always in motion and always loud. Nothing escaped his eagle eye.

Other Marine instructors were a part of the training and one in particular made quite an impression on all of them—the sober-faced class officer who had held up a small, metal, baseball-sized object with little fold-out wings on its sides.

"Do you know what this is?" he inquired in a serious voice. For once, there was no yelling. But his somber attitude was absolutely as impactful as the staff sergeant's colorful tirades.

> TAYLOR'S VERSE: THEREFORE DO NOT BE ANXIOUS ABOUT TOMORROW, FOR TOMORROW WILL BE ANXIOUS FOR ITSELF. SUFFICIENT FOR THE DAY IS ITS OWN TROUBLE. (MATTHEW 6:34 ESV)

"This is an anti-personnel bomblet designed to blast hundreds of high-velocity steel pellets in every direction with the intent to maim and kill human targets. Three hundred sixty of these are packed together into one cluster bomb with the combined capability to take out an entire enemy position with one strike."

He paused a moment to let the information sink in. Then he asked a very important question: "Are you ready to drop one of these and kill people?" Again, he paused. "Do you know why you are here? You are here to become a flight officer in the United States Navy, to protect our country from enemies far and wide, and to carry out orders that will require you to drop bombs and fire missiles at the enemy with the intent to kill. If that's not what you're here for, you need to leave. Now.

Over the next few weeks, several of Jon's classmates did exactly that. They chose the Drop on Request (DOR) option mainly because of the rigors of PT and the DI's high-pressure tactics. But Jon was no quitter and neither were 29 of his fellow candidates. They survived the first week as "poopies," completing countless circuits on the brutal obstacle courses, wearing chrome domes and ill-fitting olive-green fatigues. They pushed themselves and each other through punishing swim qualifications and monotonous hours of marching on a large patch of asphalt, lovingly referred to as the "grinder." Jon thought running through Nebraska snowdrifts was hard, but that was nothing compared to slugging through miles of Pensacola sand in the sweltering heat and humidity.

But as the weeks went by, Jon noticed that he and his companions were becoming a real team, focusing on perseverance, attention to detail, and discipline that they would desperately need if they were to succeed in the Navy environment. While each came into AOCS with a four-year college degree, they were all receiving a priceless education that would alter them forever.

As AOCS wore on, the boot-camp atmosphere transformed as more responsibilities shifted to the officers-to-be, and classes began covering topics like pre-flight training and aerodynamics. Before arriving for AOCS, each recruit had received a thorough physical and screening to see if he met the exacting requirements for flight operations. While Jon was highly intelligent and physically fit, his eyesight wasn't good enough to qualify him as a pilot, so he was assigned to be a naval flight officer (NFO) instead.

Regardless of their path, the candidates received critical sea-and-land survival training and practiced ditching out of a plane with an ejection seat. Repeatedly, they learned how to exit an aircraft underwater with the help of "Dilbert Dunker," a cockpit that is ridden down a slide and then flipped over into a deep pool, and its evil cousin, "Helo Dunker," in which students were buckled inside a simulated fuselage, lowered into the water, and turned upside down at random positions. No one, including Jon, ever wanted to experience "Panic in a Drum" for real.

Thirteen weeks after AOCS started and the course was completed, the only thing left for Jon and his classmates to do was to put on their dress whites and line up for their graduation ceremony. Jon was pleased to see that his parents had made the long drive from Nebraska to watch him graduate and be commissioned as a Navy officer.

After crossing the stage and shaking hands with his commanding officers, Jon faced DI Marine SSGT McAffee one final time. McAffee carefully looked Jon over from head to toe. The young man he saw before him was quite different from the bearded dude with the permed, curly hair that he'd met 13 weeks earlier: shoulders straight, head held high, hair carefully trimmed, and every part of his uniform perfectly in place, down to the impeccably polished white shoes. McAffee had to smile to himself. Another job well done.

"Ensign Rystrom, good morning, sir," spoke SSGT McAffee as he saluted Jon, who crisply saluted in return. "Congratulations," smiled McAffee as he reached out and firmly shook Jon's hand. Following Navy tradition, Jon reached into his pocket and gave the sergeant a silver dollar to pay for the first salute that Jon ever received. All the candidates had learned to respect this dedicated Marine, and "Dad" left an unforgettable impression on each one.

Later that day, when the new ensigns stood under the Blue Angels jet for their final class picture, Jon felt a sense of pride and accomplishment. Just that past spring, he'd been so discouraged with where his life was headed after a year of teaching and coaching football at a small-town high school in Nebraska. The meager paycheck he earned was a joke, and he'd expected better after graduating from Nebraska Wesleyan University with a bachelor's in psychology. He couldn't even afford decent housing and had to live in one of the poorest sections of this Midwest farm town. That was not the kind of life he had dreamed of, and if he ever wanted a future with his college sweetheart, he'd have to do much better than that.

When a Navy recruiter visited his school one cold winter day, Jon, who was also a guidance counselor, coordinated his visit with several of the students. Before he left, the recruiter took a long look at Jon and asked him a question.

"How good are you at math?"

Jon smiled. He was a math teacher after all. He had excelled in math during his college days and loved the challenge of problem solving. He smiled again when the recruiter offered to fly him down to sunny Florida to take the Aviation Selection Test Battery (ASTB) to see if Jon had what it took to be a naval aviator. Turns out, he did.

Should he leave the high school classroom and become an officer in the Navy? The timing seemed right. There was little to aim for where he was, and the Navy offered adventure, financial security, and a career he could be proud of. His college sweetheart was reluctant at first about this change in Jon's career and their future, but with some thought and coaxing, she eventually gave her blessing. Without hesitation, when the school year was over, he quit his teaching job, packed up his little green Triumph Spitfire convertible, and exchanged the prairies of Nebraska for the sand and sun of Pensacola.

Jon had been searching for more: more purpose, more excitement, and more challenge. He knew his Navy training had only begun, and he could hardly wait to move on to the next step of naval flight officer instruction. But if he never took another step onto

the dreaded "grinder," that would be just fine by him.

Wake Bound

While Jon was embarking on his new journey in the Navy, I was ready to launch into a new life of my own as I prepared to graduate from high school. Even though I had been mercilessly bullied in middle school, I earned the senior superlative of "most popular." But my quest for popularity had a dark side. My need for significance was like a black hole and no matter what awards I earned, what achievements I accomplished, or how many compliments I received on my appearance, it was never, ever enough.

My quest for success granted me another hard-fought-for prize: acceptance at my number one college choice, the prestigious Wake Forest University in Winston-Salem, North Carolina. While I wouldn't admit it to myself at the time, I chose this respected school more out of pride than anything.

With a low acceptance rate, tough academic reputation, and a list of respected alumni, Wake Forest was a magnet for the offspring of well-monied Southerners looking to propel their children into successful lives. I desperately wanted to be in that inner circle to finally achieve a status that my barely-middle-class parents could never give me. But my academic prowess couldn't get me in the door, as my straight A's in high school were mainly the result of hard effort and not a superior intellect. I chose to create a college resume with a long list of awards and achievements to catch their eye, and it worked. Like most young adults, I wanted to spread my wings and get as far away from my hometown as possible.

My hard-working parents didn't have the money to pay for a Wake Forest tuition but somehow, between government aid and their own sacrifice, they found a way. I was oblivious to what my college choice cost them, and I was so focused on my own success that I didn't care.

My life was all about performance and checking the boxes. Great grades? Check. Good looks? Check. Thin waistline? Check. Head majorette? Check. Most popular? Check.

My faith in God hardly made the list, except to check off the box of "Christian" as a sort of insurance policy and a way to appear respectable. I wanted to be seen as a "good girl," yet I desired the money, good looks, and successful career I saw as the yardsticks of significance. I took God off the throne of my heart and put myself there instead. I was learning how to get the affirmation I desired through my own efforts and inner drive, and I didn't need faith for that.

As I made plans for prom and wondered how to avoid the "Freshman 15" in the fall, Jon was continuing the next phase of his naval training and making choices that would have life-changing consequences for both of us.

Flying High

14 MAR 1979
0800 CENTRAL TIME ZONE
VT-10, TRARON TEN
NAVAL AIR STATION PENSACOLA
PENSACOLA, FLORIDA, USA
30.35.04 N, 87.31.00 W

The T-34 scurried down the runway under sunny skies and calm winds. Pulling back on the stick, the flight instructor coaxed the single-prop plane into the air, leaving the tarmac at Saufley Field far behind. Directly behind the experienced pilot sat Ensign (ENS) Jon Rystrom, a naval flight officer (NFO) in training. Jon loved getting out of the classroom and into the air. The T-34's bubble canopy provided excellent views of the Florida Panhandle coastline below. Even though Jon was training as an NFO and not a pilot, he wasn't merely a passenger on these instructional flights. He was learning important lessons in basic flight characteristics and navigation. Today's lesson was going to be particularly exciting.

"Are you ready to commence the stall?" queried the instructor over the headset.

"Yes, sir," Jon replied, his heart speeding up as he anticipated what would follow. In class, Jon and the other NFO students had been diligently studying the Naval Air Training and Operating Procedures Standardization (NATOPS) manual for this aircraft, and he had already taken numerous classroom tests on the material. Learning about the stall behavior of the T-34 while sitting in the confines of the classroom was one thing. Experiencing it firsthand—strapped into the backseat of the T34's tandem-seat cockpit at an altitude of more than 5,000 feet—was something else entirely.

With the throttle reduced to idle, Jon could sense the pilot pulling up the black and red-orange nose, attempting to maintain level flight. As the airspeed decreased, so did the airflow over the wings, thereby reducing lift—the force that holds an airplane up in the air. Jon looked out to his left side and saw the T-34's white wings with their red-orange wingtips catching the glint of the morning sun as the plane's rate of climb and speed rapidly decreased. Jon braced himself and clenched his fists as the plane shook a bit and then suddenly dropped, along with Jon's stomach, like a rock in the sky.

Jon, nervous yet excited, was too distracted by the unfamiliar sensations to notice the altimeter quickly rolling backwards, signaling the plane was in a full stall. In what seemed like an eternity—though it only took a few seconds—the seasoned pilot easily recovered the plane, and they were operating in level, controlled flight again. Jon took a few deep breaths and relaxed his hands. There was no way to fit what he had experienced into a manual.

"Would you like to do that again?" the pilot smiled to himself as he waited to hear Jon's response.

"Yes, sir, absolutely!" Now that Jon knew what to expect, he would be able to react properly the next time. And he did.

Straight out of AOCS, Jon and the other fresh ensigns continued their training in various squadrons, depending on their designations. All air squadrons for fixed-wing aircraft start with a "V" and as a student NFO, Jon was sent for six months to Training Squadron (VT) 10 which, like AOCS, was located at Naval Air Station (NAS) Pensacola. VT-10 was known as the Wildcats and their stated mission was to "provide world class Primary & Intermediate Student Naval Flight Officer training and prepare aircrew to fly with courage, fight with honor, and lead with commitment."

The young ensigns, all feeling pretty full of themselves, were convinced that they were prepared to do exactly that. However, they quickly discovered that they had much to learn before they could take to the skies. Hours of classroom instruction in weather, flight rules and, of course, the T-34 NATOPS, along with extended time in various computer simulators contributed to their extensive training. The ensigns didn't require Marine DIs to keep them in top physical condition; the sense of pride these aviators-in-training had in being naval officers was the only motivation they needed.

After the T-34 prop plane was mastered, the students moved on to the larger T-2 Buckeye. Like the T-34, the T-2 had a similar paint job along with a tandem seat cockpit and full-view bubble canopy, but it flew much faster, thanks to its twin jet engines. The pace of instruction increased along with the speed as the trainees had to master the T-2 NATOPS manual as well.

While Jon knew he wanted to be an NFO, he didn't know on which aircraft he would serve. During his time at VT-10, Jon was presented with several options, based on his performance during his training. After carefully considering which path to take, Jon chose the E-2C Hawkeye, a five-seater, twin-engine, turboprop plane with a large, round rotodome on top—used as an early warning radar detection and mission coordination aerial platform.

He chose the E-2C for two main reasons: One, as reflected by his avid love of chess, the Hawkeye's mission appealed to his strategic way of thinking; and two, the E-2C had the reputation as one of the safest aircraft in the Navy. Somehow being a backseat Radio Intercept Officer (RIO) in an F-14 Tomcat fighter jet wasn't as appealing to Jon as being involved in coordinating numerous aircraft and operating the latest high-tech radar gear.

Jon had yet to earn his NFO wings but after completing his six-month training with VT-10, he was one step closer. He was beginning to find the "more" he had been looking for and the camaraderie he experienced fit in well with his gregarious personality. But at 24 years of age, Jon was ready to invest himself into something—something that mattered. And as much as he enjoyed hanging out with the guys, he missed the female companionship of his girlfriend back home. Maybe when this initial training was over, he could finally marry his college sweetheart and they could begin their lives together wherever the Navy planted them.

But there was still some serious work ahead before Jon could truly launch his Navy career. For now, he had to stay focused on the task at hand and perform at his best if he wanted to escape the poverty and dead-end life he'd left behind in Nebraska.

CHAPTER 4

The Hawkeye

Demon Deacons

I was so excited when I drove through the perfectly landscaped entrance of Wake Forest University at the start of my freshman year. But as the semester began, that thrill was soon replaced with sheer panic, and I had only myself to blame. When I'd registered for my first semester, I was full of confidence and I chose the most challenging courses. But once classes started, it didn't take long to figure out that I was in way over my head. I even turned to my faith in desperation and put Bible verses on my walls, looking for divine intervention.

As the months passed by, it became painfully clear that my high-school strategy of working harder than anyone else wouldn't cut it at this highly ranked university. After only one semester, I was in danger of flunking out of my No. 1 college pick. In truth, I really didn't belong there. I was surrounded by brilliant students who were better prepared than me for this demanding environment. I loved being at Wake: the picturesque campus, the upper-class students, the Greek life, and the exciting football games. My fear of getting kicked out of my dream college and going back to my hometown in shame was quickly becoming a real possibility.

Attending those exciting football games was one of the few reprieves from my pressure-cooker study sessions. Joining the 34,000 cheering fans at Groves Stadium to watch our Demon Deacons take on their Atlantic Coast Conference rivals filled me with a sense of pride to be part of such a distinctive community. At the center of all the excitement was the Wake Forest cheerleading team, dressed proudly in Wake's traditional black-and-gold colors.

As I watched the team's routines, I envisioned me performing those same cheers and stunts. Although I wasn't a trained gymnast—I was actually a dancer at heart—I was willing to work out and train hard to learn their special skills. Finding significance academically wasn't working out, but maybe I could earn a spot on the cheerleading squad.

That idea kept rolling around in my head as I managed to eke out passing grades in all my classes and avoid the disaster of a one-way trip home. I was relieved when I could register for spring semester, and this time I had the wisdom to sign up for easier courses. Spring tryouts for the cheerleading squad weren't far away, and I ignored the voices in my head that said, "If you can't make the grades, what makes you think you can be a varsity cheerleader?" I finalized my preparations with the traditional work ethic that I applied to the rest of my life and went to the tryouts with my head held high.

When the cheerleading squad was announced, I was ecstatic to find that I had made the varsity team, but I wasn't surprised. My win proved to me that with hard work and determination, there was nothing I couldn't achieve. I no longer needed Bible verses on my wall, like "I can do all things through Christ who gives me strength," because I was proving that I could do all things myself. Finally, as a varsity cheerleader at an NCAA Division 1 school, the status and popularity that I so desperately wanted was within my grasp. Little did I know the life-long consequences that my new-found talent would cause me, but I would soon find out.

Jon was about to find out how to take his God-given talents and use them in one of the most unique-looking aircraft in the Navy: the

E-2C Hawkeye. Most people have no idea what the Hawkeye is or the important role it plays in our national defense. But Jon was proud to be a part of the Hawkeye community, and the Hummer will always hold a special place in my heart.

Eye in the Sky

11 FEB 1980
1200 EASTERN TIME ZONE
RVAW-120, CARAEWTRARON ONE TWO ZERO
NAS NORFOLK
NORFOLK, VIRGINIA, USA
36.94.25 N, 76.29.05 W

Sitting in the dark interior at the back of the E-2C Hawkeye, surrounded by some of the most advanced electronic surveillance technology on the planet, Jon felt like a kid in a candy store. Sixty million dollars could buy a lot of "candy," and Jon was enjoying learning how to operate the E-2C's highly-advanced systems. Two months ago, he had finally earned the coveted "wings of gold" and he proudly wore the title of naval flight officer. But the training never stopped.

His assignment with Carrier Airborne Early Warning Training Squadron 120 (RVAW-120) had been challenging from the beginning. For starters, students had to know the E-2C's NATOPS manual backwards and forward, all 750+ pages of it. That included knowledge of every system, the plane's specifications and capabilities, all the mechanics of the engines, propellers, hydraulics and, of course, all emergency procedures.

But that was only the beginning of Jon's education. Multiple hours logged in weapon system simulators, classroom instruction, and missions flown in the E-2C to gain experience in high-stress situations prepared Jon and his classmates to join squadrons operating around the world. This extensive preparation was crucial, because the real mission of the E-2C was what happened in the back of the plane, where the three NFOs did their jobs. But before those critical tasks can be understood, an introduction to this unique aircraft is needed.

Nicknamed the "Hummer," an E-2C Hawkeye was often heard before it was seen, due to the distinctive sound of its twin Allison turboprop engines. Thanks to the large, 24-foot-diameter, round, rotating radar dome (rotodome) on top of its fuselage and the four large vertical stabilizers on its tail, the E-2C had the most unique silhouette of any U.S. Navy aircraft. After months of training, Jon could rattle off the E-2C's basic facts without a second thought: length, over 57 feet; height, 18 feet; wingspan, 80 feet; maximum speed, 350 knots (402 miles per hour); cruising speed, 256 knots (294 miles per hour); and diameter of the four-bladed propellers, more than 13 feet.

Each Fleet VAW Squadron assigned its aircraft numbers that started at 600, so all the VAW Squadrons had planes with the same numbers—600, 601, 602, and 603—painted on the fuselage right under the cockpit. Unlike most other Navy aircraft, the Hawkeye wasn't a product of an assembly line. Each plane was constructed by hand and, therefore, had its own distinctive personality. For instance, 601 might be a true workhorse, handling any conditions thrown at it. On the other hand, 603 might be more like a high-strung Ferrari, requiring a great deal of effort to consistently maintain its fine edge.

The uniqueness of each plane meant that the maintenance team had to develop an intimate knowledge of each aircraft and work closely with the aviators who operated them. While it was true that any aviation squadron had to work as a team to be effective, this teamwork was absolutely essential in a VAW Squadron. Every service member, from the lowest ranked to the highest, had a critical role to play that benefited them all.

While Jon was a great admirer of the Hawkeye, for the non-aviator, the E-2C's $60 million price tag seemed like a mistake at first glance. To be fair, the Hawkeye was not a sexy aircraft, like its fighter jet counterparts. Its rounded fuselage, massive stabilizers on the tail, and what looked like a large gray pancake suspended several feet above the long, straight wings gave it a peculiar appearance.

After climbing up the two steps leading to the plane's door, located on the port (or left) side just under the front of the wing, impressions weren't much improved. First, there was the odor: a slightly musty, oily, hot-electronics aroma, like a cross between a car mechanic's garage and the inside of an old radio. Second, the interior was severely confined. In the two-person cockpit, conditions were cramped, visibility was limited, and the instruments appeared rudimentary. Behind the cockpit, two steps down, was a narrow, dark, low passageway, about 15 feet long, that passed through what looked like the guts of the plane. Wires, hydraulic tubes, air conditioning equipment, and various electronics were exposed on both sides.

At the end of the passageway was an undersized door that opened to the constricted compartment where the three NFOs sat. With the cramped conditions, it was hard to imagine three full-grown men having to duck their heads as they hunkered down the tight passageway and squeezed into the three high-backed seats, each located behind the other. Once seated, each NFO had a tiny round window to look out of to their right. To their left was a wall of electronic gear, which appeared in the Navy's favorite color: gray.

A civilian not trained in the Hawkeye's considerable capabilities and not observing the plane's systems in operation could be forgiven for thinking the E-2C was a relic of World War II. In truth, while much of the plane seemed to be "old school," the sophisticated electronic weapon system operated by the NFOs in the backend was more akin to "Star Wars."

The high-tech wall of electronic gear was the heartbeat of the Hawkeye's mission, and Jon knew quite well how special that capability was once the plane was launched and the mission underway. When taking off and landing, the NFOs faced forward and were secured to their emergency parachute-equipped seats with four large Koch fittings. But once the plane was airborne, the NFOs knew it was time to "turn and burn" as they unlocked their seats, swung them around 90 degrees to their left, and switched the radar from standby to operate. In this way, the NFOs sat side by side during their missions.

Once the aircraft was safely airborne and they could start performing their duties, there was often a race to see who could turn his seat around fastest. When the mission was completed, the seats would be turned back around, lowered, and locked into place. For fuel conservation, the plane flew with a slightly nose-up attitude, so the seats weren't level in flight, leading to the common joke among E-2C NFOs that your left "cheek" was bigger than your right "cheek" because of the way you always sat on it.

After turning their seats to face their electronic equipment, each NFO sat in front of a "desk" that had screens for displaying radar and various data, surrounded by multiple rows of knobs, buttons, switches, a number pad, and indicator lights. Each crewman wore a helmet with built-in speakers and headphones and used special light pens that allowed him to "hook" or interface with a screen to pull up specific data, much like people today use a stylus or their fingertip on a tablet computer.

Lying across their laps were small, flip-down trays, like mini desks, causing Jon to believe that he had the coolest desk job in the world. And it was very cool. Frigid, in fact, due to the powerful air conditioning needed to offset the high heat generated by the sizable assortment of electronics.

The tiny windows next to the NFOs' seats were kept covered during missions to block any sunlight, making it easier for the NFOs to view their radar screens and lighted buttons, and also functioning as a shield to protect them from the high level of energy emanating from the rotodome directly above their cabin. That rotodome allowed them to know where everyone else was going, be it in the air, on the land, or in the sea. It housed two antennae, one for radar and the other for Identification Friend or Foe (IFF). The systems that used these antennae allowed the E-2C to distinguish between enemy and friendly aircraft, as well as to determine their position.

Information gathered by the Hawkeye was fed into computers and that data was shared not only with the NFOs onboard but also with other ships and aircraft in their group. The E-2C's sophisticated capabilities allowed it to see everything happening for 300 nautical miles in all directions, or 3 million cubic miles of airspace, rightly earning it the "Hawkeye" moniker and the "Eye in the Sky" nickname.

The E-2C had several key roles to fulfill. Its main function was to give crucial time to the aircraft carrier and the vessels working with her, called the carrier strike group. Knowing where the enemy was and what the enemy was doing and knowing these things from a great distance gave precious reaction time to sea, air, and land forces to successfully respond to enemy threats. In addition to its early warning role, the E-2C also tracked, relayed, and helped control what its own forces were doing. This ensured that responses were well coordinated, providing priceless information and guidance in combat situations. In peacetime, the E-2C also assisted in humanitarian crises, search and rescue (SAR) operations, drug interdiction, and air traffic control.

To execute these missions and capabilities, each of the three NFOs had different responsibilities. The Radar Operator (RO) focused on identifying all the air and surface contacts and the turn-on, set-up, and maintenance of the weapon system. In the aft-most seat sat the air control officer (ACO) who had the responsibility of the air defense operation, taking planes to their mission and maximizing the situational awareness of the aircraft under their control. For example, they made sure the enemy couldn't sneak up on their friendly aircraft.

In the middle seat sat the mission commander, the combat information center officer or CICO (pronounced SEA-koh). The CICO oversaw the stationing, or positioning, of the plane and the execution of the mission, much like the quarterback on a football team. The job of the CICO was the ultimate in multi-tasking, requiring oversight and coordination of his crew and simultaneous execution of multiple missions, all while listening to six or more radios, maintaining his situational awareness of what his scope and other systems were showing him, monitoring and maximizing the performance of his weapon system, and keeping all the warfare commanders whom he was supporting in the loop. CICOs in training were warned to never take on more tasks than they could handle, because adding just one too many responsibilities could cause their entire mission to collapse like a house of cards.

Working together, the NFOs controlled fighter aircraft conducting intercepts of enemy aircraft, assisted planes refueling in the air using tankers, guided them to the marshal stack—an air traffic control pattern to direct multiple planes in for landing—coordinated airplane bombing missions, and so much more. There was almost no operation of a carrier strike group that didn't involve the Hawkeye.

Learning the Hummer from tip to tail was critical, because the mission of all the other aircraft in the air wing depended on the E-2C functioning properly. Jon had to learn what to do if certain circuit breakers were tripped and how to operate should any system fail or degrade. He also had to know the capabilities of all the other aircraft in the air wing as well as the people flying them so that he could make wise decisions about the planes that he was controlling. An E-2C NFO could never stop learning and could never know enough. Life and death—success and failure—could depend on the crew's collective knowledge and skill.

The work was very tedious and exacting, requiring great mental focus. This was made even more difficult by the mighty roar of the engines that required the aircrew to wear earplugs and the constant vibration of the quad propellers which took a fatiguing toll on their bodies. All told, it was probably a good thing that the E-2C couldn't refuel in flight, keeping the missions to a typical four-hour length. Even at that, the NFOs would be both mentally and physically exhausted when their mission was completed.

Much has changed in the Hawkeye community since Jon's era, including a near tripling of the aircraft's price tag. The four-blade propellers were eventually replaced with an eight-blade version that was easier to maintain, greatly reducing the old model's notorious vibration but also exchanging its beloved "hummer" sound with that of a swarm of highly angry bees. Effective update programs have kept the E-2C's capabilities in step with the latest technological advancements, leading to an entirely new aircraft, the E-2D, which will replace all existing E-2C planes in U.S. Navy VAW Squadrons.

But some things haven't changed. The men and women who serve in today's VAW community are still highly-trained professionals who are whole-heartedly committed to their mission. They realize that they don't fly the sexiest plane in the Navy, and with their vital role not well understood by outsiders, they don't mind flying under the radar. The modern aviators who operate E-2Cs and E-2Ds share two of Jon's loves: the love for their country and the love of flying. That's why they endure the intense training, the long separation from their families, and the known dangers of their chosen profession.

This "Eye in the Sky" has proven its longevity and usefulness over many decades of service, flying longer off the decks of U.S. Navy carriers and flying longer than any other aircraft in the history of naval aviation. With today's modern version set to remain in operation until at least the year 2050, this unique bird with its peculiar silhouette will be effectively patrolling the skies for many years to come.

As his time with RVAW-120 was coming to an end, Jon prepared to receive his orders. But he also was preparing for something else: marriage. He hoped to tie the knot with his long-time girlfriend and start their life together wherever the Navy sent him next. His first tour would be sea duty, but he would train several months with his new squadron before he would deploy on an aircraft carrier. Hopefully, that would give him and his bride time to enjoy being newlyweds before he went off to sea.

He joined the Navy, in part, to see the world. But what part of the world would Jon see first? And what would marriage be like when he and his wife would be oceans apart? If only Jon could have seen as far as the Hawkeye, he might have been better prepared for what lay ahead.

CHAPTER 5

Freedom's Flagship

500 a Day

I thought I was prepared for what lay ahead when joining the Wake Forest cheerleading squad and continuing my sophomore year. On the outside, it looked like I had it all together. I was getting noticed around campus, enjoying sorority life, and loving all the dance parties. Cheerleading before thousands of people at Deacs' football and basketball games was a total rush. Sometimes I would take a break from my hectic schedule and clear my head by taking late night runs through the historic, tree-filled university campus.

My evening runs had a darker purpose, however. For years, I was driven to control my image, success, popularity, and future. Once I joined the cheerleading squad, controlling my weight was added to the list. I remembered being careful about my weight the summer before entering college, keeping an eye on my plate and my scales. But once I became a varsity cheerleader, I set a personal goal of staying under 112 pounds, and I was determined to achieve it.

I decided to limit myself to 500 calories a day. This became increasingly difficult to maintain, especially on a college campus where pizza, ice cream, and soft drinks were the norm. I started a calorie journal, not only to track my caloric intake but also my caloric burn.

And that's where my late-night jogging sessions came into play. At the end of each day, I would tally the numbers and if I was over, I'd make up the difference by going for a run or doing aerobics in my college dorm room. If I didn't have time for exercise, I made myself throw up instead.

And my tactics worked, at least to a point. I dropped some weight, but I was never thin enough—at least in my eyes. As my body image became distorted in my mind, once I met a weight goal, I thought, "You know, I could be five pounds less," and I would double my efforts. Before long, my weight got so low that I even stopped menstruating. I found myself thinking, "Do I starve myself today or tomorrow?" I might have been cheering for the Demon Deacons, but on the inside the demon of anorexia was taking over my life.

While my life was spiraling out of control, Jon's life was taking off as he began his first sea deployment in the U.S. Navy. As I discovered years later, everything in the Navy centers around one class of ship—the aircraft carrier. As a young man, my dad had been in the Navy, but I had little interest in the military. Until I met Jon, I didn't know anything about the different kinds of ships, boats, and planes that make up the greatest naval force in the world.

Jon's love for the Navy rubbed off on me, and I developed a respect for these massive ships that impacted our relationship in so many ways. I still get a lump in my throat when I see one today.

Gonzo Station

27 JAN 1981
1400 GULF TIME ZONE, UTC+4
GONZO STATION
USS INDEPENDENCE (CV-62) WITH CVW-6, VAW-122
24.71.42 N, 58.72.47 E

Winds of 30+ knots (35 mph) swept over the flight deck as the five-man crew of 602 proceeded to their E-2C parked between elevators 1 and 2 on the ship's starboard side. Dressed in olive-green flight suits, flight boots, survival vests, life jackets, and helmets, they walked slowly around the plane, reviewing their all-important pre-flight checklist, looking for discrepancies: rivets popped, prop surfaces smooth, no fluid leaks from engines or hydraulic actuators, Pitot tube clear, etc. The ATs (avionic techs) already had the E-2C's systems running on the ship's power, so the NFOs didn't have to turn on and check every system.

As the ACO (air control officer), Lieutenant Junior Grade (LT. j.g.) Jon Rystrom, serving with the Steeljaws of VAW-122, was the first NFO to enter the plane since his seat was farthest back. He, along with the CICO (Combat information control officer) and RO (radar Operator) ascended the stairs and proceeded aft down the narrow corridor leading to their seats, being careful not to catch their gear on any of the equipment as they scooted past. Once in their seats, they strapped themselves in with four heavy-duty buckles and entered that mission's pre-flight data into the system. On word from the pilots that they were ready to taxi to the catapults, the NFOs turned and locked their seats forward and reported that they were prepared to taxi.

In the cockpit, the pilots finished their preflight procedures and steered the plane to follow the yellow-shirt handler as they started their taxi to the catapult. Even though the flight deck resembled a three-ringed circus with multiple planes and personnel in constant motion, the pilot kept his eyes on one person alone: his handler, who used a variety of hand signals to instruct and guide the Hawkeye to the launching point.

Jon could feel the lock-in and the stretching of the plane as the launch gear was connected to the powerful steam catapult system. The pilots responded to the yellow shirt's signal to ramp up the twin turboprop engines to full military power.

As a final check, the NFOs in the rear made sure that their seats were facing forward and locked and that their helmet visors were down. The pilots wiped out the cockpit, looking around to make sure all was set for takeoff.

The CICO in the back reported to the pilot that the NFOs were ready. The pilot silently signaled readiness to launch to the yellow shirt with a salute. The catapult officer returned a salute, the shooter touched the deck, and they shot down the flight deck, accelerating from zero to 150 miles per hour in 2.5 seconds. The force of the acceleration slammed Jon and the other crewmen back into their seats, but this was a procedure they had all experienced many times, and seconds after launch, Jon won the contest for unlocking and turning his seat around first.

Disappearing rapidly behind them was USS Independence, a Forrestal class aircraft carrier serving in the Gulf of Oman Naval Zone of Operations, otherwise known as Gonzo Station. The Gulf of Oman, located between the Arabian Peninsula and Iran, led to the Persian Gulf to the northwest and to the Arabian Sea to the east. This northern section of the Indian Ocean could be a hotbed of activity.

A week earlier, USS Independence was one of several Navy vessels on watch as the Iran Hostage Crisis finally came to an end. Within minutes of Ronald Reagan taking the presidential oath of office on January 20, 1981, the 52 American hostages in Tehran were released, ending their 444 days of captivity. Though the hostage exchange didn't require their assistance, USS Independence was prepared and ready to step into action, if needed.

As a lowly "nugget," an aviator on his first sea tour with the Steeljaws of VAW-122, Jon's days rarely had a high level of excitement. But there was one important job that Jon and all the other nuggets in the air wing shared: adjusting to life in their new home away from home, the aircraft carrier. To fully understand what Jon, or any other naval aviator, did in his career, you must understand what defines the greatest display of military power on Earth—the modern supercarrier.

Coming out of World War II, the aircraft carrier was the central piece of naval power and strategy. Considering that the world's oceans cover 70 percent of the planet, possessing the ability to access international coastlines unhindered with massive military force is a tremendous advantage. Carriers allow the United States to place a movable airbase off the shore of any country in the world at will—no permission required.

As multiple presidents have discovered, the first question commonly asked in times of international crisis is, "Where is the nearest aircraft carrier?" Often the mere presence of a U.S. naval carrier is enough to put the damper on rising tensions, while other times carriers help protect critical shipping lanes, assist in humanitarian crises, or deliver Marine forces.

But what exactly is an aircraft carrier? First, think about its size. Imagine the Empire State Building—minus its antenna tip—lying on its side, and you can begin to grasp the scale of her length. Now picture that ship is 24 stories tall, from her keel at the bottom to the top of her mast and nearly 260 feet wide at her broadest point.

Now think about her crew. Nearly 6,000 people are required to run this floating city on the sea, which has a world-class airport, kitchens that crank out thousands of meals a day, a fully-functional hospital, a post office, laundry services, a daily newspaper, stores, a chapel, a library, and even a jail. With a vessel so massive, it's easy to see how a Sailor attached to the carrier could serve on one for more than a year and still not have seen the entire ship.

The people on board are what bring this wonder of engineering to life. The carrier's crew is split up into two main divisions: over half the Sailors are assigned to the ship, with the other 2,400 or so attached to the air wing. The ship's crew is responsible for running the "city" itself, while the air wing supplies the planes and the people who fly and service them.

When asking the men and women who serve on these modern marvels what a carrier is all about, the responses are enlightening. Some say that the carrier is the heartbeat of the fleet. Everything in the Navy exists to serve and support the carriers. Others might say the carrier is a symbol. For a Sailor, the carrier can represent his or her office or jobsite. For that Sailor's family, the carrier is a point of pride, knowing their loved one is serving their country on a remarkable vessel. For an American, the carrier is a symbol of the power of a nation. For those suffering and oppressed in foreign lands, the carrier can be a symbol of hope.

What is it like to live on an aircraft carrier? For those privileged to serve on this symbol of power, pride, and hope, the experience of working in this unique and, at times, peculiar environment is hard to put into words. Some say you can't. The only way to know what it's really like is to experience it firsthand.

One thing everyone agrees on is that living on a carrier is noisy—constantly, incessantly. Jet engines being tested, catapults launching, planes landing—an everything-humming-24/7-kind-of-noisy. Imagine living inside a huge machine in perpetual motion along with 6,000 other people. The carrier is truly the city that never sleeps.

Some sounds can be anticipated but not avoided. Everyone on board knows the unmistakable initial sound of when a plane is about to be launched by a steam catapult, called a cat shot. But when you first hear it, there isn't enough time to plug your ears before the blast hits. You simply know you're in for it and there's no escaping it.

Sleeping in such an environment could be a major challenge, especially for lower-ranked Sailors who share larger berthing areas with bunk beds, called racks, stacked three high. Even the officers' staterooms, which are more spacious yet still modest in size, are located right under the flight deck, with planes launching and landing at all hours. Not the best sleeping conditions. But after about two weeks onboard, it doesn't make any difference. You're so tired that you learn to sleep through anything.

When stepping aboard a carrier, one of the first things observed, after being overwhelmed by its massive size, is the obvious odor. Called the "ship smell" by some, this aroma caused by all the lubricants, fuels, paints, working machinery, and 6,000 bodies living in close proximity to each other permeates everything that comes into contact with it. The smell is not unpleasant, but it is distinctive. Some Sailors would have two sets of clothes: one for wearing at home, another for wearing on the ship. No amount of laundry soap could remove the ship smell from clothing.

Living together on a carrier creates a unique bond between all who serve on her. Whether they are brown-shoe aviators or black-shoe mechanics, whether they are attached to the ship or to the air wing, whether they are a low-ranked petty officer or a high-ranked rear admiral, everybody depends on everyone else. What affects one affects all. But rank does determine much about your life on the carrier: where you sleep, where you eat, where you work, where you go, who you talk to, and who your friends are.

Everyone onboard is affected by the extended time away from families that life at sea requires. Deployments usually last around six months, preceded by a period of training and preparation called "workups," where the carrier and crew are put through their paces for weeks at a time. Some handle deployments like it's a walk in the park—a fact of Navy life. Others find the separation extremely difficult, especially when young children must be separated from a parent.

When a carrier is at sea, there is another unseen crew that is deployed: the families and loved ones back home in CONUS (continental United States). Spouses become single parents, children miss the presence of their mom or dad, and loved ones face holidays, celebrations, and life events apart. Many marriages crumble under the stress, and rates of depression are high. Today's Navy makes a concerted effort to mitigate these challenges, but we should never forget the sacrifices that all military families make for our freedom.

The aircraft carrier does not do her work alone. She is a part of a carrier strike group or as it was called in Jon's day, a carrier battle group, a potent combination of vessels that can include cruisers, destroyers, submarines, and supply ships that carry ammunition, fuels, and supplies.

But the formidable force contained in the air wing is the tip of the spear of the carrier strike group. The air wing only comes onto the carrier during workups and deployment. Various squadrons from home bases all over America make up the air wing, including fighter jets, electronic jamming aircraft, helicopters and, of course, E-2C Hawkeyes. Each squadron includes its own maintenance personnel along with the pilots and NFOs.

The upper levels of the carrier are mainly occupied by the air wing. Unlike a house, a carrier doesn't have a first floor, second floor, etc. Instead, it has decks and levels, each with its own unique number. If you were to fly high over the ship from behind, you would look down to see the flight deck, numbered the 04 level, marked with a 650-foot, off-angle runway that starts from the stern (back) and ends far down the port side.

Near the back end of the runway you'd see four, heavy-duty steel cables, called arresting wires, which are caught by tail hooks on the landing planes to help them stop. The deck would be covered with various aircraft and you might see the four catapults in operation that launch the aircraft: Nos. 1 and 2, parallel to each other near the front, and catapults 3 and 4 located farther back on the port side. When the flight deck is operating at full capacity in daylight conditions, two planes can be launched and one landed every 37 seconds.

On the starboard (right) edge of the ship, about one-quarter of the way forward of the stern, would be the all-important island, a narrow, multileveled structure that houses critical command centers, including the ship's bridge from which the captain commands, steers, and controls the ship and Primary Flight Control (Pri-Fly) that controls the launching and landing of aircraft and the movement of planes and crew on and off the flight deck. The sides and top of the island house numerous powerful radar and other antennae.

(By the way, if you're a landlubber and have trouble remembering the difference between port [left] and starboard [right], remember that port has four letters like the word left, and starboard has more letters, like the word right. For bow and stern, remember you bow forward, so that is the front of the ship, meaning the stern is the rear. Port and starboard mean the left and right sides when facing the bow. So if you're facing the back—or aft—toward the stern, the port side would be on your right.)

One thing you would notice about the flight deck, especially if you were a mother with small children, is that there are no railings on the sides to keep the deck crew from falling off the edge. With planes

54

landing and launching at 150 miles per hour, such a structure simply isn't practical, so those working on the deck must be exceedingly careful about everything they do.

A carrier's flight deck has been called the most dangerous place to work in the world and for good reason. Unfortunately, many a Sailor has been blown off the side by the blast of a jet engine, killed or maimed by snapping cables, burnt alive by blazing jet fuel, or blown apart by exploding ordinances. It's the job of the air boss, working with a birds-eye view from Pri-Fly atop the island, to keep everyone down below safe and operations flowing.

The first three levels directly under the flight deck, numbered 03 through 01, house the offices for those in charge of the carrier strike group, the ship, and the air wing, along with the ready rooms for the various squadrons. Also found here are the aviators' staterooms, mess rooms and wardrooms (cafeterias), command centers to control missions during combat, and various maintenance shops.

The second most impressive area of the ship after the flight deck is the massive hangar bay on deck 0. At 3.5 acres, the hangar bay, with a width of 110 feet and length of 685 feet, is about three-fourths the size of the flight deck. Its open structure and 25-foot-high ceiling, which extends up to the bottom of the 03 level, makes it the perfect place to store aircraft, spare engines, heavy equipment, and more.

Four heavy-duty hydraulic elevators deliver planes back and forth from the hangar bay to the flight deck. The best valet parkers in the world operate in the hangar bay, using mini tractors and the guidance of handlers to park numerous multi-million-dollar aircraft within inches of each other. A fully operational hangar bay is a wonder to behold.

"Fossil burners," like USS Independence, had to be refueled on a regular basis, compared to more modern nuclear-powered carriers that require refueling every 20 years. But regardless of the carrier's fuel needs, the air wing stationed on the carrier couldn't go anywhere without jet fuel, and today's nuclear aircraft carriers can store over 3 million gallons of it.

In Jon's day, only men were allowed to serve on carriers. The long deployments made each day at sea seem much like the day before. The ship-based crew that worked below the upper decks could go weeks at a time without seeing the light of day. The only way to communicate with folks back home was through snail mail, with the emphasis on "snail." The monotony of carrier life was broken up by a few ports of call, Saturday pizza nights, or the occasional steel beach party where the flight deck turned into a mega barbecue picnic. But these distractions were few and far between.

One bizarre distraction for Jon and the entire ship's crew happened when USS Independence sailed over the equator. Following naval tradition dating back hundreds of years and common to Sailors from around the world, King Neptune and his court "arrived" on the ship for the Line Crossing Ceremony where new Sailors (called "slimy pollywogs") had to endure humiliation, like crawling through nasty food scraps and wearing clothes inside out, before they could become trusty shellbacks and Sons of Neptune. On their next cruise, the newly christened shellbacks could enjoy dishing out the fun to slimy pollywogs.

While passing through the Suez Canal on the journey home, called doing "The Ditch," Jon reflected on his first tour at sea. His time in Gonzo Station had shown him a part of the world that he'd never known before. He sure knew more about being an NFO than he did when he was training with RVAW-120. He had no regrets about switching careers and joining the Navy and could see himself rising in the ranks and achieving the success he'd always wanted. But what would life hold for him when he returned home?

He'd been married for less than six months before the Indy started her Indian Ocean cruise, and for much of that time, he was away on workups for days on end. Letters from his new bride were terse and critical, and the separation was causing serious strains in their fragile relationship. His wife had to handle unexpected storm damage to their roof and manage to make ends meet on Jon's meager ensign salary while far from family and all alone. Hopefully, when he returned, he could make up for his six months at sea and get his marriage back on track.

But USS Independence still had a few weeks of sailing left before the air wing departed the carrier in mass for the traditional Fly-In and welcome home. He was already making a list of what he would need to do when he returned, but for now, Jon could list at least two major accomplishments from his first deployment—he was no longer a slimy pollywog or a nugget.

CHAPTER 6

Single and Searching

As I finished my senior year at Wake Forest, I was faced with several harsh realities. For one, even though I left the cheerleading squad behind, my eating disorder still had a grip on me. Because I had starved myself for so long, my metabolism ratcheted down, so I needed less and less to keep going. Once I began to eat normal amounts, I gained weight and gained it quickly, becoming chunky and unattractive. I turned back to my calorie-counting ways, but with my body screaming for food, it didn't last long. Sometimes I tried to break free from the madness and eat whatever I wanted in a bingeing craze, but depression and disgust came crashing in and once again the anorexic/bulimic cycle consumed me.

My job prospects after college didn't look promising either. My Wake Forest education was top-notch, but to be more marketable in my chosen major, mass communications, I needed additional experience and skill. A master's program seemed like a logical solution, but where?

This raised another issue: I hoped to find someone to love me along the way, but not just any man. I wanted a man of faith to love me—someone like my own father—a godly man who would be devoted to me in the same way that my dad was devoted to my mom. But I needed to find a place that had more men of the marrying type and ones that shared my Christian faith. My relationship with God, which had taken a backburner to my pursuit of happiness, was something that I was being drawn to again. I was ready to return to my spiritual roots and try to find the peace that had eluded me for so long.

When I looked for master's programs in mass communications, one choice seemed to check all my boxes: CBN University, associated with the Christian Broadcasting Network, in beautiful Virginia Beach, Virginia. Their program looked extremely promising, and the student body would be packed with eligible Christian men. And surely my failing faith would flourish in the university's spiritual atmosphere.

Despite my struggles, I loved my years at Wake Forest, but it was time to turn the page on my crazy college days and step into a more mature future. I only hoped, as I left the "Demon Deacons" behind, that my own personal demons wouldn't follow me on my new path.

Jon's path at the time was leading him to a new assignment, a task that he found challenging, yet fulfilling, and would bring him one step closer to me.

Put to the Test

06 JUNE 1983
0900 EASTERN TIME ZONE
COMOPTEVFOR
NAS NORFOLK
NORFOLK, VIRGINIA, USA
36.92.59 N, 76.29.22 W

Once again, Jon felt like a kid in a candy store. After his stint with USS Independence and the Steeljaws of VAW-122, Jon left his three-year sea duty behind and started his next shore tour at the Navy's Commander Operational Test and Evaluation Force (COMOPTEVFOR) in Norfolk, Virginia. Working down the road from

where he had started his E-2C training years before
with RVAW-120, Jon remembered how excited he had been
to get his hands on the Hawkeye's advanced technology
as an NFO in training. Here at COMOPTEVFOR, Jon had
a similar feeling but even more so. This time, he
didn't just get to enjoy the candy; he was working
behind the scenes at the candy factory, getting to
taste the latest flavors and deciding if they were
good enough to share with the other children.

COMOPTEVFOR performed a critical job for the Navy
and the Department of Defense. Its mission was to
test and evaluate ships, systems, weapons, and other
essential items under real-life conditions and judge
their effectiveness, durability, and affordability.
Everything the Navy needed to carry out its mission
was tested, from the latest destroyer ship to ordinary
life vests. Every tester asked three basic questions:
1) Is what we're testing better than the system that
it was designed to replace? 2) Can we support it? and
3) Can we afford it?

COMOPTEVFOR's green light was like the Good
Housekeeping seal of approval. Without it, nothing
could be rolled out or receive funding. Testers of
any rank, even though they briefed high-position
Pentagon officials, had the power to say whether
something passed or failed. To fulfill its mission,
COMOPTEVFOR required the efforts of both civilian and
active-duty personnel. Jon's role as an E-2C NFO was
as an Operational Test Director of the E-2C Airborne
Early Warning Projects, and his work was considered
classified.

He'd been thrown into the deep end when his
deployment with COMOPTEVFOR began back in April. He'd
left the Steeljaws feeling highly confident, having
earned his CICO designation and rising in rank from a
lowly O-1 ensign all the way to an O-3 lieutenant and

ranking No. 1 out of 14 lieutenants in the squadron. But when he arrived at the testing center, a major operational test was already underway, and he had to jump in and get up to speed much faster than was usually expected of junior Air Warfare Division officers. But Jon buckled down. He leaned heavily on his Nebraska-farmer work ethic and problem-solving skills to become a valued participant in the test, earning the respect of his commanding officer as well as other military support and civilian personnel.

In this demanding environment, Jon's natural tactical skills were unleashed. Instead of playing chess with a king, bishops, and knights, he was using advanced radar and other technologies to maximize the E-2C's unique capabilities in an active wartime environment. He relished the opportunity to benefit the entire VAW community, knowing the fruits of his efforts would be rolled out across the entire fleet. He also cherished the fact that his opinions were sought out and respected, giving him affirmation that he was a valued asset to the testing team.

If only Jon were as successful in his personal life. After his first sea duty, Jon had hoped he could patch up things with his wife before he went to sea again, a year down the road. But as his second cruise on USS Independence drew near, his optimism faded—the strain between his wife and him increased. The Navy life wasn't easy and his wife was struggling with Jon's long absences. This time the Indy was headed to the Mediterranean Sea with several ports of call planned along the way, and Jon and his wife decided to arrange for her to meet him at one of them. Perhaps being able to spend some time together in the middle of his deployment would make the six-month separation easier to handle.

Those ports of call were suddenly put into jeopardy when Israel invaded Lebanon as the Indy put out to sea, forcing the U.S. Navy's Sixth Fleet to change the Indy's mission. They were tasked to support a contingent of U.S. Marines sent to the region as part of a multinational peacekeeping force. USS Independence spent many weeks in this southeast part of the Med known as "Bagel Station," remaining vigilant and prepared to assist the Marines based onshore at a moment's notice.

By the time USS Independence could finally enjoy their ports of call, Jon was anxiously anticipating a much-needed reunion with his wife. But instead of welcoming him with open arms, she greeted him with divorce papers in her hand. The weeks that Jon was away on workups and the long months at sea were too much for her to handle. The stresses of Navy life had taken a toll, and their young marriage lasted over two years. Jon was crushed. He knew their relationship was in trouble, but he certainly hadn't expected this.

When the cruise was over, Jon returned home with a heavy heart and tried to convince his wife to change her mind, but his efforts were in vain. She had already moved on with her life and had no interest in being married to a man who was rarely home. Jon was the first person in his family to get a divorce, and he found no pride in this distinction. Months would go by before he even told his family the sad news.

Perhaps that was why the respect and affirmation Jon received during his tour of duty at the Navy's testing center meant so much to him. Jon felt like a failure, and the success he had working on the various important projects for the E-2C was like applying salve to an open wound. At age 28, this unattached Sailor was lonely, but he didn't want to rush into another long-term relationship. Jon realized that not every woman was cut out for the stress of Navy life, but he hoped that somewhere out there was a woman who could earn his seal of approval and, in turn, he could earn hers.

Plans Gone Wrong

While Jon was enjoying his tour at COMOPTEVFOR, coming to CBN University was a calculated step I took on my path to success. I was convinced that surrounding myself with Christian professionals would give me a better chance of finding a husband and help me get my chaotic life back on track. But things didn't work out exactly as planned. At age 21, I was the youngest student enrolled in their master's program. Most of my classmates were considerably older than I was, and many of them were married with kids. Not exactly the best husband-hunting environment.

I also didn't count on feeling uncomfortable in this Christian-saturated culture. Some fellow students would participate in late-night Bible studies and multi-hour prayer sessions, but I simply wanted to focus on my studies, earn good grades, and make enough money at odd jobs to cover my expenses. These super-Christians were so much more serious about their faith than I was, and I just couldn't relate.

One positive change that I experienced was the healing power of contemporary Christian music. It was a new world to me, and I surrounded myself with the songs of Amy Grant, Russ Taff, DeGarmo and Key, and the Sweet Comfort Band. My eating disorder followed me to Virginia Beach, but the music of these artists, along with many others, planted the seeds of healing in my shattered soul.

I finished my master's degree in communications in a record 18 months. The only thing left to do was to complete my dissertation, but there was no rush to do so. I needed to focus on finding a job—a real one—not the dead-end side jobs that I'd had to pay my way through grad school.

But finding a decent-paying job in the mass communications sector proved difficult. I searched earnestly for jobs in Charlotte, North Carolina, where many of my Wake Forest friends had relocated, but my attempts proved futile. Then a job opened in Virginia Beach at a weekly fashion publication called Port Folio. Owned by the Landmark Corporation, its market covered the area from Williamsburg to Virginia Beach, also known as Hampton Roads. Port Folio featured local political issues, sections for arts, entertainment, and travel, along with restaurant and movie reviews, personal and classified ads, and the like. They were looking for an advertising account executive, and working on commission for a magazine that was only two years old was attractive to me.

As Charlotte was clearly a closed door, I decided to take the Port Folio job in spring 1985. Finally, years of classes, studying, and test-taking were behind me, and I could focus on one full-time job. Surely with the pressures of school and job hunting behind me, my long-term eating disorder would become a distant memory.

But my inner despair only worsened. While many of my college friends were sending me wedding invitations, I was giving up on ever finding true love. Disgusted with my distorted body image and growing weary of my eating disorder, I briefly despaired of life itself. I was the lowest that I had ever been, and my internal demons had replaced my fun-loving personality with brokenness and distress. Life was not turning out as I had planned.

My job at Port Folio, while not the high-profile one I'd dreamed of when I was younger, was a bright spot in my otherwise drab life. I was finally making real money and started a savings program to give myself a more secure financial future. I enjoyed the office atmosphere and many of my fellow workers were young, single women like me. We'd laugh and joke around with each other, and after working there a few months, we became good friends. But I had no idea that these friends would do me the biggest favor of my life.

I wasn't the only one striking out in the love department. Not far from me was a lonely Sailor who was about to make a significantly fateful decision.

Blind Date Gone Wrong

25 MAY 1985
2315 EASTERN TIME ZONE
HAMPTON ROADS, VIRGINIA, USA
36.88.68 N, 76.23.40 W

"I'm glad that's over," Jon sighed in relief as he pulled his little silver pickup truck into his driveway and turned off the ignition. He shook his head in disbelief as he thought of the evening's disappointing end. Yet another blind date gone wrong. From the start it was clear that he had absolutely nothing in common with the latest fix-up from a well-meaning friend. She was attractive enough, but why his friend thought the two of them would be a good match, Jon had no idea.

He'd been hopeful when he first noticed his slender and nicely dressed date, as she entered the restaurant and joined him at their corner table. But as soon as she opened her mouth, all hopes were dashed. She didn't ask him a single question the entire evening. She talked nonstop about how much she hated her ex and how she thought football was totally ridiculous. And as a die-hard Cornhusker fan, Jon didn't need to hear another word to know she wasn't the one for him.

At least the painful date was over, but it didn't bring Jon any closer to what he was looking for. Jon knew there had to be a better way to find meaningful female companionship. He had tried the bar scene, and that didn't go well either, even when he had a trusty wingman by his side. How could a highly trained NFO like himself know how to detect all types of aircraft from 300 miles away and not be able to find one compatible woman in a metro area of nearly a million people?

Perhaps he'd been going about this dating thing all wrong, Jon realized. It was time for him to put his extensive training and problem-solving skills to work once again. How could he decrease the false hits of incompatible dates and increase the probabilities of successful ones? As he entered his house and flopped down on the couch in dismay, something lying on the coffee table caught his eye. He reached over and picked it up. It was the latest edition of a free weekly paper called Port Folio, the magazine of Hampton Roads. As he thumbed through the pages, he paused when he reached the personal ads in the back.

Long before there were Internet matchmaking sites and dating apps, people looking for love turned to the trusty personal ads found in the classified sections

of nearly every newspaper. These short and simple notices used a special code to quickly communicate essential information: "S" stood for single, "F" for female, "M" for male, "D" for divorced, "W" for white, "B" for black, and so on. A DWM was a divorced, white male who might be looking for an SWF. Jon wasn't sure what he would find in the personal ads, but he couldn't do worse than his latest blind date.

"Cross-eyed cutie, DWF, 37, secretary, seeking attractive, SWM professional to share summer days and nights. Must be good with children and love cats. If it lasts, great; if it doesn't, it wasn't meant to be. Photo and letter please. Box 8345."

Jon frowned as he read it. He couldn't believe that someone would actually describe herself as a "cross-eyed cutie." Definitely not the one for him. He read the next one:

"I'm not a movie star, but I'm a tall, slim, blue-eyed blond, 28, looking for a tall, sensitive SWM 26-36, non-smoker, who enjoys dancing, dining out, and sports. Gentlemen with brains and sense of humor preferred. Photo appreciated. Box 8134."

That one sounded more promising. As he continued reading through the ads, he began to smile. Here was exactly what Jon was looking for: a concise list of nearby available females, along with their descriptions, occupations, likes and dislikes, and specifics on what they were looking for in a man. This reminded Jon of his role in the E-2C where his radar would identify aircraft, and his light pen would pull up the "bogey dope" on each target.

Jon wasn't sure about the accuracy of the "bogey dope" each "target" provided in the personal ads. Was "Incurable Romantic" really in great shape and was "Streisand Eyes" witty and affectionate? Who knew, but it had to be better than his current companion-seeking process. He'd rather sit on the couch and sort through these personal ads than hang out in a bar and hope the right one strolled by. All Jon had to do was send a letter and a photo of himself to the paper, reference that ad's box number, and wait to see if he received a response. It sounded like a plan.

Jon was ready for his personal life to match his professional one. At work, Jon felt confident, competent, and valuable. And he was growing in his skills and responsibilities. He was scheduled to receive training as a casualty assistance calls officer (CACO). These were the officers that had to personally notify the next of kin when a service member was injured or died in the line of duty. A CACO walked alongside the affected families, helping with funeral arrangements and guiding them through the necessary paperwork to receive the benefits they were due. It was a solemn responsibility that Jon hoped he never had to carry out. For now, Jon's work hours were often spent on a United States Air Force (USAF) E-3A AWACS, a modified Boeing 707, flying sorties as a weapon systems operator during operational testing missions.

In spite of his Navy achievements, Jon was growing restless. His job couldn't give him the internal satisfaction he desired, and at age 30, he was ready to share his life with someone special. Almost two years had gone by since his painful divorce, and the bachelor life was getting old. He took another glance at the Port Folio personal ads and decided it was time to act. The first decision was easy: "Cross-eyed cutie" clearly would not make the short list.

CHAPTER 7

Green-Eyed Lady

Summertime came to Virginia Beach, and my coworkers and I were looking for a little fun to liven up the atmosphere around the Port Folio office. It all began when one of our coworkers confessed that she had been thinking of running a personal ad in our paper. We were all a bit surprised, as this gal seemed to have no trouble finding dates. I was even more surprised when she suggested that all of us girls should run our own personal ads at the same time!

We looked at one another and, instantly, several girls were very enthusiastic about the idea, but I wasn't one of them. I always thought those ads were so cheesy. Only losers resorted to such tactics, and I told them so. Their stories of happy couples who had met that way didn't change my mind. But when one of the copywriters offered to write my ad, after I gave the excuse that I wouldn't know what to say, I finally gave in.

Before the day was over, the other four girls had their ads ready to submit. My copywriter friend smiled broadly when she handed over a draft ad for me. I scanned through it quickly, making sure she had the facts straight, but it wasn't quite what I expected. There was a word she used to describe me that I didn't think guys would understand, so I asked her to remove it. But she insisted that it stay. She explained that it would make me sound "exotic and mysterious." I reluctantly agreed, as I was not putting much confidence into the whole experiment anyway. What could possibly come from a tiny personal ad other than a handful of "sorry" letters from a few desperate men?

"Tawny"

17 JULY 1985
1845 EASTERN TIME ZONE
HAMPTON ROADS, VIRGINIA, USA
36.88.68 N, 76.23.40 W

Sitting on his couch, Jon was ready to kick back and relax after a long day at COMOPTEVFOR. He'd been working extra hours on the E-2C Update Program (UDP), including preparing briefs for high-level meetings, based in part on his evaluations. The assignment was important and required Jon's detailed focus and his total commitment to delivering quality weapons systems to the fleet. But the work left him exhausted, and he was looking forward to clearing his mind before he hit the rack.

He ran his fingers through his short, bowl-cut, blond hair and rested his elbows on his knees. On the coffee table in front of him, he noticed that week's edition of the Port Folio news magazine. He knit his brow as he hesitated to pick it up and look inside. His new strategy for finding a mate had not gone as planned. He'd sent several letters in response to various personal ads, and the two dates he'd gone on had left him feeling miserable and discouraged. Perhaps it was time to rethink his strategy. He sighed and figured that it couldn't hurt to at least determine if an ad merited his attention.

Most of the ads printed in the personals section were by men looking for women, and some of them were hilarious. Jon laughed when he read, "Adam gave up a rib to get Eve, but with today's inflation, she'd be worth two thigh bones." He wondered how many responses SWM, 26, had received for that entry.

He passed over the ad posted by "Outer Banks," the SWF who was 40, 170 pounds, and needed lots of TLC, and the "Peninsula Beauty" seeking an educated, professional gentleman between 40 and 55. Then he saw one that piqued his interest. He read it once, and then he read it again:

"GREEN-EYED LADY. SWF, 23, advertising account executive, tawny, athletic, energetic, and fun. Looking for SWM, 26-35, who has "IT," that elusive quality that can only be recognized, never defined. He should also be educated, artistic, funny, and attractive. No machos, no wimps need to apply. Box #6575."

Jon scratched his head and said to himself, "Tawny. What the heck does that even mean?"

He read the ad a third time and did some simple calculations. This gal was the right age, and she had a job. She was tawny, whatever that meant, and it sounded like she would be a good match for his own high-energy personality. He was in the age range she specified. He didn't know if he had "IT" or not, but he was college educated and well known by his friends for having a great sense of humor. No one had ever accused Jon of being a wimp. As an avid cyclist, he often rode his bike 25 miles one way to work, but he doubted that biking or his one-armed pushups would qualify him as macho. He wasn't sure about the artistic or attractive requirement, but maybe she'd be so overwhelmed with his "IT" factor that she wouldn't notice.

Tawny. That word intrigued him. He still wasn't sure what "tawny" meant, but he'd like to find out. He fought the doubts of writing yet another letter to a mysterious woman on the other end of a personal ad but decided to give it one more try. He leaned forward to compose his response. He found a recent picture of himself with some friends and grinned as he wrote a quick note to tell her which one was him. As he looked for an envelope, he hoped that, although he'd struck out twice before, maybe the third time would be the charm.

Jackpot

A week went by and then one morning as I walked through the door at the Port Folio office, I could see the other girls giving me funny looks and grinning from ear to ear. What was their problem, I wondered. Did I have dog hair on my skirt? I had a new puppy at home, a black terrier mix that I'd rescued from the pound, named Sophie. I adored my little puppy giving me love and affection. But I had been so preoccupied with house training her that I had dismissed the personal ad completely.

When I got to my desk, I found out why they were smiling so much. For there, stacked in a pile, was a massive mound of letters. More than 60 of them. I had hit the jackpot. I wasn't the only one with a stack of responses, but my ad had brought in the most. My copywriter friend was all smiles.

We eagerly began opening the envelopes and reading our letters. We soon realized that we had quite an advantage over the regular Port Folio subscriber, since we could compare each other's responses. Did some guys respond to every ad? Yes, they did, in fact, with the very same letter. I threw all of those out, along with any respondents with kids. Having a puppy was a big enough job without adding children to the mix. Over our lunch break, we compared photos and letters and helped each other prioritize responses.

For me, I was looking for an established, professional type and decided to start with a graduate from West Point, an Army officer. On my girlfriends' advice, I suggested that we first meet at a public place, and he agreed. The guy was very nice but not really my type. Although I was impressed with his West Point education and career possibilities, he seemed a bit dull and uninteresting. He definitely did not have "IT." There was no chemistry between us at all. I could mark him off my list.

My second choice was another Army officer and West Point grad, but all he wanted to talk about that evening was politics—not my favorite subject. And to top it all off, it turned out that he was good friends with date No. 1. Out of 60 letters, how did I end up picking the two of them? Another matchmaking blunder.

But I wasn't a quitter, so I was willing to give it another try. Living in a military community, I had quite a few servicemen who responded to my ad, and I decided to choose a different branch of the service. I sorted through the letters and found one from a Navy officer, an aviator, who also owned several homes for rental income. At least this one had some business sense. He had included a photo of a group— three guys, looking impressive in their Navy dress whites, along with a girl in a fabulous dress. Obviously, they were attending some formal function. The attached note said, "I'm the good-looking one." I smiled. So he had a sense of humor as well. Of the three guys pictured, none of them were bad looking, so I might as well give him a chance. His name was Jon.

When I dialed his number, Jon wasn't home. Not quite ready to give out my name, I left a message that said the "green-eyed lady" called and I gave my phone number. It wasn't long before "the good-looking one" gave me a call. After my lackluster experiences with the Army officers, I wasn't as eager to go on a date, so we talked on the phone several times, taking time to get to know a little bit about each other.

It turned out that Jon loved dogs, and with his past experience as a Norwegian elkhound dog breeder, he gave me helpful advice for my new puppy. A few weeks later, when Jon asked to meet in person, I agreed. Like before, I asked to meet somewhere in public first, which also provided opportunity to duck out early if I decided that this was another dating disaster. We chose the next Monday evening to meet at Darryl's, a casual restaurant in Virginia Beach. I was hopeful, yet at the same time wary.

When I arrived at the restaurant, I caught my reflection in the glass of the entrance door. I had dressed cute for the evening, but I was still a little heavyset from my eating disorder. Hopefully, Jon wouldn't notice. To this point, I still hadn't seen Jon in person, so I wondered how I would find him. But when I walked inside, there was a man sitting at the table nearest the door. One look at me and he stood up, walked over, and held out his hand.

"Kris?" he smiled.

"Yeah. Jon?" I asked, as we shook hands. As he led me to our table, my first impressions of him were somewhat promising. To be honest, the "good-looking one" wasn't that attractive, but his athletic build was noticeably appealing. He had dressed nice for our meeting, and I was flattered by his effort. His clothing choices of a short-sleeved, baby-blue pinstriped dress shirt with white, summer cotton pants were a flattering look. I tried to look past his distinctively sharp nose, slight facial scarring, and military-bowl-cut blond hair in an effort to perhaps make a new friend.

Our lengthy conversations on the phone over the past few weeks had stirred my curiosity, and I wasn't going to dismiss him this early in the evening simply because he didn't look like a GQ model. What happened next, however, took me by surprise. As we sat down, he looked at me, turned his head slightly to the side, and said, "You know, you remind me of someone," he paused, thinking of the name. "Brenda Vaccaro."

"Who?"

"You know, the actress with the husky voice?"

Jon could tell by the confused expression on my face that I had absolutely no idea who he was talking about, and if he meant it as a compliment, he was failing miserably. I realized that he was 7 years older than me, which meant it must be a generational thing that I wasn't familiar with the actress. Anyway, it was an awkward moment for both of us.

Jon realized his social blunder, and after a few painful seconds, he simply said, "Hold it." He stood up and calmly walked out of the restaurant. I was so taken aback—I didn't know what to do—but as I turned around, I saw him walk straight back in, cool-headed and unflappable, with a smile on his face. He approached me and held out his hand.

"Let's try this again. Kris?"

I had to laugh as we shook hands for the second time, and Jon took his seat. Not only did he have a sense of humor but also a sense of confidence. The ice finally broken, we started talking, introducing ourselves to each other. And we kept on talking. We even closed down Darryl's and moved on to a beach restaurant that stayed open later.

I learned a lot about Jon that night, like how his parents were humble farmers in Nebraska, which probably explained Jon's pickup truck. How he'd been a state runner-up in wrestling, twice, in a state where wrestling is everything. His year of teaching high school math and how he'd made the decision to join the Navy. His failed marriage with a college sweetheart who wasn't cut out for the Navy life.

But the most important things I learned weren't about Jon's background but about who he was. From the first moments we met, his humor and confidence were obvious. And as the evening went on, I was able to look past the bad haircut and acne scars to see a genuinely kind, personable, intelligent, and wise man. By his appearance and his vehicle choice, Jon was clearly a down-to-earth guy. As we got to know each other on that late-summer night, I couldn't help but wonder if I had met the man who had "IT," that elusive quality that can only be recognized and never defined. I did know, however, that for the first time in my life, I had met a man who cared more about others than himself.

I liked him, but he wasn't really the successful, handsome, professional man of my dreams. At the time, I had no idea what it took to become a naval flight officer, and I certainly had no clue about Jon's specialized skills. He was a true professional in every sense of the word, but I was looking for a man in a suit and tie who ran a successful business or had a C-Suite title. After so many years of searching for my preconceived idea of "Mr. Right," I had trouble seeing Jon as my "Prince Charming." But then, how did Jon view me? Could he see a chunky, somewhat dysfunctional 24-year-old as his dream-come-true? I wondered what caused him to respond to my ad in the first place, so I asked him.

"It was that word you used, 'tawny,'" he replied with a grin. "I found it intriguing." I confessed that my copywriter friend at the office had come up with the word, and it was fitting as my summer skin had taken on a golden tan from the weekend beach days. He seemed to like what he saw.

Even though I had some reservations, I didn't resist when he kissed me as we finally said our goodbyes and went our separate ways. The evening was far better than any I'd had in some time, but this was not love at first sight. As I drove home through the nearly empty streets of Virginia Beach, I decided that if he asked me out again, I'd probably say "yes." But I wondered exactly how far this relationship realistically could go?

Everything's Coming Up Roses

20 AUG 1985
0912 Eastern Time Zone
COMOPTEVFOR
NAS Norfolk
Norfolk, VIRGINIA, USA
36.92.59 N, 76.29.22 W

"What's up with Rystrom?" whispered one young officer after Jon walked by, whistling a little tune. "I've never seen him like this before."

"Me neither," another responded. Jon's jovial spirit wasn't anything new, but today he'd taken it to a whole new level. As Jon sat down at his desk, he took a deep breath and smiled. On his morning bike ride in to COMOPTEVFOR, the birds were singing louder, the sky was bluer, and all seemed right with the world. At last, after months—no, make that years of fruitless searching—he'd found a woman that touched his heart. August 19, 1985, would forever remain one of the best days of his life.

He couldn't explain it, but from the moment he'd looked into her big, green eyes, Jon knew that Kris was a gem. And by the time the evening ended, he knew that "the one" he'd been looking for was "green-eyed lady." He'd also found out what "tawny" meant, and he decided he liked it. He liked it a lot.

There was no way Jon that was going to let this one get away. Now that he had a fish on the line, it was time to set the hook. What could he do to show Kris how much he had enjoyed their evening together? And how could he do it for maximum impact?

A light bulb went off in Jon's mind as he grabbed the Yellow Pages and began his search. He hummed to himself as he flipped through the pages: fencing, flooring, florists. He scanned through the florist ads, picked one, and grinned as he dialed the number.

"Yes, I'd like to place an order, please."

He's a Keeper

Due to the late night, I was a little tired at work the next day, but all my friends wanted to hear about my date with Jon. They all cringed when I told them about the Brenda Vaccaro comment but smiled when I told them how he'd handled it and how we'd talked until the wee hours of the morning. At our lunch break, they pressed me for more details, and they agreed that he seemed to be a genuinely nice guy. But I told them that he really wasn't my type and that I didn't think we could be much more than friends.

I had to rethink those words later, when a gorgeous vase of a dozen, long-stemmed, red roses was delivered to my desk. His attached card read: "Thanks for the special evening. Jon."

As my coworkers oohed and aahed over the lovely bouquet, I realized that Jon had been wise to send the roses to my office instead of my home, knowing that my fellow office workers would be impressed at his romantic gesture and sing his praises. But it would take more than a dozen roses to win my heart.

Jon wasted no time in asking me out again, and before long, Jon and I were spending more and more time together. Sophie became a part of our relationship, and through our common love of dogs, I could see more and more of Jon's tender, loving nature. I was beginning to warm up to this lively, funny, pick-up-driving Nebraskan, but I still had my reservations. However, Jon's influence on my life was having effects on me that even others began to notice.

A coworker pulled me aside one day and asked me if I had been losing weight. When I got home, I hopped on the scales and saw that I'd lost 10 pounds without even trying. I was amazed. My anorexic/bulimic cycle had been fading away as my relationship with Jon grew deeper. Soon after we started dating, I had confessed to him my struggle with a distorted body image.

"Don't you think I'm fat?" I fearfully asked him.

"No," he replied, shaking his head with a smile. "You're sturdy."

His matter-of-fact response made me realize that Jon didn't have an issue with my weight and, in time, I began to see myself the same way. Jon's approach to food was freeing as well. He was an excellent cook and sometimes, instead of eating out, he'd fix delicious meals for the two of us. Before long, I was eating three regular meals a day and joining Jon for bike rides, beach walks, and tennis games. But it was Jon's unconditional love and acceptance that made all the difference. Now that I was feeling valued and no longer focusing on achieving and performing, the weight came off. The grip of my six-year eating disorder was finally being broken by the gentle love of one special man.

In the same way that Jon helped me with my eating disorder, I helped Jon get back in touch with his faith. I invited him to join me at First Baptist Church Norfolk on Sundays, and I could see how his heart was being awakened by God's love. Growing up as a weekly church attendee, I knew much more about the Bible and spiritual truth than he did, and yet so little of that truth had penetrated my own heart. As we experienced God together, both of us were finding new meaning in our spiritual lives.

Even with all of the good that was happening between us, I still wasn't sure that Jon was the man for me. Giving up my long-held image of "Mr. Right" was proving hard to do. I needed some clarity and an objective opinion on our relationship. We'd been dating for a few months now, and Thanksgiving was approaching. Perhaps it was time to take Jon back to Charleston, West Virginia, to meet my parents. Maybe they would see Jon in ways that I couldn't. And I could introduce my parents to Sophie as well.

Jon, a very relational guy, was enthusiastic about meeting my parents and looked forward to having Thanksgiving with my family.

My dad had been an enlisted Sailor in the Navy in his younger days, so I knew the two of them would have plenty in common. But I didn't know quite how much.

My parents met both Jon and Sophie with open arms, and right away Jon and my dad hit it off like long-lost buddies. Mom and I came up with a nickname for them: "the friends." For the rest of the weekend, the friends spent hours playing chess and cribbage and reliving Dad's old Navy days. They couldn't have gotten along any better.

As the weekend wound down and Mom and I were in the kitchen together, I asked her what she thought of Jon. She got a misty look in her eyes and smiled.

"Krissy, the first time I saw him hold your puppy, I knew that he was a keeper."

Mom had an innate sense of people that I cherished, and her words helped me see Jon through her eyes. Jon's bonding with my dad wasn't something he was pretending to do just for my benefit. Their connection was genuine and warm, and the way he honored my father and enjoyed his company spoke volumes about Jon's character. And I couldn't deny that since Jon came into my life, I'd experienced peace and contentment as never before. It was as if I were allowed to have my "ugly" stage so that I could meet Jon. And I was so thankful I had. That Thanksgiving trip to Charleston provided the clarity that I needed. Jon was a keeper. On the way home, I could finally tell this blue-eyed, down-to-earth Swede: "I think I'm falling in love with you."

CHAPTER 8

Welcome to the Navy, Mrs. Rystrom!

Bicycle Ride

07 DEC 1985
1500 EASTERN TIME ZONE
HAMPTON ROADS, VIRGINIA, USA
36.88.68 N, 76.23.40 W

Jon bent down to check the air pressure in his bicycle tires as he prepared for a late afternoon ride. He had a lot on his mind, and it would feel good to burn off some nervous energy in the cool December air while he sorted through a jumble of thoughts and emotions. His tour at COMOPTEVFOR was very successful but coming to an end. He'd been a major force in the development of the E-2C Updated Development Program and the testing of APS-138, 139, and 145 radars. He'd written the final report on a highly classified, sensitive project, all while fulfilling his myriad of other duties. Other fleet E-2C aircrews were coming to him for advice on tactics and how to best utilize the Hawkeye's unique weapons system. His high-performing unit had been awarded the Naval Unit Commendation a few months earlier.

But now it was time to look to the future. In six months, Jon's shore duty would end, and he'd discussed his options with his detailer. Only yesterday, Jon received his new orders. It seemed the Navy needed him to transfer to San Diego, California, beginning with RAG (Replacement Air Group) refresher training at Miramar Naval Air Station and then on to sea duty with VAW-114 Hormel Hawgs and the carrier USS Carl Vinson.

This was no surprise to Jon. Navy careers alternated between three years of sea duty and three years of shore duty, but the timing and choice of assignment weren't the best for Jon's personal life. He'd met Kris less than four months ago, and he'd much prefer to allow their budding relationship to grow gently over time. If his sea duty had been based out of Norfolk, very little would need to change in their relationship at least for the next year. But having to move thousands of miles away to California meant that Jon had to consider some significant issues much sooner than expected.

As Jon mounted his bike and his legs worked through the gears, his mind worked through the situation. He didn't even question whether he wanted to continue his relationship with Kris. He couldn't imagine life without her. Could he and Kris maintain a bicoastal relationship? That didn't seem practical or desirable. But would she be willing to leave her job and friends behind and follow him to California? That would require a higher commitment from both of them. And were they ready to take their relationship to the next level, or was it too soon to ask Kris for that kind of commitment?

Kris had several qualities that would suit her well as a Navy wife. She was independent, strong, self-assured, and outgoing. She knew how to handle her own finances and had the beginnings of a promising career. She was always ready for new adventures and knew how to establish a network of close friends. Even her parents were amazing, and Jon had instantly connected with Kris' father when he'd visited them over Thanksgiving. To top it off, Kris was absolutely gorgeous, and she even shared his love for dogs. If a NATOPS manual had been written for the perfect Navy spouse, Kris would have met every requirement. What more could he ask for?

But Jon knew how hard the Navy life could be. Kris didn't. Was it fair for him to ask her to make that level of sacrifice? He loved her deeply, and the last thing he wanted to do was hurt her. He had experienced the intense pain of a broken relationship caused by extended deployments, and he didn't want to put himself or anyone else through that again. Was the love they shared strong enough to endure the stresses that his career would bring?

Not only would Kris have to choose to join Jon's life, but also he had to choose to join hers. From the beginning of their relationship, Jon understood that faith was clearly a priority for Kris. But was Jon willing to make faith a priority as well? Over the weeks and months that they had known each other, Jon had felt a rekindling of faith in his heart. He remembered going to a church camp when he was a teen and responding to a tug inside of him, pulling him toward God and His grace. While that was a genuine experience for Jon, years of neglect and outward focus had diminished that flame to a dim flicker.

But that little spark had been rekindled after being with Kris, attending church services with her, and hearing once again of God's amazing love and mercy. And while Jon still had many questions about spiritual matters, he could not deny the growing desire in his spirit to grow closer to Christ. Could a relationship with God be a part of the "more" that he had been looking for all along?

As the sweat ran down Jon's face and his feet spun the pedals, he knew it was decision time for him and for Kris. The path forward wasn't completely clear, but he couldn't deny the growing love in his heart. And whatever the future may hold, was she the woman to join him in the journey?

Jon came to an intersection and faced a fork in the road. Which way should he go? And that was the question he had to answer: Which way should he go?

40 or 50 Years

As we rang in the New Year of 1986 together, Jon and I both had a lot on our minds. Was he serious about me joining him in California as his wife? And if so, was I ready to say yes? Those questions were put aside briefly when Jon suffered a slipped disk in his back, forcing him to lie flat on the floor for several days until the disk recovered and the pain subsided. With Jon out of commission, I tried to help him with practical things, but he didn't appreciate my attempt at making him breakfast. With my "hard eggs," I knew that if Jon decided to ask me to marry him, it wouldn't be because of my cooking skills.

Jon's back issues came as a complete surprise, given how physically fit he was. But uncertainty was something no one could avoid. Nothing brought that fact home to me more than an incident that happened soon after Jon recovered from the slipped disk. It was January 28, 1986, when the news came that the space shuttle Challenger had exploded seconds after liftoff.

Like the rest of America, I was deeply saddened to hear about the loss of seven astronauts less than two minutes into their historic mission. NASA had such an outstanding safety record that successful launches and recoveries were taken for granted. Everyone was stunned that something like this could happen, and I could only imagine the pain and suffering that the families of those astronauts must be experiencing, especially when their grief would be on public display. This tragedy hit a little too close to home, knowing that the Challenger's pilot, Michael Smith, was a naval aviator.

As sad as the Challenger tragedy was, life goes on and a special holiday was fast approaching. Being a new couple, I was anxious to see what Jon had planned for our first Valentine's Day together. The morning of February 14 came, and I was sitting at my office desk, as usual, going over my accounts. I heard some of my coworkers whispering together, and I glanced up to see Jon, dressed in his Navy khakis and holding a big box of chocolates in his hand.

He must have been on his way to work and dropped by to wish me a Happy Valentine's Day. That was sweet of him, but it wasn't the first Valentine's Day gift as a couple that I'd been dreaming of. Maybe he had something more exciting planned for that evening. But a big box of chocolates was a good start. I smiled as he came around my desk.

"Would you like a chocolate?" he asked playfully, handing me the large, heart-shaped box.

"I don't mind if I do," I grinned back, removing the lid so that I could see the selections inside. As I gazed at the assortment of truffles, caramels, and fudges, my eyes went to the center section where one chocolate confection had been removed. A beautiful diamond ring had taken its place!

The surprised expression on my face signaled Jon that I realized this was no ordinary box of chocolates, and to the delight of all my coworkers, Jon promptly got on one knee, held my trembling hand, and said, "Krissy, will you marry me?" His twinkling blue eyes met mine in an eager gaze, and my heart skipped a beat as my own eyes began to fill with tears.

"Yes! Yes, of course, I will!" I fervently replied, as several coworkers began wiping away their happy tears. He gently took the chocolates from my hand, lovingly placed the ring on my finger, and the office staff applauded as we sealed the sacred moment with a passionate kiss.

What a surreal moment it was to know that in six months I had gone from sitting in this same office debating on whether I should place an ad in our magazine to now being asked to spend the rest of my life with my personal-ad love. And to think that some people say "advertising doesn't work." I beg to differ.

For years, I'd been trying to put a square peg in a round hole, looking for popular, successful, upper-class guys to fill the void in my soul. But what I'd really needed all along was a man of character and substance—someone who could love me the way my father loved my mother. I'd been envious of all my old friends tying the knot right out of college and despaired of ever finding a soul mate of my own. But I'd found true love at last, and I couldn't have been happier.

Now that I'd said yes, a whirlwind of activity quickly ensued. Jon had to report to his new squadron in California by mid June, so we picked May 3 as our wedding date. This would give us time for a honeymoon and to move across the country. But that gave us less than three months to prepare. To keep things simple, we chose a full military wedding at Dam Neck Naval Base, which had a beautiful gazebo right on the beach for the wedding ceremony, and the nearby officers club was perfect for the reception.

My mother and friends helped me pull all the details together in record time, but I felt like I was living in a dream. After all the years of my personal struggles to find significance and value, I was experiencing for the first time the promise of security and unconditional love from a man who would soon be my husband. Everything was happening so quickly—I wasn't just getting married, I was leaving behind my job, the East Coast, and my old life. Everything would be different right away for Jon and me but, with Sophie in tow, we were anxious to begin our new adventure together.

After our whirlwind engagement, our wedding day arrived. The cool, spring breeze coming in from the ocean was so strong that the musicians had to hold their music in place with clothes pins. Jon's Navy groomsmen, all dignified in their dress whites and sabers, looked comical as they tried in vain to lay down the flimsy bridal aisle runner on the wooden deck leading up to the gazebo. We were surrounded by our close friends and family from different parts of the country. Jon's niece, Sara from Stromsburg, was our adorable flower girl. Jon's Nebraska family joined us to welcome me as the newest Swedish Rystrom. His brother, Martin, and his family made the long trip from Boston for our special occasion as well. It was so sweet seeing Martin's twin boys, Adam and Nick, proudly carry our rings on white pillows down the aisle as my soon-to-be nephews.

JORDYN'S VERSE: ... BUT THEY WHO WAIT FOR THE LORD SHALL RENEW THEIR STRENGTH; THEY SHALL MOUNT UP WITH WINGS LIKE EAGLES; THEY SHALL RUN AND NOT BE WEARY; THEY SHALL WALK AND NOT FAINT. (ISAIAH 40:31 ESV)

As I took my father's arm and walked slowly down the aisle, I could sense his pride and excitement. I was gaining a husband, but my father was gaining not only a son-in-law but also a son. I hoped that my hat wouldn't blow off in a sudden gust, but once I locked eyes with Jon—standing confidently on the gazebo stage and looking so handsome in his Navy dress whites—I forgot all about the wind and the hectic weeks leading up to this special day. This was a moment that I wanted to cherish forever.

As my father took my hand and placed it in Jon's, the robed minister reminded us of the solemn oaths we were about to take.

"Wherefore," he began, addressing all of those gathered, "those who purpose to enter this holy estate should do so with a profound sense of the seriousness of the obligations they are about to assume." He paused and then continued, "A vow and covenant once made should not be broken."

Before he continued with the ceremony, the minister took us by surprise. He lowered his voice so that only Jon and I could hear him, and he shared with us a special story. It was taken from the Gospel of Luke, Chapter 15, and it was the parable about the old lady and the lost coin.

"In those times when you got married, a husband would give his wife 10 coins as a personal act of faithfulness and love—a way to show there's a certain perfection about the marriage that he wants to retain. So when this old woman, who'd been married for many years, lost one of those coins, she was very disturbed and looked for it constantly. And when she found it, she rejoiced because something that was lost was found again." He paused slightly before continuing his remarks.

"The point I want to make is twofold. First, today we're setting a standard of perfection for each other. That's what your vows are all about. You're talking about ideals, the way you'll behave and relate to each other in love and faithfulness for the rest of your lives. It's a standard you want to keep returning to, because in life we tend to lose a coin or two along the way." He smiled, obviously having experienced this himself.

"The second point is this," he continued earnestly. "In the parables of Jesus, we recognize that the main characters are a reflection of God Himself. In this case, God is like the old woman, seeking out a certain perfection, looking to bring back a relationship which He cherishes. God will seek you out throughout your whole marriage and bring you back to that which you confess and share today." The minster smiled as he prepared to bring his private sermon to a close and make his final, most crucial point.

"The key is that we recognize that God has not abandoned us—that He is constantly working to bring us to the point where we share in His joy and happiness as we are today. Because of His death and resurrection, He remains your God and He cherishes you as much as you cherish each other."

His comments were like his own personal wedding gift to us, and both Jon and I were touched by his kind and sincere gesture. His words were still echoing in my heart as Jon and I took our wedding vows.

"Jon, will you have Krista to be your wedded wife to live together after God's ordinance in the holy estate of matrimony? Will you love her, comfort her, honor and obey her, and keep her in sickness and in health and forsaking all others keep unto her so long as you both shall live?"

"I will," Jon promised. I promised the same. The minister had us make one additional vow to each other. Jon went first.

"I, Jon, in the presence of God and this assembly, take thee, Krista, to be my wedded wife and give myself to you in every way, not to part from you till death do us part."

"I, Kris, in the presence of God and this assembly, take thee, Jon, to be my wedded husband and give myself to you in every way, not to part from you till death do us part."

The minister was right. There should be a "profound sense of seriousness" in the vows that we take. As a dewy-eyed bride, I had little idea of the true weight of the promises that Jon and I were making to each other.

After the exchanging of rings, the minister pronounced us husband and wife and gave the final prayer.

"And now, Father, give them strength to keep the vows that they have made to be loyal and faithful to each other and to support each other throughout their lives. May they bear each other's burdens and share each other's joy. Help them to be honest and patient with each other and to be loving and wise parents one day. In all their future together, may they enjoy each other's lives and grow through each other's love. Keep them faithful to You, and at the end of this life on Earth to receive them and us all into Your Heavenly Kingdom. Amen."

The minister turned to Jon and spoke the words we'd all been waiting for.

"You may kiss the bride!"

Jon wasn't one to question orders, and he willingly complied. I was so happy to be Mrs. Krista Rystrom and also relieved that my hat hadn't blown off during the final prayer. With military precision, Jon's fellow officers marched down the aisle before us and created a saber tunnel for us to walk through. As we were about to pass the last two officers in the line, I could feel Jon slowing down, and I was surprised when they lowered their sabers and wouldn't let us pass.

"Welcome to the Navy, Mrs. Rystrom," one groomsman called out, and I felt a sharp, little slap on my bottom as one of them gently swatted me with a saber. Jon laughed with a twinkle in his eye, delighted that I was completely surprised by this traditional introduction to the Navy. I laughed along with him and knew it would be the first of many revelations to come. I had not only married Jon, but I had married the Navy as well. I didn't know at that moment exactly how much that commitment would cost me.

Our reception was filled with congratulatory toasts and joyous smiles. And there were also tears as we were saying goodbye to dear friends before we moved across the country to California. After Jon and I used a saber to cut our wedding cake, he shared his thoughts on this special day with our guests.

"One thing I can tell you," he said with a smile, "is that eight months ago, I wasn't thinking about getting married. And it wasn't until I met this wonderful lady that we clicked, and I'm looking forward to the next 40 or 50 years to have a great time with her."

I felt the same way, as we stepped into our getaway car and headed out on our weeks-long honeymoon at several bed and breakfasts across America. The winds were blowing—blowing us into marriage, out of

Virginia, off to a life together. We were both so certain that after 40 or 50 years, we would only be getting started on loving each other.

Jon and Kris watching a Blue Angels air show at Miramar Naval Air Station.

CHAPTER 9

Highway to the Danger Zone

The earth-shaking rumble of jet engines jolted me from my sleep. In frustration, I glanced over at the alarm clock beside the bed: 2:36 a.m. I looked over at Jon who was sleeping like a baby beside me. How did he do it? I put a pillow over my head in a failed attempt to shut out the noise as another jet passed overhead.

I hated that sound—the sound of F-14 fighter jets going through their paces in the desert air over our new home, a small apartment at Miramar Naval Air Station. Thankfully, we only had to live here a brief time before we could move off base and into a duplex that we had purchased. But until then, I had to endure the constant cacophony of all sorts of aircraft as they carried out their training, day and night, at this massive military airport. Welcome to the Navy, Mrs. Rystrom.

Jon was assigned to Miramar for what he called RAG, or refresher training, required for all aviators before they could reenter active flight. In four short months, Jon was scheduled to join the Hormel Hawgs of VAW-114, which served on the aircraft carrier USS Carl Vinson. Not having much time to enjoy being married before he went to sea was frustrating, and living on base was causing sleep deprivation for me, which caused even more irritation.

Jon knew that I needed an evening out, so he suggested the movie "Top Gun." This popular action flick about Navy fighter pilots had been released while we were on our honeymoon, and Jon was eager to see it. Much of it had been filmed at Miramar, also known as "Fightertown, USA." In real life, Top Gun, the name of the United States Navy Fighter Weapons School, trained naval aviators in fighter and strike tactics. Every day as I drove from work back to our apartment on base, I would pass by the hangar where the real Top Gun was operating. I wasn't nearly as excited as Jon was to see the movie. I'd had my fill of jets, thank you very much. But I didn't want to disappoint him, so I agreed to go.

Surprisingly, from the opening scene of a bustling carrier flight deck, I was hooked. As the high-energy music of Kenny Logins' "Danger Zone" filled the theater, I was seeing Jon's world for the very first time. This was his life. The danger and drama of the missions, the Soviet MIG intercepts, the intense training, the bravado of the men, and, of course, the romantic love story totally transformed the annoying rumble of late-night flyovers into an intoxicating aphrodisiac for this new bride. Of course, Jon flew in the E-2C Hawkeye and not the F-14 fighter jet, but when he was dressed up in his flight suit, he was as handsome to me as Tom Cruise.

After the movie, I asked him about the death of Tom Cruise's radar intercept officer (RIO) in the movie, nicknamed "Goose," and the dangers of flying. He tried to reassure me.

"Don't worry, Krissy, I fly the safest plane in the Navy."

Jon fibbed a little on that one, because it wasn't really true, but it was the safest plane on an aircraft carrier. "Goose" was an NFO like Jon, but he told me he couldn't eject in the E-2C like Goose did in the F-14. Instead, they had parachutes attached to their seats in case of an emergency, along with other survival gear. That helped alleviate my fears a little, but his joke about CACOs certainly didn't.

"If you see a white car parked on the street and naval officers in their dress blues coming to the door, you'll know that I didn't make it." He said it with a laugh, but I didn't see the humor. He went on to explain that at one time he had been a CACO officer, someone who notifies the next of kin in case of death or a severe accident. Jon said he never had to notify anyone himself, but he went through the training and knew the drill all the same.

I tried to get the image of naval officers coming to my door out of my mind, especially as Jon's RAG training ended and the time came for him to go to sea. While he was packing his bags for his Indian Ocean tour, I was unpacking boxes from our cross-country move now that we had relocated to our two-story duplex. I found it comforting to know that while Jon was away, I wouldn't be all alone. I had made friends with the squadron wives from the Hormel Hawgs and with co-workers at my new job selling newspaper advertising in San Diego. Also, Jon and I had joined the College Avenue Baptist Church and choir, and we were forming new relationships there as well.

The carrier was already out to sea, and Jon would be joining USS Carl Vinson (or as he called it, the "Chucky V") mid tour, meaning he'd be gone only four months instead of six. "Only" wasn't the right word, because I couldn't imagine going one day without Jon. I was tremendously dreading the separation, especially since we'd be missing many firsts as a married couple, like my birthday, Thanksgiving, and worst of all—Christmas.

I could tell that Jon was getting stressed too, mainly by the smell of chocolate cake. In our few short months of wedded bliss, I'd discovered that even optimistic, upbeat Jon had a bad day once in a while. And on those rare occasions, he often would bake a chocolate cake to unwind. While my cooking was improving, it was Jon's efforts in the kitchen that kept me eating three square meals a day, which held my eating-disorder tendencies at bay. I would miss Jon's cooking, along with his smile, his voice, and his kisses—but most of all, his presence. Being around Jon made me feel so safe and secure and loved. I knew his first marriage hadn't survived because of the stress of his long deployments. I couldn't help wondering how it would affect us.

Because Jon had to meet up with the carrier sailing somewhere in the Indian Ocean, we said goodbye at the San Diego International Airport. I drove away in a puddle of tears, barely able to function, and ended up taking the afternoon off from work. Opening the door and entering that quiet, empty house—all alone, except for my little dog Sophie—was too much. I was only hours into the first deployment of my Navy-wife life, and I wasn't sure that I could make it.

Dear Jon

But before I could check off the first day of Jon's 1986-87 Chucky V cruise, I needed to write Jon a letter. Before the days of cell phones, email, texting, video calls, and the Internet, the only way to regularly communicate with a Sailor at sea was through mailing letters. And if you think snail mail is slow, imagine trying to get letters back and forth to a ship out in the middle of the ocean. The time lag between when a letter was sent and received could be as little as a few days or as long as a month, with the average around 10 days. The sending and receiving of mail was affected by the weather, the ship's location, the mission of the carrier strike group, and even postal bags falling overboard!

But that was only part of the challenge. The other problem was that letters could stack up for days, both on the ship and at shore, before a plane (called a COD) could land on the carrier to transport them. As a result, letters never came in the order they were written or mailed. Numbering letters was critical; otherwise, you'd never be able to read them in order or know which ones were still to come.

With two prior cruises under his belt, Jon knew all about writing letters, but this was a new experience for me. Before he left, we made a solemn "Rystrom promise" to write one letter to each other every day of his deployment. We were determined that our marriage would be even stronger when he returned, and this daily investment of time and love was a token of our commitment to one another.

As I got out pen and paper, I thought about what to say. I didn't want Jon to worry about me, so should I put on a brave front and act like my first day was a breeze? Or did I risk making him feel guilty by letting him know how much I'd cried and how awful our first day apart had been? I decided on the latter. I knew Jon wanted me to be completely honest and open with him, and there was no way that we'd grow closer if I tried to hide my inner feelings and deepest struggles. Knowing my words would travel around the world and to my husband's heart, I sat on the den couch, turned on the television to relax, and began to write.

Oct. 6, 1986

Hi sweetie!

Well, here goes my first letter of many to my dear, sweet, wonderful, strong, sexy Navy husband. It is 10 p.m. Monday night and Sophie is digging in the trash can and scratching her fleas. I'm sitting in the den watching Cagney & Lacey. It's been a rough day...

Four pages later, I signed my letter and put it in an envelope, making sure to add a circled number "1" on the back just like Jon had showed me. I went a step further and started a letter log of my own to track the dates of letters and packages that I sent him during his cruise. This wouldn't bring him home any sooner, but it helped give me a sense of accountability and a way to count down the days.

When I got home from work on Tuesday and checked my mailbox, I nearly jumped for joy when I found my first letter from Jon. The postmark said Los Angeles, and with the next postmark coming from overseas, I knew it would be several days before I could expect another. I ran inside the house and flopped down on the den couch. Sophie cuddled next to me as I ripped open the envelope and read my very first letter from Jon, written in his unmistakable scribble.

6 Oct. 86 1335

(Of course, Jon would use the military form for dates and time. I needed to subtract 12 to remember that 1335 was 1:35 p.m.)

Hi Krissy,

Here is letter 1 and I hope you can read my writing. First off, I love you!

(This part was written in larger letters and underlined three times. His words were like a warm hug.)

Now that I have that off my chest, I am sitting in LAX (Los Angeles International Airport), it is 1335 and I had to wait over one hour to get my ticket. I am not stopping in Korea. I am stopping in Tokyo, then to the Philippines.

(So there had been a change in plans already. I'm sure it wouldn't be the last.)

There were over 100 people in line for tickets. What a zoo. It still hasn't really hit me that I won't be seeing you for a while. I don't think I will mention actual numbers as it will depress me.

(That's how I felt. I couldn't bring myself to look at the calendar— February seemed so very far away.)

I am a little nervous about going to the boat cuz of not knowing anyone, but I guess after several days the newness will wear off. It will be interesting to meet the guys in the squadron and then match up the wives. We will see if we think they match.

(Jon had such an outgoing personality that I doubted he'd have any trouble fitting in. But I could feel his anxiety just the same.)

They just loaded the aircrew, over 20 people, must be a full flight. I hope my flight gear makes the flight but if not, oh well. LA was foggy but seemed very pleasant, at least what I saw of it. Would you pick up my passport and mail it to me ASAP? Never know when one would use it.

(Sure, Jon, I'll get it in the mail to you right away.)

I just hope and pray that nothing major happens very soon and that you are allowed to develop a routine.

(How sweet of him, though I wasn't sure how I'd ever get used to this Navy life.)

I have no idea what type of weather to expect, only that Australia is opposite of the U.S. So when we stop in December, it should be summer there. I am in the waiting area and it is packed. I will close soon so that I can find a mailbox.
I promise one thing—that you will meet me next cruise if it is at all possible (I am a sloppy writer). Something to shoot for.

(I could tell his "possible" was a little hard to read, but I didn't think his writing was sloppy at all. And I found any grammatical errors that he made and his little abbreviations, like "cuz," endearing. It would be a dream-come-true if I could meet him on his next cruise. There was no way to arrange it for this first one, but I wished we had.)

Well sweetie, time to close so that I can mail it before I leave. I will write every day of my fears, joys, expectations, friends I meet and my favorite topic, my girl (I should say woman), Krissy.

I miss you,
Love, Jon

I sighed as I finished savoring his heartfelt words, and Sophie lay her head on my lap as though she shared my sorrow. Receiving this letter was a blessing, but knowing this was how Jon and I would be relating to each other for the next four months was a sobering thought. I was glad we wouldn't only be sharing facts with each other but also our deepest feelings too. Perhaps that would be one silver lining to this dark deployment cloud. I scanned through the letter again, realizing that he should be meeting up with USS Carl Vinson any day now, and I wondered where on the other side of the world was my sweet husband and what was he doing.

```
DIEGO GARCIA
16:42 IOT TIME, UTC+6
10 OCT 1986
USS CARL VINSON
00.05.57 S, 65.32.28 E
```

Jon glanced right, out the small porthole window, to see the blue waters of the equatorial Indian Ocean as 601 made its final approach to the flight deck of USS Carl Vinson. The E-2C Hawkeye was the last aircraft to land, and Jon was glad to have his first flight of the cruise under his belt. On this boring hop with minimal tasking, Jon had sat ACO (air control officer) in the very back, the coldest seat in the plane. Maybe that's why he'd been shivering so much during the flight.

With the NFO seats facing forward, locked and lowered, and visor down, Jon double-checked his four-point harness. The two pilots dropped their hook and began their counter-clockwise holding pattern over the carrier. Coming into the break, they did a 60-degree bank as they lowered the throttle, let down their landing gear, and continued around the oval about a mile from the ship as their speed and altitude gradually decreased. As they took their turn to the final approach heading and the stern of the ship, Jon could finally spot the white, frothy waters of the carrier's wake, which was his cue that in a few moments he'd be back aboard "Mother," the naval aviators' traditional nickname for the carrier that was their home away from home. "Mother" was turned into the wind and moving forward at nearly 30 knots (35 miles per hour) to increase the amount of wind coming across the deck.

> ... *I WILL NOT LEAVE YOU OR FORSAKE YOU. BE STRONG AND COURAGEOUS ....* (*JOSHUA 1:5-6 ESV*)

"601, Hawkeye ball, 4.2."

Now that 601 was in the groove, radio silence was broken as the copilot called the "ball," meaning they had sight of a lighted device on the deck's port side that helped the pilot keep the plane on the perfect glidepath to safely land. The "ball" was a Fresnel lens light system with a row of green horizontal lights intersected with a vertical column of yellow lights with red ones beside it. The pilot also gave the fuel state, communicating they had 4,200 pounds left in the tanks. If something went wrong during the landing, the crew coordinating the plane's recovery would know how many landing attempts 601 could make before getting too low on fuel.

This could happen for several reasons. One was a wave-off due to pilot error, where the pilot wasn't lining up correctly and was directed to abort the landing to avoid a possible plane crash. Another was a foul deck wave-off, where the landing area was deemed unsafe, either because the carrier had a problem, like with the arresting gear or wires, another plane was in the way on the deck, or some knucklehead not paying attention walked past the foul line and into the path of an oncoming aircraft. A plane could also bolter—a situation where the aircraft's tail hook skipped over and failed to grab one of the four arresting wires.

Those arresting wires, called cross deck pendants, were long, thick, steel ropes that were stretched about 50 feet apart across the landing area. These cross deck pendants were held up a few inches above the surface of the flight deck by several thin, metal, arched supports. Part of a larger system of cables and hydraulic cylinders located under the flight deck, the arresting gear system could bring a jet plane going 150 miles per hour to a complete stop in about two seconds.

With the pilot's eyes on the "ball," the landing signal officers (LSOs) had their eyes on 601 as she prepared to land. Standing in an area on the port side of the landing area, this specially-trained group of air wing pilots watched each aircraft's approach, gave guidance as needed, and recorded a grade and critiquing comments for every landing. Those recorded grades and comments were used later for a face-to-face debrief of each pilot's landing performance.

"Roger ball, 26 knots slightly axial," came the call from the LSO, telling 601 the conditions of the wind relative to the landing area. The pilot's hands and feet were in constant motion, making minute adjustments to the speed and pitch attitude, using the Hawkeye's control yoke, rudder pedals, and throttles to keep the aircraft on the perfect glidepath. Pilots' heart rates were often highest within seconds of landing on the carrier, as opposed to being in the middle of combat.

"Little power, easy with it," called the LSO in a calm, even voice, helping 601 stay on the correct glidepath. As the Hawkeye flew onto the angled landing deck, the pilots cranked the twin turboprop engines to full military power in case of a bolter. But its hook caught the third wire, a perfect trap, and Jon and his companions experienced a 3 to 4G pull forward against their harness straps as 601 came to a sudden and violent stop. Jon often described landing on a carrier as a controlled crash and that's exactly how it felt.

Within seconds, the Hawkeye raised its hook, and Jon could hear the plunk of the wire hitting the deck as the engines throttled down and then back up as yellow-shirt handlers guided 601 out of the wires and to its parking place near the island tower. The Hawkeye had to rotate around in the landing area before backing into its parking place with wings folded to save space.

The time from when 601 entered the groove until it landed was less than 20 seconds. During active missions with multiple aircraft recovering, the goal was to land planes on the same 650-foot-long runway every 45 seconds. Pilots had to carefully gauge how they conformed to the other planes in the recovery pattern, because if they exceeded the proper intervals and caused a delay, it meant the total time to recover all the aircraft would be longer.

That would require the ship to maintain a set course and speed into the wind for a longer time. Steaming ahead at a steady speed and heading made the carrier's movement predictable, a vulnerability in times of combat. If a pilot had an off-day and the LSO had to wave him off to try again or if his poor landing technique resulted in a bolter, the ship would have to continue its steady course until the plane could successfully land. With every landing graded, pilots were under pressure to land successfully the first time for good reason.

Once 601's wheels were chocked, the crew deplaned and 601 was secured to the deck with tie-down chains. Coming from the arctic chill of the Hawkeye's cabin to the 100-degree tropical heat of the flight deck did little to slow Jon's shivering. Maybe he was coming down with something after all. A flight deck was a dangerous place, and Jon and his fellow crewmates kept their heads on a swivel as a cursory post-flight walkaround was completed and the crew went below deck.

With his new job in the maintenance department, Jon reported on the 601's weapon performance and any mechanical issues that needed to be addressed by the maintenance crew. Then it was on to the parachute rigger, or PR shop, to hang up his flight gear. Next was the ready room, the squadron's headquarters aboard ship, where Jon checked for mail, did paperwork, and maybe later watched a movie.

But a visit to the ready room always brought a smile to Jon's face, for there, pinned to the bulkhead, was one of his favorite sights: a large four-foot-square, homemade calendar for that month, created by the squadron officers' wives back stateside. Each day featured a different picture from one of the ladies, and on October 14 there was a gorgeous photo of Kris in honor of her 25th birthday.

Jon wasn't the only one who'd noticed Kris's attractive portrait. Jon had joined up with USS Carl Vinson when she was docked at Diego Garcia, or D-Gar, a small horse-shoe shaped atoll near the equator that was owned by the British and served as the only naval base in the Indian Ocean. The last day before the Vinson left D-Gar to head back to Gonzo Station, the enlisted men and the officers of the Hawgs had a softball game. The O's beat the E's by a score of 7 to 3 but not before a tropical downpour made the last few innings a slippery mess. When the game was over, one of the enlisted troops came up to Jon with a grin on his face.

"Lt. Rystrom? Is that your wife that's turning 25 on the calendar this month?"

"It sure is," Jon smiled back, surprised at his comment.

"If you don't mind me saying so, sir, she's absolutely beautiful."

"I couldn't agree more. She's one beautiful creature, and I miss her like crazy already." The enlisted guy shook his head in understanding. Deployment was hard on everyone.

Jon loved having other guys be envious of him for a change. His aches and shivers brought him back to the present as he left the ready room and made his way through the maze of passageways and hatches and back to the stateroom he shared with another Hawg officer. As he crashed in his rack, Jon knew he had his work cut out for him to get the maintenance crew whipped into shape. But he enjoyed a good challenge and this billet would provide it.

After nearly a four-year hiatus from carrier life, Jon found that for the most part little had changed, including the food, unfortunately. He was happy to find more cereal choices for breakfast and a return to his old standbys—peanut butter and jelly sandwiches and milk. But he sure missed Kris's home cooking.

Joining his Hormel Hawgs Squadron mid cruise was different, having missed getting to know them during the months-long workup period prior to deployment. Guys were polite enough, but Jon would have to take the initiative if he wanted to become one of the gang. Before long, he'd be back into the swing of things and be readjusted to carrier life.

The one significant change from his last cruise was the flight schedule. A cut in military funding meant they would sit at anchor for a few days after 5 to 6 days of flight operations. While the Hawkeye could be launched when the carrier wasn't moving, jets could not and the no-fly days made the cruise seem even longer. Jon would have to be creative to keep boredom away with a schedule like this.

After hitting the rack early, Jon was wide awake at 3:30 a.m., due in part to jet lag but mostly because of his worsening cold. The stresses of travel, playing softball in the rain, the humid tropical air, and the air conditioning on the Hawkeye and the ship certainly weren't helping him recover. Jon had heard that most of the new guys caught this Indian Ocean illness, the "cruise crud," and if that was the case, he might end up med-down for a few days and unable to fly until he recovered.

Jon figured that since he couldn't sleep, he might as well write Kris her daily letter. He was anxiously awaiting his first letters from her, but he knew they were on the way. In the meantime, he couldn't wait to tell her about the compliment she'd received and to wish her a happy birthday.

Krista,

I just want to wish you the happiest birthday you could ever have. I know I am not there with you, but I love you and care for you more than I ever thought I could love any one person.

Jon glanced over longingly at a framed wedding picture he had on his desk and sighed.

I never want to lose you, he continued the letter. If only he could be there to celebrate with her.

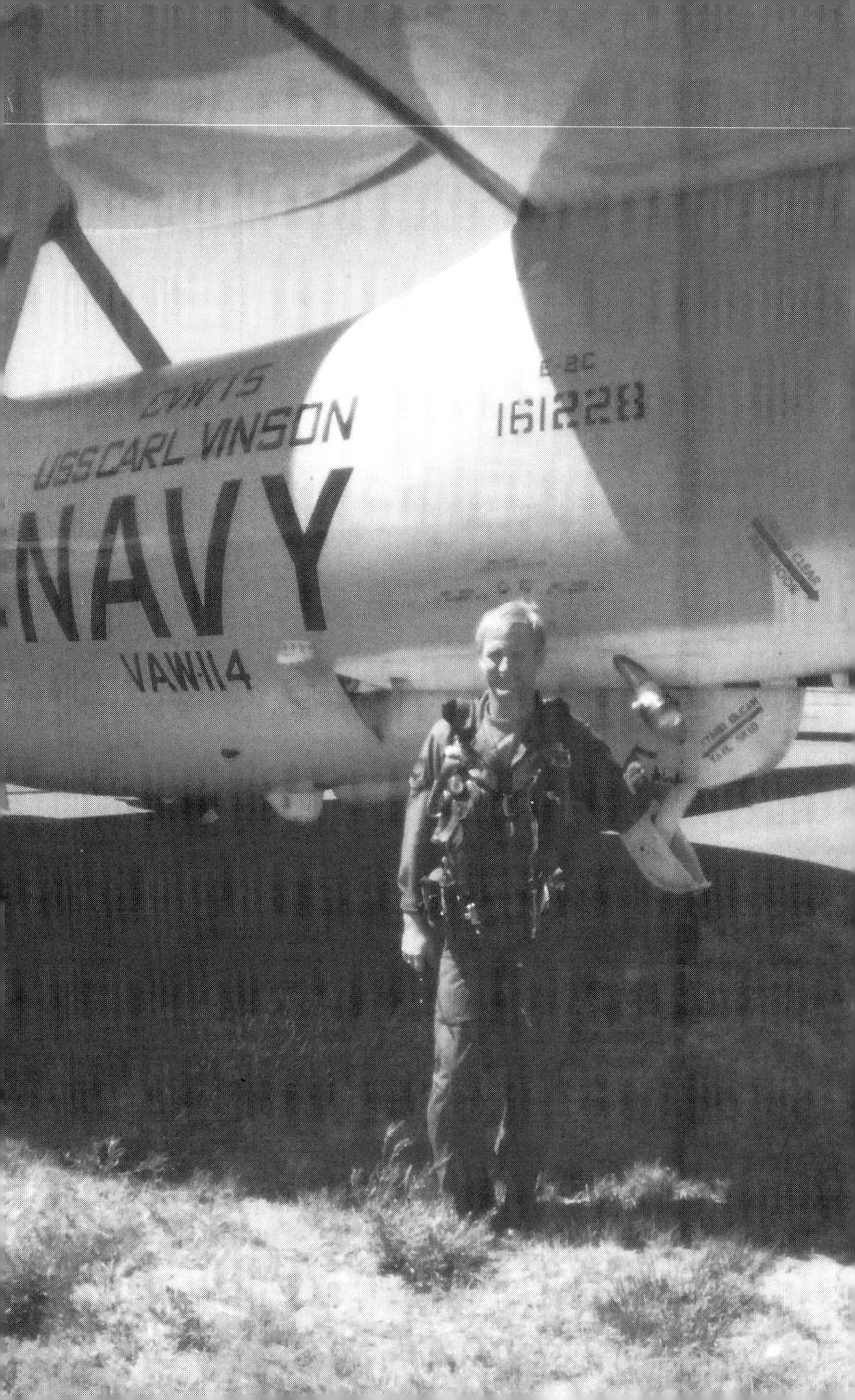
CVW 15
USS CARL VINSON
E-2C
161228
NAVY
VAW114

CHAPTER 10

Love Letters Across the Sea

issing special days together was one of many adjustments I had to make to the Navy-wife life. But the letter-writing ritual created by our separation was one of the greatest gifts that I received from this season of my life. At the beginning of our first cruise, I didn't realize how much our letter writing would mean to both of us. I never dreamed, as I started collecting Jon's letters in shoeboxes, that the love captured in their pages would continue to minister to our daughters and me decades later.

The letters not only sustained us in our months apart but also provided a history of our relationship and a legacy for my daughters today. How glad I am that I kept them all these years tucked away out of sight, waiting to be rediscovered—waiting to unlock their enduring messages of devotion, faithfulness, and affirmation.

Our world today is so different with our instant gratification of text messages, emails, and social media posts. We rarely invest our time to physically write a letter or repeatedly check our mailbox, longing to hear from a distant loved one. Our electronic messages so easily slip through our fingers and fade away. Even trees record the years of their lives in the rings of their wood. What testament will remain of our precious relationships decades from now, if we rely solely on the latest techno device to transmit our love?

Looking back, I realize that these daily letters deepened and solidified my love for Jon. Don't get me wrong—I certainly loved him before—but even in our short dating time and even shorter engagement, I wasn't filled with the "mushy" kind of love for my Cornhusker Swede. The security he gave me from the beginning of our relationship is what drew me to him. But the man I discovered, as we entered marriage and endured this forced time apart, went well beyond that basic need and touched a deeper part of my soul that I never knew I had.

After my birthday, letters from Jon began arriving in my mailbox and sometimes at work. But it took a few weeks before we could tell that we were receiving each other's letters. I found it funny that Jon received my first letter on my birthday, eight days after I'd written it on October 6.

What a great day, my honey turned 25, I am feeling better and I, Jon Rystrom, got my first letter from you, I love it. I didn't realize how one person can make me feel all gushy inside. I swear I have read your letter 10 times already. Oh, I truly love you.

As you told me in your letter how your first day went, my heart wept when you did. I could feel the same emotions that you were feeling. I bet you were really out those four hours that you took for sick leave too.

Jon didn't receive the letter I'd written on my birthday until 11 days later. With the inconsistency, I'd find myself closing a page with, "Please write me!" even though Jon had no control over when his letters would come. Both of us struggled with the irregularity of letters, and Jon understood my frustration.

I promise you, hon, that I have written every day and that I will continue to write one letter (minimum) a day to my favorite person in the world. I guess getting letters is the hardest part for you cuz no one is around to let you know if they have received letters from the ship or not. I feel great about your letters, cuz every time we have had a mail call, I have received a letter and that means the world to me.

I am so glad you are finally getting my mail. As you can see, I have been writing every day. Now that you have had several days of no contact with me until the letters came, you may be able to understand what I was talking about when I said how important mail is on the ship. In reality it is a two-way street—mail is just as important to you. Oh, how I love you.

My heart would explode with joy when my mailbox was full.

What a fabulous day ... FOUR letters from my handsome, sexy, adorable, rugged, educated, artistic (woops, starting to sound like a personal ad!) husband. I about flipped right in the street! They were wonderful—you are wonderful. Whew, I was worn out after reading all those letters, and I cherished every letter, word, and punctuation mark on those pages!

Those are the warmest, most love-filled words you have ever given to me. I will cherish them for the rest of my life. Thank you, Jonathan, for loving me. That has made my life fulfilled, because you have made my life complete! You are my world, and I will do anything for you, always and forever.

As a young newlywed, I eagerly shared my warm feelings, reaching out across the miles to let Jon know what his love meant to me.

Before you go to sleep tonight, I want you to read this letter again and think of me. Know in your heart that you have a woman who cherishes you, Jonathan, adores you, worships you and will always be there, waiting for you, loving you, giving you a happy home, having your children, supporting you and your career and living beside you, taking every step with you as you live your life. Remember that as you close your eyes, my love, for your wife sends you these truths across the miles to your pillow.

I'm in love with this man. He is out on an aircraft carrier right now, protecting our country. He is the "coach" up in the air. He has strong legs, beautiful eyes that sing with fun and happiness when he smiles, and a loving and kind heart that no other man in the world has. His name is Jon and I am his wife forever ... I love you, Jonathan, more than you could ever, ever know. I think about you constantly. I give you the best I could ever give. No conditions, no demands, no expectations ... Just me, with all of my faults and flaws, just the entire package ... And it is all yours forever.

Jon was not a poet, but he had his own unique way with words, especially when they came straight from his heart.

I think about you more than I should, cuz when I do I just realize how long I have to wait before I have you in my arms. But to bring me back up in spirits, I think in relative terms—what is four months out of 40-50 years—and also knowing how we feel about each other just makes me feel GREAT! Now I can face anything.

I have gained so much knowledge and wisdom about you through your letters. Sometimes I can feel your pain, your hurt, your joy, your intense desire to please me in your letters. When I read your letters, I read between the lines and just marvel at what an incredible woman I have married. Kris, I knew from the first day I met you that you were a special person in my life and you have not disappointed me in the least. I have grown to love and care for you more and more every day. I just love it!!!

I guess you realize that my two favorite things in the whole world are loving you and college football. And in that order!!!

Missing Jon was one of my consistent letter topics, but writing him helped me process my feelings of loneliness.

It seems so strange without you. I've really been doing very well keeping myself busy but at night when I lock up the house, turn on the alarm, and tuck Sophie in, I look beside me at this empty space and I long for you … It's only been six days, but it seems like forever. …

It seems like you've been gone forever. It is almost like I'm married to a man, live in his house, sleep in his bed, watch his TV, and drive his car, but there is no man around. I know it sounds weird, but everything around me seems like you are here but the laundry I do is mine, the messes I clean are mine, and the conversations I have are with me too. Now, don't worry, I'm not freaking out. I'm just explaining my feelings as I am going through this the first time. Sometimes I call home just to hear your voice on the answering machine ... What a laugh! I missed you more today because I didn't get a letter ... But you know I'm so patient these days, thanks to the Lord putting us through our frustrations and wait. He was really preparing me for what was ahead. Pretty neat, don't you think?

You seem so far away now. It is amazing that out of the billions of people in the world, there is one little boy on one side of the world loving one little girl on the other side and vice versa, and all because of one little 2" by 1" ad that ran in August 1985. Amazing, isn't it? I love you sweetheart, more and more each day.

I was thinking about you so much yesterday evening that I got in your closet, smelled your clothes, and even put on one of your flannel shirts so that I could smell you all evening!

Anytime someone we love is far away, we worry about their safety. But imagine how much you'd worry if your husband was flying off a busy aircraft carrier thousands of miles across the ocean. My anxiety even showed up in my dreams.

Hi, hon. It is Friday morning (7:30 a.m.) and I'm at work. I woke up this morning at 5:00 a.m., because I was having a terrible dream about you. That you were killed in an accident. It really shook me up, so I started praying for your safety. I love you! I love you! I love you! You ARE my happiness and life. Krissy

Maybe it was because Jon had a degree in psychology, or maybe it was his optimistic personality, but he seemed unflappable and cool-headed in every situation. He didn't stress out like I did, and he could handle my wide range of emotions.

I just today got your little note written on the 17th and honey I hope you do not have any more nightmares, cuz I am fine, honest, and I won't let anything happen to me, OK?

Even when Jon was far away, he still tried to care for me, especially after I wrote about my poor meal choices and weight loss.

GO TO THE STORE! I knew you would eat badly while I was away. When I was by myself, I would eat cereal or SpaghettiOs. But please try to eat a balanced meal. Buy a lot of balanced frozen dinners. I don't have an answer but try to eat more balanced meals and get some vitamins. Enuf said.

117 lbs. is great, but Kris one serious note. You are not becoming anorexic, are you? If you are eating but still losing, OK, but I love you and I want you healthy. I worry about you, OK? Let me know.

Kris, I am so happy and proud about your weight. But remember that I fell in love with you over a year ago, when you were sturdy.

From across the ocean, Jon knew how to love me and motivate me. I heeded his words and started eating regular meals. And my weight stabilized without my anorexia rearing its ugly head.

While Jon had been worried about my weight, I'd been worried about how our marriage would handle the separation, especially since it contributed to his first marriage ending in divorce. Now that I was experiencing some of the same stresses, I understood the situation better, considering how young his first wife was, having to live on very limited means, and being separated from her family and friends back in Nebraska. Jon was coming to terms with it as well.

Kris, I never loved her the way I feel about you, because she never let me. I never felt the love from her that you give me. I am not sorry about my divorce any more cuz I got the better deal. I am in love like I have never been, with Krista Kaye Rystrom, the woman I want to be the mother of my children and who I want to be with for the rest of my life. Krista, I love you like I have never loved before. Never forget that cuz you are my love and my life. I love you for you and always will.

During this first cruise, we learned the importance of consistently encouraging each other in our letters. Words of hope and affirmation would be read time and time again when the days were hard and your lover was nowhere near. At least I had family and close friends that I could call for a pick-me-up, but Jon had only the words in my letters, like these:

... I just finished watching "An Officer and a Gentleman." Boy, did that ever give me goose bumps. I am so proud of you every time I think about what you've had to go through and what you are going through now. I am so lucky to have found someone so dedicated, hard-working, loyal, and loving as you. I will love you till the day I die, and even then I'll still love you because we will be together in heaven. ...

... I love you more and more every day, Jon, and there are a lot of people praying for your safety. Keep up the good work and just remember that you have a happy, safe, and loving home to come home to this time and forever. Loving and missing you but coping fine. Your wife, Krissy.

Jon's warm words helped carry me through times of doubt and frustration, especially when appliances broke, my car needed repairs, or the lawn mower had issues. I would ask myself: What would Jon do? How would Jon handle this? As the weeks and months went by, I found myself taking on more household repairs and growing in confidence. His natural optimism began to rub off on me and gave me a healthier perspective on life.

... If you didn't have a terrible day every once in a while, you wouldn't be able to feel so great when a great day happened. I hope this makes sense cuz I am trying to be upbeat about life in general. I also feel and know that when I am feeling low, I just think of you and the love you have for me, and I immediately feel better and know I can face anything with that type of love and caring. Kris, I have never wanted to be loved by somebody so badly in my entire life as I do with you. I think of past times of us together, plus the excitement of the future, and it just gives me a rush like you wouldn't believe. Knowing that I have most of the next 50 years with the woman I love, I just can't have a bad day knowing that.

I always had the utmost confidence in you, Kris. I knew what a gem you were the moment I met you. I don't remember ever doubting that you were the one for me. I just knew. Love is grand, isn't it!! You realize, the more you like yourself and believe in yourself, the more of you that you can give me. ...

You can do it, Kris. I have faith in you!

Jon was great at giving advice, but there were times that he was forced to follow it himself. Even unflappable Jon had a bad day once in a while. And this time, his bad day affected both of us.

Good News, Bad News

04 DEC 1986
23:32 IOT TIME, UTC+6
DIEGO GARCIA
USS CARL VINSON
7.18.11 S, 72.24.38 E

If only every day on the cruise had gone by as fast as this one. Jon started the day with a debrief on his department's mid cruise inspection and received a passing grade. That included airframes and their corrosion inspection. Salt water environments and metal airplanes didn't mix well, and fighting the never-ending battle of corrosion, known as crud control, was one of the most important tasks of Jon's maintenance department.

With that duty behind him, Jon was free to join the rest of the Hormel Hawgs of VAW-114 for an onshore picnic and softball game. USS Carl Vinson had been docked at Diego Garcia for several days, and the squadron was taking advantage of the opportunity to have some much-needed R & R.

But many of the men were moving a little more slowly, thanks to a marathon relay run on the lush tropical island a few days earlier. Jon was humbled by having to walk a few times before finishing. But after talking with several of the other guys, he realized he wasn't alone in dealing with the intense tropical heat. Jon knew that his nightly push-ups and sit-ups weren't helping his endurance at all, and he needed to change up his exercise routine.

Later that evening on the boat, Jon was approached about being on the Anti-Aircraft Warfare Board, where he would help plan how best to defend the carrier strike group in a war scenario. On top of that, he'd officially been qualified as a CICO with the Hawgs and could finally get his own crew. Jon was definitely one of the gang now and a valued member of the team.

As he sat at his desk to write his daily letter to Kris, he smiled in satisfaction at his situation.

Everything is falling into place, my beautiful wife and marriage, and work is good for me. God takes care of everyone who wants to let God into their lives. I am so glad that we found each other. I have never been more happy or content in my entire life.

The small, framed picture of their wedding—that Jon had on his desk—caught his eye.

Thank you, Kris, for saying "yes."

Jon concluded his letter, before he turned out the lights.

I am bushed, so it is time to close. I love you, I do, I do, I do.

The next morning, he expected to be a bit sore from the previous day's activity, but he didn't anticipate the aching in his right foot. He started his morning routine, but before he could finish his daily shave, his foot was hurting so badly that he could hardly take it. His roommate called medical, and after a quick evaluation, it was determined Jon needed to go to the onboard hospital for a thorough examination.

By now the pain was so intense that Jon couldn't stand, let alone walk. A wheelchair wasn't an option, not with the gauntlet of hatches, ladders, and stairs in the way. That only left one choice: putting Jon on a backboard—carried by four muscular Marines and taking him up to the flight deck so that he could ride the bomb elevator down to second deck, one deck below the hangar bay where the hospital was located. As Jon passed the curious faces of workers on the flight deck, he wondered if it might be a while before he saw the sun and sky again.

Once in the medical ward, the flight surgeon confirmed Jon's suspicions. The same slipped disk that plagued Jon's back in January, pinching his sciatic nerve, had flared up again and the treatment was the same: bed rest for at least one week and then reevaluate.

Life had seemed so perfect the night before. How quickly circumstances had changed, and Jon was humbled by the suddenness of it. But he didn't panic. If his last bout with back pain was any indication, he'd be in severe pain for three days and then be back to normal in less than

> *... BE STRONG AND COURAGEOUS. DO NOT FEAR OR BE IN DREAD OF THEM, FOR IT IS THE LORD YOUR GOD WHO GOES WITH YOU. HE WILL NOT LEAVE YOU OR FORSAKE YOU.*
> *(DEUTERONOMY 31:6 ESV)*

10. Until then, he and the only other patient would have the 40-bed ward all to themselves.

How would he break the news to Kris? This wasn't a true emergency, so no need to send her a scary Red Cross message. His daily letter should do, and probably by the time she received it, he'd be on the mend anyway. As he found a semi-comfortable writing position, he had a sudden realization: Today was the half-way point of his cruise. It would be all downhill from here, but he hoped that didn't apply to his back as well.

Hi, Krista Kaye.

How is my No. 1 lover and friend? I have some good and bad news. The good news is I love you more and more every day. In fact, I can't get you off my mind. It's great. The bad news is that I am flat on my back in the hospital ward with my back acting up again. Now don't worry. At first I wasn't going to tell you until I was flying again, but I knew I should be honest with you. It is no worse than before, and the flight surgeon said the same thing: one week of bed rest, and then we will go from there, so let's keep our fingers crossed. ...

The next few days brought little improvement to Jon's condition. Jon had little to distract him from his discomfort, except for a quick bed-side visit from famous country music singer Loretta Lynn who was making a celebrity stop at the ship that day to encourage the troops. He even had his picture taken with her.

Now Kris, don't get too worried over this. I am not going to die, it is not life threatening, it is just like what happened in January, and I have seven doctors looking out for me, so I am in good hands.

But Jon showed a chink in his confident armor. He wrote,

I wonder if I will have this for the rest of my life, not like a broken leg that heals, but this won't totally go away, so include me in your prayers as I will pray for you.

After 11 days of care, the flight surgeon gave Jon his options: 1. get better—Jon's obvious choice; 2. bed rest for another week—the ship's last day of their port of call in Perth, Australia; or 3. if Jon still couldn't stand without pain—fly him to the military hospital in the Philippines for further testing and possible surgery.

He dreaded Christmas more than ever, forced on bed rest, being stuck on the ship when they docked at Perth, and not having Kris nearby to comfort him. To make matters worse, there had been no mail call for six days, which meant the mail to Kris was delayed too. Did she even know about his back trouble? And how would she handle it when she found out?

Jon's letter No. 62 came nine days before Christmas. The first two lines took me by complete surprise:

It is now day 2 in the Carl Vinson hospital suite. If you didn't get my last letter No. 61, I hurt my back again but I'm just fine.

I had no idea how Jon hurt his back, because I hadn't received letter No. 61 yet. I quickly wrote a reply and tried to not worry, but I couldn't help it. Several days later, Jon called me out of the blue from a military hospital in the Philippines. What a miserable Christmas it would be with Jon being stuck in a hospital bed at Clark Air Force Base and me being stuck in San Diego feeling sorry for the both of us. The day before Christmas Eve, I wrote him this heart-felt letter.

Dear Jonathan,
It is Tuesday night and I talked to you today. Oh, how I needed to hear your voice, just to reassure me that you were OK. I cried for an hour after we hung up, out of hurt for your pain, your loneliness, your

frustration, your boredom, for you. I went straight to bed and fell asleep out of exhaustion from my emotions.

I guess it all hit me today, the fear, the worry, the frustration and wanting to be beside you to comfort you, to make you laugh and smile. To know that you will be spending Christmas alone, in a hospital bed, tears me apart. If only I had the money, I would fly right to your side just to hold you and tell you how much I love you. But I can only do that in my thoughts, prayers, letters, and dreams.

There must be a reason for all this. What is it? Only the Lord knows. We can always second guess it. Maybe we've gotten too secure and cocky with the Navy and your success. Maybe this is directed at me for taking your career for granted. I just don't understand how we could have so many problems in our first eight months of marriage. Why? What have we done? Is this to make us stronger? Secure our love for each other? Prepare us for major hardships in the future that normally could be devastating—only not for us, since we have survived through so much? Is this to make our faith in Christ stronger?

No one really knows, only that the sun comes up every day and there are three sure things going for us: 1. There is always tomorrow; 2. God loves us very much; 3. We love each other more than any husband and wife ever could. With these things, Jon, we can do anything! Believe me, I'm telling myself this more than you, because after today, I need it! I love you honey, and I'll keep living one day at a time looking for the day when our lips can meet again. ...

Loving you,
Kris

The very next day, on Christmas Eve, I called Jon back. What a way to spend our first Christmas as a married couple. How I wished I could travel through the phone lines and be there with Jon in that hospital room. When he wrote me his letter that night, it was clear he felt the same way.

When you called today, I just wanted you to whisk through the phone so that I could hold you in my arms and cuddle and pamper you. Kris, I just want to bawl. I wanted to be near you so much. Your voice and your love mean so much to me. Words will never be able to express how totally in love with you I am but I try. I want to take you in my arms so that you never have to worry again. I realize that is impossible, but please don't worry as much cuz God is looking out for me.

I'll never forget that January day when Jon came home. He didn't arrive to a hero's welcome at the squadron's celebratory Fly-In. Instead, he was rolled in a wheelchair from a small military plane to our car. This was not the image that either of us had imagined back in October when we said our goodbyes at the San Diego International Airport. While we were thrilled to be reunited, the homecoming was bittersweet with Jon lying flat on our den floor and us questioning our future. But as the days went by, we were blessed, as Jon's back made a full recovery, and he rejoined his full duties with his Hormel Hawgs Squadron when they returned home later in February.

The cruise was not at all what I had expected, but I was thankful for the experience. Had we changed—Jon and me? Absolutely. Our goal to strengthen our relationship was met with flying colors. Our love and understanding of each other had grown even deeper. As for me, I gained tremendous confidence and independence as I found that I was capable of much more than I had ever known. As Jon said, you never know what you can do until you have to. As it turned out, this Navy wife could do quite a lot.

Sophie and Max Deacon

CHAPTER 11

The Hormel Hawgs

Falling Into Place

J on and I grinned at each other as we put on our snorkel gear and slipped over the side of the boat and into the magical world below us. The crystal-clear waters along the San Diego coast and bright afternoon sun combined to deliver a showcase of vividly colored tropical fish, dancing among the variety of corals as if on parade. The breathtaking beauty of this underwater paradise was so inspiring that when we got back into the boat, we decided to become certified scuba divers.

And why not? With the scare of his back injury in our rearview mirror, Jon and I plunged straight ahead making up for lost time and enjoying life to its fullest. We were still newlyweds after all, and with the stress of the cross-country move and Jon's first deployment behind us, we finally had the luxury to simply enjoy each other. After working during the week, we'd travel all over on the weekends often finding ourselves somewhere near the beach or on the water. We also added a new member to the family, Max Deacon, an adorable Norwegian elkhound puppy. Sophie and Max would often join us on our beach adventures.

Now that Jon was home, he rejoined me in the church choir, and we attended an in-depth Bible study together. Jon had never been discipled in his faith, and this season of solid Bible study and meaningful relationships with fellow Christians founded him in his beliefs. We relished experiencing this important part of our lives together after his months at sea.

Jon's Navy career was moving forward according to schedule, as we looked forward to his planned promotion to lieutenant commander (Lt. Cmdr.) coming up later in the summer. Jon and the rest of the Hawgs would start workups in the fall—the "hello-goodbye" training period where Jon would be gone for weeks at a time in preparation for USS Carl Vinson's 1988 cruise. Jon was well acquainted with his squadron, and the stress of being the new guy was over. He was nearing an important milestone as an NFO. Two thousand flight hours logged in the E-2C Hawkeye was considered quite an accomplishment.

Everything was falling into place for us, and my box-checking personality enjoyed tallying the results of our perfect life. Perfect marriage? Yes, most definitely. Perfect home? We certainly had a much nicer home than most of our friends and family. Perfectly fit? Our active beach lifestyle kept us both in great shape and beautifully tanned and tawny, at least I was. Financial security? Jon was an investing wizard who didn't like having debt. His Navy friends were intrigued by this lieutenant that had his own stock portfolio, and they began asking for his financial advice. Perfect job? I was enjoying climbing the ladder of success in the advertising world, and Jon loved his Navy career.

I Smell Chocolate

Months went by as our "perfect life" played out perfectly. That's why I was confused when I came home from work one day and opened the door to discover an old but familiar smell—the aroma of a freshly-baked chocolate cake—a sure sign that Jon wasn't having a good day. I walked into the kitchen to find Jon with a despondent look on his normally cheerful face. My stomach tightened as I asked him what was wrong.

"The results from the lieutenant commander promotion board came out today," he said softly. "I didn't make it."

I couldn't believe what I was hearing. How could this be? I'd never seen Jon devastated like this before. We held each other tightly and I tried to comfort him, but I was crushed too. When I shared our disappointing news with a choir friend later that evening, she seemed sympathetic, but as a civilian she didn't understand the seriousness of our situation.

This was more than a missed promotion. While the Navy's officer structure was like a pyramid and promotions were not automatic, they were somewhat predictable. As they climbed the ladder, the percentage of officers promoted decreased and fluctuated each year based on the Navy's needs and budget. But the percentage of lieutenants promoted to lieutenant commander was still fairly high.

Those passed over, like Jon was, had until the time the next promotion board convened to improve their fitness reports and performance. And if they failed to make promotion the second time, in most cases they'd have six months before the Navy forced them to take an honorable discharge, ending their Navy career. We never thought Jon would be faced with this possibility after only nine years of service.

Promotion boards, bound by strict rules, were very formal and were only allowed to look at service records to make decisions. While Jon's confidence was severely shaken, he wasn't going to let his Navy career go without a fight. He became obsessed with poring over all his old fitness reports. And he contacted previous commanding officers to ask them to amend any reports that had "regular promotion" to show "early promotion" instead.

Other higher-ranked officers gave Jon advice on how to handle the situation, and he wrote various letters to plead his case. But this missed promotion was like a dark cloud that hung over our perfect life until the board met again. And that wouldn't happen until USS Carl Vinson was on its 1988 Pacific/Indian Ocean deployment.

We turned to our faith for answers and hope, but trusting God wasn't easy to do. Both Jon and I had a deep-seated need for significance and security, and we struggled to turn it over to God and let Him handle it. From our beautifully decorated home to my top-quality business suits, it was obvious that I still had desires to surround myself with the trappings of success. Jon's career difficulties hit at the core of my own dysfunctional value system and my driven nature. But we both knew, at the heart of it all, we had no real control over our lives and the only way to move forward was to find our significance in our relationship with Christ.

As the June start to Jon's 1988 cruise approached, we finalized our plans for his six-month deployment. We were excited about meeting each other in Hong Kong where the ship had a port of call in November. A friend of mine would be my housemate for the first several months, so I wouldn't be living alone. And to stay connected and growing in our faith, Jon and I would be reading through the same marriage devotional while he was away.

For the first time, I experienced a proper sendoff of the squadron, gathering with other families at the Miramar VAW-114 hangar to watch our guys fly away to meet USS Carl Vinson at sea. But I knew Jon's first few days of deployment wouldn't be on the aircraft carrier—but on one of the ships in the battle group.

Big Fish, Little Pond

THE TEXAS
GULF OF ALASKA
USS TEXAS CGN 39
20 JUNE 1988
1700 AK STANDARD TIME, UTC-9
58.09 N, 147.26 W

Jon braced himself against the blast of the helicopter wash as he stood on the pitching deck of USS Texas, as he prepared to be airlifted for his return to USS Carl Vinson. Dressed in a cumbersome orange Gumby survival suit in case he fell into the chilly waters of the Gulf of Alaska, Jon watched eagerly as the Sikorsky SH-3D Sea King, hovering 30 feet overhead and in sync with the forward-moving ship, lowered the horse-collar rescue strop harness that wrapped under his arm pits so that he could be hoisted up into the copter's hold. At 585 feet long and with a crew of 600, USS Texas, a nuclear-powered guided missile cruiser, was by no means a small vessel. But she wasn't equipped with a landing pad, so this was the only way for passengers to come and go when at sea.

After exchanging thumbs up with the hoist operator above, Jon's feet left the deck and the Texas behind. Once safely inside the helicopter, he strapped into a seat as the only passenger and the helo banked from the ship and headed out. Jon thought the unique pickup was a thrill, but the excitement wore thin when the crew proceeded with a three-hour anti-submarine warfare (ASW) mission looking for subs. All that time, Jon didn't have a headset, he couldn't move because of his uncomfortable Gumby suit, and to make matters worse, he desperately needed to use the bathroom.

The hours spent helplessly strapped in his seat gave Jon plenty of opportunity to reflect on his wonderful experience serving as a tactical action officer (TAO) on the Texas. Jon gave lectures on the E-2C, discussing the upcoming Soviet overflight threat and how to counteract the Soviet cat-and-mouse games. He acted as an advisor during ops, or operations, and helped the Texas perform well during a critical B-52 escort and intercept exercise.

Jon was the star of the show, and as the resident expert, he was like a big fish in a little pond. The captain of the Texas had a private meeting with Jon before he left, and in plain language said he didn't want to let Jon go and that he'd done an outstanding job. He even gave Jon a Texas ball cap and an 8 by 10 photograph of the ship, signed by the captain along with this special message:

"Jon, with deep appreciation from your shipmates in Texas. You're a great professional, and one of our best TAO's. You're welcome here anytime."

Jon thrived on positive reinforcement and the captain's affirming words made his return to peon status on USS Carl Vinson easier to swallow. The promotion board would be meeting any day now, and Jon would know his fate once and for all. But whether he'd receive his long-desired promotion or come to the end of his Navy career, he'd always have his days on the Texas to hold on to.

When Jon finally got back to his stateroom on the carrier, he taped the signed picture of USS Texas on his wall, as a reminder that someone of significance valued Jon and respected his talents. His roommate, Steve, commented on it and laughed when Jon told him about his long helo ride. Jon could already tell that he and Steve were going to be great roommates.

The next morning, Jon hoped that a letter from Kris might be waiting for him when he got back on board, but mail was slow in coming. Light-weight deliveries to the ship—mail, boxes, parts, and personnel—were flown in by the C-2 Greyhound, a cousin of the E-2C Hawkeye, called a COD (carrier on-board delivery). The arrival of this workhorse for the carrier was eagerly anticipated by everyone on board, as they hoped a "mail call" announcement would be made soon after its landing. The first COD of the cruise landed later that day, but only five guys got mail. Everyone was antsy to get their first letter from home and find out if their families were OK.

Jon wrote to Kris to let her know that he'd be calling her when the ship stopped in the Philippines, around July 8 or 9. Surely by then they would know the promotion board's decision and, hopefully, they'd be able to share the good news together.

The next day, another COD arrived and, at last, Jon received his first letter from Kris. Jon's attitude always perked up after reading one of her letters, and this time was no exception. He was glad they were reading their devotional together and, so far, his favorite Scripture had been from Galatians 6:7: "Do not be deceived. God cannot be mocked. A man reaps what he sows." Jon looked at the picture of the Texas on the wall and said a silent prayer of surrender and trust.

Cloud Nine

The Fourth of July arrived a few weeks after Jon left. Even though I attended a huge party, I felt very much alone and missed Jon terribly, especially on such a patriotic day. The meaning of the day was still on my mind when I wrote Jon my daily letter that evening.

Happy Fourth of July!!!

I love you and am so proud of you. I thought of you all day today—knowing that because of you, we are able to celebrate freedom every day and especially today. Thank you for allowing me to have freedom, sweetie. You are a very special and honorable man to give so much for your country ...

One of our friends was telling people how wonderful you are. She said that you are so special, the kind of guy you meet once every 20 years. I agree with her all the way! You radiate with warmth. That is why I married you and most of all why I love you— because to me you are the kind of guy you meet once in a lifetime. I love you. Thank you for choosing me to live your life with you.

The promotion board met, but it usually took a few weeks before the official list was released. Jon said he would call me when they docked in the Philippines, but I wasn't expecting the phone to ring so early in morning. I was still half asleep when I answered the phone.

"Jon? Is that you?"

"Just call me Lieutenant Commander Rystrom!" he exclaimed excitedly, and even the static from the overseas phone call couldn't diminish the joy in his voice. This sure beat his last phone call from the Philippines when his back was injured.

We were both so relieved that he'd been promoted, but that wasn't the end of the good news. He'd also been involved in the first Soviet MIG jet fighter interception of the cruise and—best of all—Jon was nominated for the Hawkeye of the Year award, a high honor in the VAW community. Jon was on cloud nine, and I was so proud of him and so happy for us. Now we could both relax and look forward to our Hong Kong reunion.

But we did have another matter to consider and a major decision to make. Jon's tour with the Hormel Hawgs would end a few months after this cruise was over. Where Jon served next was very important, because he had the goal of commanding a VAW Squadron someday, and to do so you needed to follow a certain path. He was very strategic in his thinking, and he carefully weighed his options in the months to come. In the meantime, Jon still had his daily duties to perform. But sometimes those duties reminded Jon that the one thing that was certain in the Navy life was uncertainty.

Needle in a Haystack

SAR
14 JULY 1988
1725 UTC+8
USS CARL VINSON
NEAR SPRATLY ISLANDS
N 1200 E 11400

Jon sat CICO in the E-2C Hawkeye, Hormel 602, as it continued its station high over the South China Sea, listening in vain on the guard frequency for an emergency signal. Two days earlier, VRC-50, a Fleet Logistics Support Squadron, had lost one of their planes in the ocean. A T-39, similar to a small Learjet, was flying from Singapore to Clark Air Force Base in the Philippines and got lost due to an equipment failure with its navigation system. The crew sent out a distress signal before the bird ran out of fuel, and the three-person crew—including a female pilot who was two months pregnant—had to ditch the plane at sea.

There had been no radio contact since, and many planes, including 602, had been flying around the area of last-known contact trying to raise a signal. While other planes flew low to look for a life raft or emergency flares, the E-2C flew high and "looked" with its powerful radar. If a plane went down during a mission, its general location was usually known, and another plane nearby would be designated as an on-scene commander until a helicopter could be vectored in to pick up any survivors.

But in this case, the SAR (search and rescue) team was starting with their foot in a bucket, because they didn't know where T-39 went down. Searching hundreds of square miles of open ocean and coming across one small life raft was like trying to find the proverbial needle in a haystack. Being in tropical waters, there was still a chance of survival even after three days. Had this same mishap occurred in much colder waters, the story would have been very different.

As Hormel 602 concluded its part of the search and headed back to USS Carl Vinson, Jon thought about Kris waiting on him back home. He couldn't wait to see her in Hong Kong, and being involved in sobering SAR missions like this one made him miss her even more.

Hormel 602 made its final turn toward the ship and rolled wings level into the groove. At the same time, an arresting gear petty officer on the flight deck noticed an issue with the No. 2 arresting wire and reported the problem to Primary Flight Control up in the tower in the island, who promptly called a foul deck. The arresting gear office released the pickle switch, causing the Fresnel "meatball" lighting system to flash red.

"Wave off foul deck," the LSO transmitted over the radio, just before 602 was poised to land. The E-2C pilot instantly throttled up the engines, pulled back on the yoke, and climbed out past the ship.

"Take angels one point two, when level, cleared downwind report abeam heading three six zero," came the directions from Approach, with Control telling 602 to climb to an altitude of 1,200 feet and in which direction to fly.

While foul deck wave-offs weren't very common, they'd all been through this routine before. And it probably wouldn't be the last time.

Everyone was relieved to hear the news the following day that the three-person crew of T-39 had survived and was picked up by a Vietnamese fishing vessel. If only every SAR had such a happy ending.

Deep, Deep Down

While Jon was flying over the ocean, I was diving into it. One of my strategies to get through Jon's cruises was to give myself projects to complete and to keep myself busy with activities. On Jon's second cruise, I took a class to earn my advanced scuba certification. One of my favorite dives was off Catalina Island. We were 110 feet underwater where a buoy was anchored to the ocean floor. The water was cold and clear, but there wasn't much to see that far down: no fish, no sharks, no corals, no wrecks like we'd seen on other dives; nothing of interest, except that our blue wet suits turned a deep purple at that depth.

I was surprised at how comfortable I was in the water and at how much I'd enjoyed earning my advanced scuba certification. Even our safety training was a blast. We practiced rescuing a victim both from the surface and from deep underwater, where we had to dive down, release their weight belt, and bring them to the surface. I couldn't wait for Jon and me to scuba together when he returned home.

Another thing I couldn't wait for were letters. After experiencing typical letter delays during the first cruise, you'd think I'd be fine when Jon's letters were slow in coming the second time around. But that wasn't the case. Sometimes, I could get downright mean about it. But other times, the lack of letters made me depressed.

Another day without a letter, but today I was more prepared ... Think of submarine families that go without mail for months ... You seem so far away, almost like you must be a man in my dreams. I'm finding that in order to deal with this horrible emptiness, since I haven't had any contact with you, I put my really deep feelings way back in my mind so that I can get through day by day.

When I'm alone, I think a lot about our future, our next year, and the next few months before I see you again. I really, really miss you ... Why are we putting ourselves through this? Does it all really make sense? Boy, not getting letters from you has to be the toughest thing yet. The thought of losing you, your love for me, or even your desire for me would literally break my heart.

Of course, the letters came eventually, and over time I learned to have faith that even if I wasn't hearing from Jon the way I desired, he still loved and cared for me. Besides letters, we would also send recorded messages back and forth with cassette tapes, and on this cruise, Jon got his hands on the latest technology—a video camera.

The back of Jon's flight jacket.

CHAPTER 12

A Day With Jon and Steve

"Live and Direct"

7 AUG 1988
1010 GULF TIME ZONE, UTC+4
USS CARL VINSON
02 DECK
INDIAN OCEAN
12.32.53 N, 64.46.71 E

Beep beep beep beep—beep beep beep beep. The sound of an alarm clock cut through the constant, background low hum in the darkened room. A feeble light appeared behind a closed curtain, illuminating a bottom bunk as the alarm shut off. The curtain was pushed back to reveal a waking, blond-haired man rubbing his eyes, while a dark form on the top bunk switched on his light and groaned. Then he laughed.

The man on the bottom bunk leaned up quickly on his elbows, looked out across the room, and broke the silence.

"Well, good morning, ladies!" he announced in his best cheerful stage voice. His bunk mate joined in with what was clearly a somewhat-rehearsed, back-and-forth, and overly eager recitation.

"Hi! Live and direct ..."

"From ..."

"USS Carl Vinson ..."

"On Sunday morning, 7 August 1988 ..."

"In the middle of the Indian Ocean, live and direct, your husbands!" The top rack occupant couldn't help but laugh at this point.

"Jon!"

"Steve!"

"Good mornin'!" said Jon as he hopped out of his bottom rack.

"Good morning, Mary!" said Steve, addressing his wife, who, along with Kris, would no doubt be bent over in laughter in a few weeks when the video tape that the roommates were making would finally arrive in Kris' mailbox. Jon and Steve had borrowed a video camera from a squadron mate and had enjoyed learning how to operate it the night before, as they planned to make an entertaining show to film for their wives back home. Of course, Jon had taken the lead in creating the script, but Steve, also a good-natured and fun-loving guy, was enthusiastic to play along.

"Lights on!" Jon quickly continued in a chipper voice as he ran across the floor dressed only in his boxers. Reaching the wall near the recording camera, he switched on the lights, exposing a tiny, two-person living quarters with two stacked racks, or bunk beds, on one end. The top bunk was still occupied by dark-haired Steve, who was lying down and grinning like a school boy at the camera—that is, if school boys had full-grown, dark mustaches.

A makeshift curtain on a rope was pulled open on the bottom rack with both beds identical in shape and type: metal sides with the middle portion cut out to make exits and entrances easier, and a small, metal shelf attached on the outside near the right end. Both shelves held a small alarm clock showing the hands at 10 past 10—the men's morning rehearsal time had taken a little longer than expected.

"This is how we wake up every morning," Steve explained, placing a hand on the ceiling to steady himself as he dropped his nearly six-foot-tall frame down to the floor below.

Jon, sporting a blond—but more demure—mustache of his own, chimed in, "And I'm down here on the bottom rack. I don't like to sleep with the lights on, so I close my curtain." Jon—noticeably paler and a good three inches shorter than his rack mate—demonstrated the closing and opening of his rudimentary light-blocking device—much like a model on "The Price Is Right." He was obviously enjoying the camera time.

"This is our humble abode," Jon exclaimed with a flourish, gesturing with his hands, "and we're going to take you on a guided tour of a normal day in the lives of ..." and at this point Jon took in a deep breath, puffed out his chest and continued in his most manly voice, "Jon," then playfully patting his friend on his stomach, he added, "and Steve!" Both men broke into laughter. They were going to get a kick out of making this tape, whether their wives would enjoy watching it or not.

"Let's start the tour with the 'O-4 executive bunk room,'" Jon grinned, referring to the fact that both he and Steve had only received word that they had been promoted, though it wouldn't be official until November. Looking around the "O-4 executive bunk room," one thing became very obvious: The Navy's paint palette was quite limited. Everything in the room—the walls, the racks, the metal storage units, the floors, even Jon's makeshift curtain—were all varying shades of gray, gray-brown, or gray-green.

"We figured that since this was mixed company, we should have some kind of manners," Jon explained as he and Steve put on their dark bath robes and retrieved their shaving supplies from the compact storage locker under the tiny, metal sink and matching wall mirror located near the door. "We wanted to bring back the memories for you ladies of how we'd get ready for work back home."

What Day Is It?

Steve took his turn shaving first. "You know, we have a lot of ways of counting down the days 'til the cruise is over. I brought three of these with me," he explained, holding up a baby-blue can of Noxzema shaving cream as he began to lather up his face, "and it's almost empty. So two cans to go 'til I come home, 17 pizza nights, and I'm thinking maybe five or six more bars of soap."

"Now for me," Jon added, "I like to count pizza nights. That's a biggie event around here, every Saturday night. And Steve has it down to a science." Steve grinned under his beard of white foam and commenced shaving as Jon explained the ritual. "You have to participate by eating at least one pizza in order to count that as a bona fide Pizza Night. So last night, at about 10:30 after Big Bucks Bingo, we went by the mess and had our normal ration. I normally have two, and Steve stopped counting at 32." Steve turned to the camera and gave a big grin and laughed. "No," Jon continued. "I don't know how many Steve had, but he sure enjoyed it."

"And it's a pretty good method," Jon went on, "because every day is pretty much the same around here, Monday through Sunday. Most of the time we don't even know what day of the week it is." Steve, nearly finished shaving, nodded his head in agreement as Jon kept talking. "But you always know that Pizza Night is Saturday night and another week has gone by."

Steve finished rinsing out his blade and dried off his face. "All the water here is spring loaded. See?" Steve demonstrated how the water turned off as soon as you let go of the handle. "It's like washing your hands in a public restroom. You never can get enough water."

After the men finished shaving, they headed out of their room and down a narrow hallway to the showers. Some of the doors they passed were rounded instead of having corners and didn't quite meet the floor, which allowed them to be sealed watertight with "dogs" that gave added structure to the ship. But that also meant you had to step up and over these "knee knockers" to avoid tripping as you walked through. The shower room had one of these doors.

"We always use the fourth stall," Jon continued as he focused the camera into the opening and pointed up to the ceiling. "See that fluorescent lamp up there? We can put our shampoo or whatever up there, and it doesn't fall down on the deck."

For their wives' enjoyment, the men took turns capturing carefully cropped yet family-friendly images of each of them entering the shower. Once back in their room, they showed off their desks and storage units.

"You can see my space, Kris, and all the pictures you've sent me," Jon stated as he scanned the camera over numerous photos of Kris, their dogs, other family, and friends, all taped to the fronts of the metal drawers and cabinet doors. "And here's my desk, a little messy," which was true. His cubbyhole, about 10 by 18 inches with a miniature safe on the right end, was filled with books, papers, and office supplies.

"And here's my favorite picture," he said as he pointed to their wedding photograph in a small, metal frame with a heart opening, tucked inside the cubby hole. "It's easy to clean up my desk, because all I have to do is flip it up and close it, and it's all put away. And this is all the space I get, right here. That's it. All my personal space."

"Let me back up and show you the whole room," Steve continued as he slowly scanned the cramped space. The beds, storage unit, small open closet, a VCR and micro television, and a sink filled a space that was less than 100 square feet.

While these quarters might have seemed spartan to land lubbers, it was the Taj Mahal compared to those of the enlisted men attached to the ship. Many of them slept in large berthing areas with racks stacked three high that held up to 100 Sailors. Their only personal space being the storage locker that fit directly under their rack.

As an "ops" or operations guy, Steve dressed in his washed khakis and brown, airdale shoes. As a maintenance officer, Jon dressed in a long-sleeved, green, flight-deck jersey and his black lox boots.

Hawgs and Auto-Dog

They decided to pass by their ready room on the way to the dirty shirt mess where they ate their regular meals. They climbed up a flight of metal steps, more like a rung ladder set at an angle with stainless steel handrails on each side, to reach the 03 deck,

located directly below the flight deck. The ship opened up slightly at the top of the stairs where several other hallways came together. As other airmen walked by, Jon made them stop and pose for the camera.

"Hey, here's Carl and Bill, looks like they just came down from a workout on the flight deck. Look at those shorts on Carl! Man ..." Jon let the camera scan the length of Carl's white legs, sporting the latest in 80s athletic wear as he grinned shyly for the camera. The guys were well accustomed to Jon's playful jesting. Jon and Steve walked into the busy Hawg ready room marked by a black door with a single, diagonal red stripe.

"Here's where we get mail," Jon said, pointing the camera to a filing unit against one wall where a senior officer was standing nearby. "Have I got any mail?" Jon asked, as his boss did a quick check and found Jon's slot empty. But not missing a beat, he grabbed a large stack of paperwork from another slot and jammed it into Jon's. Everybody laughed.

"Here's the ready room from the back," Jon continued, showing four rows of blue flight seats with a center aisle leading up to a wooden lectern, white board, bulletin board, and television monitors hung from the ceiling in the corners. Above it all was a mounted head of a hog with the words "Hawg Country" emblazoned on both sides.

On the blue tile floor in front of the lectern was an intricate "Hawg" image inlaid in the tile and cut out from red, white, and black floor tiles in great detail. The men were clearly proud of it. Behind the flight seats on the right side was the large, hand-drawn calendar for August that was made by the squadron wives back home.

"Come on. Let's go eat," said Steve, who had missed his breakfast to work on the wives' video, taking over camera duties from Jon. They exited the ready room and turned left and down a narrow passage to the "dirty shirt mess" where any officer from the air wing could eat, regardless of how they were dressed. Unlike the enlisted Sailors, officers had to pay for their food, buying a "meal share" at the start of the cruise, followed by a monthly food bill.

As the men entered Wardroom 2, Jon and Steve grabbed white cafeteria trays and went through the hot-food line. Steve called out that day's offerings.

"Looks like grilled cheese sandwiches, hot dogs wrapped in bacon, macaroni and cheese ..."

"And broccoli cooked very well," interrupted Jon as he was handed a plate featuring a mound of the limp, pale-green vegetable. They passed on through to the final room that featured a stainless-steel salad bar.

"This is where I normally eat," Steve said, hoping that Mary would be glad to see he was eating his vegetables.

"Uh-oh, there's the bad guy. See that machine over there?" said Jon, pointing to a stainless-steel, box-like contraption sitting on a platform against the wall. The machine, with two handles to operate it on the front, looked innocent enough.

"That's the auto-dog machine," Jon stated, in a serious tone.

"That's like custom-made ice cream cones, all day, every day, all the time," Steve explained in an almost dreamy voice. For those unfamiliar with the auto-dog machine, it only took the first feeble attempt at making the perfectly shaped soft-serve chocolate cone to understand the origins of the name.

Jon showed Kris the 24/7 supply of bread, peanut butter, and jelly, which had powered Jon through more than one late night shift. He and Steve took their food-laden trays to one of the back cloth-covered tables.

"This is the Hawg's table where we sit together every day and just like at home, we read the daily paper." Jon grabbed the latest copy of The Eagle, the ship's onboard newspaper, as he and Steve took their seats. Within minutes, the room filled with hungry officers. But by the lukewarm reactions of the men toward the day's menu, there was a high chance that Jon and Steve might want to visit the auto-dog machine later.

FOD Walk and Coffee Talk

No tour of an aircraft carrier would be complete without a stop at the flight deck, and that's where Jon and Steve headed next. Steve continued being the camera man and Jon the tour guide as they walked through a stiff wind and by rows of planes parked only a few feet apart.

"They just called for a FOD walk down," Jon explained loudly, referring to the foreign object damage walk done every day before flight operations began. "That's where a large group of whoever is available walks shoulder-to-shoulder on the deck, from the bow to the stern, looking for any little piece of metal, paper clip, paper, rag, anything that could be sucked up or blasted by a jet engine or rotor or prop wash and damage a plane or a person."

"It's the highlight of our day to come up here and do a FOD walk. It's the only time you can be on the deck to enjoy the sun and get a good look at the ocean," Steve continued.

As they passed by F-14A Tomcats, A6 Intruders, and a helicopter with its rotors folded to make it more compact, Jon pointed out the various colors of flight-deck jerseys and what they meant.

"The white shirts are worn by a lot of folks, like Steve in Ops, and landing signal officers. Green means maintenance workers; brown-shirts are guys from the line and plane captains; red is for the guys who stop the fires or control the bombs and ordinance; and purple guys—we call them the grapes—fuel the planes. Blue-shirts help park the planes, and yellow-shirts help to taxi the aircraft and operate the catapult arresting gear."

The men walked aft and toward the ship's island, the multistoried structure on the starboard side of the ship that housed the bridge and flight control decks, then to the ship's port side to give their wives a view of the white-capped ocean.

The flight-deck tour complete, Jon and Steve returned to their bunk room to take turns recording personal messages to their wives. Jon was up first and referred to a handwritten list of topics.

"Thanks so much for all your letters. Yes, we still adhere to the 'Rystrom promise' of writing a letter a day. I'm sorry you didn't get letters for 8 or 9 days in a row," Jon mentioned, in response to one of Kris' recent letters. "I have no control over the mail, but I have been writing every day. Steve can verify that and, Mary, he's been writing to you too." Steve gave a little laugh off camera. He knew Jon never skipped a day on his letter writing. "So keep your head up and your heart together, and the mail will come."

"As you can tell, I know you don't care for it, but I've started my cruise mustache. It gives me something to do—one less part I have to shave every morning—and no problem, I'll shave it off once cruise is over," Jon winked at Kris through the camera. "It's a change—something else to do on the ship."

"That 110-foot scuba dive you took sounds incredible," Jon grinned as he shook his head. "I can't imagine being that far down in the water."

"This Sunday, I'm going to sign up for a chess tournament, and I give Steve a hard time about this, but I keep telling him I'm undefeated." Jon winked at Kris again. She was very aware of Jon's love for the game and his reputation as a strong chess player.

Jon referenced a few of the books Kris had given him that he was reading. "I'm through the first few chapters of the New Testament," he added. "It's hard. It's long reading, and I have to re-read parts of it, but it's one of the things I read before I go to bed."

"And we've got four types of International Coffees," Jon continued. "We've got double chocolate, chocolate mint, Swiss mocha, and cappuccino. If you've got other flavors to send us, we'll try them all. That's our letter-writing coffee. We have one cup each night when we sit down to write the two most important people in our lives."

Jon sat down his list and turned his gaze back to the camera for his final message.

"I know you don't always like that I have a list, but I like to keep organized," Jon explained and gave a final smile. "God bless, and I pray that God will watch over you two. And, Kris, I love you very much. You are my reason for being."

Kris visiting Jon's stateroom on USS Carl Vinson.

CHAPTER 13

Hong Kong Homecoming

Front-Page Widow

Mary and I had the best time watching Jon and Steve's antics. My favorite part was watching the guys get up, shave, and go to the showers. What a riot! I thought it was the greatest, most creative, funniest, and most fulfilling thing that Jon had ever done for me during a cruise. Jon was right: I kept my head and heart up, and the letters came. But some of what Jon wrote me later was downright disturbing and brought fearful images to my mind that were hard to shake.

What a day! I was involved in a lost aircraft. VF-111 lost an F-14 jet tonight. In fact, just three hours ago, and my crew was involved in the rescue. Both the pilot and his RIO are OK. We were flying an exercise with me in the RO seat to help train the other NFOs. I was controlling two eagles, 101 and 110, against two A-7s and had completed one hour, when all of a sudden, we heard an aircraft in the water. It was 204, an F-14 from VF-111. So I took over as CICO, had one guy go to a small scale and maintain a good pic, and the other guys to take notes and get two

S-3 Viking jets over to the area and two helos outbound to pick them up. From start to finish it only took 55 minutes.

The F-14 had gone down about 45 miles from the Carl Vinson. One of them, the RIO, had back injuries—we don't know how serious—and went into shock aboard the helo, but he's stable now. The other one, the pilot, was in good shape. The cause of the crash? No one is talking. I'm sure we will hear more in the next day or two. Well, that's the big news and, no, we weren't heroes - just doing our job.

Regardless of what Jon said, I considered him and the men he served with to be heroes, but I feared for his safety all the same. The letter he sent not long afterwards made my apprehension grow even more.

Now for the sad news. We lost another F-14 today. Both guys are OK but that is two in less than two weeks. He had smoke and fire in the cockpit, so they ejected 10 miles from the Carl Vinson. The Ops officer of VF-111 was the pilot. This is three aircraft from VF-111 lost in less than six months.

But there was another image that appeared to me in this same time period—one that would haunt me for years. It wasn't in a letter from Jon, but on the cover of a local newspaper. Living in a military community, I was accustomed to seeing articles on planes and service people all the time. But something about this image grabbed me by the throat and wouldn't let go.

It was a picture of the young widow of a Navy aviator, holding a folded flag presented to her at her husband's funeral. The F-14 fighter jet had been on a training run when it developed mechanical trouble. Both the pilot and the RIO ejected, but the RIO got tangled in some power lines and broke his neck. He died of his injuries the next day. The plane itself crashed into a local airport, causing several injuries on the ground and a fire that destroyed several buildings.

As I looked at that mournful image and the grieving face of the Navy widow, this thought went through my mind: One day, that will be me. Why would I think such a thing? Her husband had flown one of the most dangerous fighter jets in the Navy, the well-known F-14 Tomcat. Jon was in the "safest plane in the Navy," the slow and lumbering E-2C. I shuddered at the thought and tried to erase it from my mind. But the memory of that front-page photo seared into my subconscious, and I found it resurfacing when I least expected it.

Once in a Lifetime

I pushed these dark premonitions aside and focused my energies on something much more delightful: our upcoming reunion in Hong Kong. I couldn't wait to be safe and secure in Jon's arms again. The long-anticipated November day came, and while experiencing the exotic wonder of this bustling city gave me a rush, it could not compare to the thrill of being reunited with my beloved Jon.

With the luxurious Kowloon Hotel as our home base, Jon and I spent nearly a week together, touring the harbor, shopping for pearls, purchasing custom-tailored silk suits, and experiencing Hong Kong's

unique cuisine. We shared many activities with other couples from the squadron but still had plenty of alone time to reconnect and rekindle our love. During that week, we had Jon's official frocking ceremony at one of the rooms in our hotel, where I was proud to place Jon's new lieutenant commander stripes on the shoulders of his dress whites.

Jon seemed as excited about discovering and buying Hong Kong treasures for me as I was to receive them. Jon didn't have a selfish bone in his body, at least not where I was concerned. He went to great lengths to make sure I had plenty of meaningful mementos from this once-in-a-lifetime adventure.

At the end of our visit, all the wives rode the liberty boat out to USS Carl Vinson where our husbands gave us a guided tour of the carrier, including their personal staterooms. How surreal it was to be sitting in the same "O-4 executive bunk room" that I'd seen on their hilarious home video months earlier.

Saying goodbye to Jon—for the second time this cruise—wasn't any easier than the first. But we knew we had less than one month to go before Jon and the rest of his shipmates returned home in time for Christmas. When I arrived home, I was thrilled to find a letter from Jon in my mailbox:

> *Krista, without a doubt you will get this after H.K., so I am simply writing because I love you and for no other reason. I want mail to be waiting for you when you get home after our wonderful adventure in H.K. Definitely don't overextend yourself and get plenty of sleep (that's an order!).*

At the end of his two-page letter, I noticed his P.S.:

> *I had a great time in H.K.!!!!!!!*

I realized that he had written five days before our trip. How precious! Even then I felt embraced by his tender love and thoughtfulness for

164

me. Now that our trip had actually happened, I had to agree with Jon: I had a great time in H.K. too.

The Friends

The last highlight of the 1988 USS Carl Vinson cruise for Jon was the Tiger Cruise, a special event where selected friends and family come onboard and experience life at sea. My father, Chuck Windham, was Jon's special guest. As a former Navy enlisted man, having a Navy officer as his son-in-law was a point of pride for him. Dad flew out to Pearl Harbor, where "the friends" met up with the ship, then onto the carrier for several memorable days at sea.

As the ship neared its San Diego port, the air wing prepared for the Fly-In, where all the planes left the carrier and returned to their home bases across America. I joined the other VAW-114 Squadron families at the Hawgs' home base in preparing a special homecoming for our aviators. With our San Diego home so close to Miramar Naval Air Station, I had grown accustomed to the engine blasts of F-14 jets and the thrilling flyovers of Blue Angels in tight formation. But nothing stirred my heart like the unmistakable sound and sight of Hummers in the sky.

As the planes landed, I tried to hold back the tears. But as Jon and his squad mates walked across the tarmac, dressed in their flight jackets and matching straw fedoras, this was the homecoming I'd always hoped for—the one I'd dreamed of. As Jon and I embraced, our kisses mixed with tears of joy and relief.

You Make Me Complete

As I thought back over our first full six-month cruise, we were not only able to maintain but also grow our close relationship. Outside of our fairytale trip to Hong Kong, my most special memories of that cruise could be encapsulated in how we expressed our love to one another in our daily letters.

To Jon Alvin Rystrom:

Three years ago tonight I met a man that would change my life. This man would teach me about the Navy, about finances, about buying a house, about using a drill, about Nebraska football, about Norwegian elkhounds, about moving cross country, about operating two VCRs, a stereo, and a TV at the same time, about patience, about listening, about giving, about accepting, about lovemaking, about snuggling, about responsibilities, about security, about waiting, about flexibility and positive attitudes, about marriage, about ... love.

I will cherish the wonderful memory of our meeting for as long as I live. Oh, to think that it has been three years and look at how much we have been through and what lies ahead. What a thrilling thought. I love you with all my heart. Thank you for being the man I prayed for all my life, and most of all for giving love a try again in your life. Because this time, babe ... it worked!

You changed my life and taught me how to live it. Thank you, Jon Alvin. I will love you for eternity.

Your "Green-Eyed Lady"

Dear Krista,

I am so lucky to have you as my better half. I absolutely adore you. I love it when guys complain about me getting so many letters, but they don't realize it is a two-way street. If I didn't write as often as I do, you would find it tougher to write to me so much. I am glad we agreed to try to write every day, and I think that overall we have done very well.

I'm not sure I handle the pain of things correctly (like losing in wrestling or missing the 0-4 promotion the first time). But because of you in my life and opening my eyes again to God, I can accept the little things that go wrong—as long as God is on my side and I have my faith and our love for each other.

I love you,
Jon

My sweetheart Jon,
Oh how I love you and long to be totally wrapped in your arms tonight. Only a moment is all I need to satisfy my intense craving for you. How can one man have such an effect on one woman? Do we take these feelings for granted when we are together? Oh, shame on us if we do, because you are the only man in this world that makes me feel alive, special, loved, and like an entire woman. I'm into you, Jon, for a lifetime. I want to go everywhere you go, do everything you do, be everything you are, and never, never do I want to be without your love.

Tonight, I cried for you and opened your closet to just wrap my arms around your clothes, because I needed you next to me to sense the warm, secure, and totally content feeling I have when I am with you. I love you, Jon Alvin, more than you will ever know, and tonight when I close my eyes, I will dream of only you.

Goodnight babe,
Krista Kaye

Hi Good Looking,

I really enjoyed reading your lovey-dovey letter. But I have to disagree on one thing: You want to go everywhere I go? Well the bathroom is off limits (ha ha). Always remember: You never—I repeat never—will be without my love. We may be apart physically but never emotionally or spiritually. I agree, Krista, I miss the warm, secure, and totally content feeling I have when I am with you. You make me complete. Jon Alvin Rystrom loves Krista Kaye Rystrom FOREVER!!!

Jon and Kris at Balboa Park, San Diego.

CHAPTER 14

Go Big Red

Decemeber came and Jon and I started a Rystrom family tradition of decorating our Christmas tree together. With the New Year came the time to make our final decision on Jon's new orders. A Joint Service tour, where Jon would serve alongside service members from other branches of the military, would be the best move for Jon's career and would likely increase the chances of his future promotion to commander. That narrowed our options to two polar-opposite tours of duty. The first was the obvious choice—a job in the beautiful paradise of Hawaii.

The other was in of all places, Nebraska. The National Emergency Airborne Command Post (NEACP), or the "Flying White House" plane, was based at Offut Air Force Base, just south of Omaha. Jon would need special clearances to qualify for the position, but Jon had been told that NEACP was the best-kept secret for tours of duty because of the time you were able to spend at home.

Hawaii and Nebraska couldn't have been more different from each other. Either place would be fine for Jon's career—but which one to choose? When I thought of Hawaii, I could see Jon and me frolicking on the exotic beaches of Oahu, scuba diving off the coral reefs, and soaking up the year-round tropical sun. When I thought of Nebraska, all I could see was shoveling through chest-high snowdrifts, being awakened by tornado sirens, and being surrounded by endless acres of corn.

Nebraska had one thing going for it, and it was a big one—family. Jon's Navy career meant visits with his family were few and far between. The possibility of being based so close to his parents and most of his siblings and their families made Nebraska a harder option to dismiss. Relationship was very important to both Jon and me, and with NEACP on the table, we both prayed long and hard about the direction we should take and asked God to give us clear guidance on which way to go. To be honest, Nebraska was not my first choice, but I was prepared to go if that was God's will for us. I even went so far as to ask God for a sign—like putting out a fleece—something I had never done before.

I sorted through my conflicting thoughts about our future as I drove into downtown San Diego to meet with one of my advertising clients. As I entered a parking lot, my eyes settled on the license plate of a parked car that I passed by. It was from Nebraska. I caught my breath, and then shook my head. I had Nebraska on my brain for sure, but what a coincidence to see a Nebraska tag here in sunny San Diego. Later on, while driving down the freeway, I looked over to the other lane, and there was another car with a Nebraska tag! This time the sign was harder to ignore. But I wasn't one to be flaky and follow random events as if they were gospel. I prayed a quick prayer and said, "God, if it's You, give me one more."

In a matter of seconds, a car passed me, sporting a "Go Big Red" bumper sticker, a sure sign of a Nebraska Cornhusker fan. I was floored. I'd asked God to give me one more, and He had! As soon as I got to my office, I called Jon at work and said, "We're going to Nebraska!" Jon was surprised when I told him my story, but we both had peace about God's guidance and our decision. My Cornhusker husband was going back home.

Bellevue Baby

Many times in our lives, we don't understand the significance of events as they occur. Choices we make and what happens around us can seem random or purely coincidental. But as I look back over my life, I am convinced that my days are preordained by God. He knows our future, and He prepares us for what is to come.

As we prepared to say goodbye to our San Diego home and our backyard with its citrus trees and rosebushes that Jon had planted for me, God's sovereign hand was in motion in ways that we could not yet see. Pulling up the roots of the life we had established in San Diego was another harsh reality of the Navy life that I had chosen, but that truth was made much sweeter when I discovered something else right after we accepted the NEACP tour—I was pregnant! The next chapter of our lives would include Baby Rystrom and God's guidance to ditch the beaches of Hawaii for the cornfields of Nebraska now made complete sense. Starting our family living so near Jon's would be perfect.

We spent the last few months in San Diego tying up our loose ends before we moved to Jon's new post in May. We decided to rent out our duplex instead of selling it, keeping it as an investment in the rising real estate market. As boxes were being packed, my own personal checkboxes were changing. Great house? Leaving it. Great job for me? Leaving that, too. We decided that, until Baby Rystrom arrived, I would be a stay-at-home mom. I could go back to my career afterwards.

Great marriage? Yes, that one box was still checked. Faith? We'd loved our church home in San Diego, and I was comfortable with my relationship with God. Finding a new church home would be a priority. Great family? My growing tummy was a constant reminder that life was about to change for us, forever. Whatever adventures lay ahead, Jon and I would face them—together.

Moving into our new home in Bellevue, Nebraska, a suburb surrounded by cornfields about 30 miles away from Omaha, was nothing like the fast-paced, beach-centered lifestyle to which we were accustomed. Several other military families lived in our neighborhood, and I was thankful that they quickly accepted me into their circle. As the birth of our Baby Rystrom approached, we found it easier to slow down and embrace a simpler, calmer lifestyle. We traded in our Jeep for a minivan, our vacations for trips to see Jon's family, and late nights out for cookouts and barbecues with Jon's new squad mates.

In September, four months after moving to Nebraska, we experienced one of the best days of our lives—the arrival of our firstborn, a baby girl, named Jordyn Deay Rystrom. Her middle name came from the maiden name of Jon's mother, and sharing her birth with Jon's family made this milestone moment even more precious.

As I held my newborn daughter in my arms, my entire life was transformed. In the same way Jon's unconditional love for me brought healing to my eating disorder, becoming a mother and experiencing the affectionate bond that I shared with Jordyn brought healing to my need for significance. My intention had been to return to work soon after delivery, but once Jordyn was born, my heart was full, and my desire to gain affirmation by climbing a career ladder diminished. Jon was shocked that his once highly competitive, business-woman wife was now content to stay home with our baby girl and hang out with other moms and their children. If someone had told me back in San Diego that I'd be embracing the mom life, I wouldn't have believed it.

Jon and I found a meaningful church home at Christ Community, a Missionary Alliance church in nearby Omaha. There, at Jordyn's baby dedication, Jon and I promised—before God, the congregation, and each other—to raise our daughter in the faith and in a home that honored Christ, to surround her with God's people, and to teach her the truths found in God's Word.

The President's Nightwatch

Jon's new work schedule was total bliss for a Navy wife who had spent nearly half of her marriage apart from her husband. Jon served on one of three NEACP crews that rotated responsibilities on a weekly basis. Jon was gone the first week. For security reasons, Jon could never tell me where he was, but with one plane always staying within 200 miles of President George H. W. Bush, it didn't take a genius to watch the news and figure it out.

The second week, Jon's crew was home and on-call but had to stay within a 12-hour travel time of the base. On the third week, they had to stay within a four-hour recall time while training and serving as backup for the active crew. For a civilian, this might seem very restrictive, but for this Navy wife, it was heaven. Jon being gone one week out of three was much easier to handle than him being gone six months at a time.

That didn't make the week that he was away easy, especially when I couldn't contact him or know where he was, but Jon made up for it when he was home. He was used to working all hours of the day and night, so helping with baby Jordyn's care in the wee hours of the morning was a pleasure for him. And his schedule allowed us to travel and have fun, as long as we didn't drive too far away. We both agreed that the NEACP tour was indeed the best-kept secret in the Navy.

Much like the sounds of Miramar jets gave me a thrill and the humming of the E-2C tugged at my heart, now the sound of the NEACP's 747 flying overhead turned my thoughts to Jon and the significant duty he was fulfilling. The sight of that massive jet as it prepared to land—so low it seemed it might fall from the sky—made an unforgettable impression. But seeing it close-up was even more remarkable.

A Whole New World

FALL 1989
0900 CENTRAL TIME ZONE
JOINT STAFF NEACP
OFFUTT AIR FORCE BASE, BELLEVUE, NEBRASKA, USA
41.13.08 N, 95.91.85 W

A sense of excitement filled the air as family members gathered for the open house at Offutt Air Force Base. Standing out on the tarmac, Jon's extended family joined the crowd of other service members' relatives awaiting their turn to take a rare tour on one of the military's most highly-classified aircraft: the E-4B of the National Emergency Airborne Command Post, or NEACP.

Better known as the "Doomsday" plane or "Nightwatch," the military version of the Boeing 747 performed a critical role in the United States defense strategy. In case of a nuclear attack or other national emergency, the president and the secretary of defense, along with the Joint Chiefs of Staff, could carry out their duties safely from the air without having to land to refuel for days at a time, if necessary.

To accomplish this mission, the massive jet was packed with the latest top-secret technology and operated by a team of highly-skilled crew. Four of these jets made up the NEACP fleet, with crews rotating watches so that one plane was ready to go 24/7. Service members from the Army, Navy, Air Force, and Marines all worked together to accomplish this weighty mission.

Jon was proud of his assignment with NEACP, working primarily as a strategic operations officer. As such, Jon had detailed knowledge of the Single Integrated Operational Plan (SIOP), the United States' comprehensive strategy for nuclear war. Understandably, the SIOP was one of the most sensitive and secretive documents that the United States government possessed. To say Jon's job was classified was an understatement.

"So, Jon," questioned his brother-in-law, "what exactly do you do here?" Jon paused a moment, took a deep breath, and then a serious look came over his face.

"Well, Jim, I could tell you everything," Jon replied as he put his arm on Jim's shoulder. "But then, I'd have to kill you."

"Never mind, then!" Jim quickly responded and he and Jon both broke into laughter. Jon was enjoying sharing his "other" life with his relatives.

"I guess I'll have to be checked out before I can board the plane," Jon's dad, Mervin, joked with a smile.

"To be honest," Jon grinned, "all of you were checked out before they cleared me for this assignment." His family looked around at each other in disbelief, beginning to appreciate how serious Jon's job was.

The family felt a sense of patriotic pride as they approached the sparkling-white jet plane, with "UNITED STATES OF AMERICA" in bold capital letters emblazoned on the side above a single, blue stripe. The plane looked very similar to Air Force One, which is what it would be called should the president ever be on board. Jon smiled as he watched his family's reaction to seeing the enormous plane up close for the first time.

"She's over 230 feet long, with a wingspan of nearly 200 feet, and powered by four massive engines that produce nearly 53,000 pounds of thrust," Jon explained.

"What's that funny little bump on the top of the plane?" inquired his sister, Barb.

"That's a radome, like on my E-2C Hawkeye. It houses a SATCOM antenna, so we can talk to anyone anywhere in the world."

"Except me," Kris interjected. "I'm lucky if I get a single phone call when Jon is deployed on the plane." They all laughed, and Jon smiled. They both knew the plane's sophisticated communications systems couldn't be employed for personal use.

"Yeah, it's funny to be surrounded by the most advanced communications gear in the world, but we all scramble to find a payphone to call home when we land somewhere." Jon made many overseas trips to places like Turkey, Spain, England, and Japan, but letter-writing didn't work with the logistics of being on the plane.

"Looks like it's our turn to start the tour. Let me show you my office," Jon beamed as he took his mother's arm, leading the way through the starboard door near the front of the plane and into a whole new world.

Once inside, the first thing they saw was a spiral staircase, much the same as the ones on the commercial version of the 747.

"Now, it gets a little tight in here, so follow me up the staircase and I'll show you the main deck first. We'll come back to this lower deck later." Wide-eyed, they filed up the stairs, not knowing exactly what to expect. Once they made their way up to the next level, Jon ushered them to a small room toward the front of the plane.

Those who couldn't fit inside looked in through the doorway at four swivel seats around a shared table. Several phones were located throughout the drab room, with several clocks on the wall, along with a few well-worn airline seats and two basic bunk beds. The back of the room housed a typical airplane lavatory and a tiny closet. After all the anticipation leading up to the tour, this spartan space was a bit of a letdown.

"Can you guess what this room is used for?" Jon asked his family, relishing his role as the tour guide.

"Not very fancy, is it?" his mother, Jo, responded.

"Believe it or not," Jon answered, with a slight mischievous look on his face, "this is the personal space for the president and the secretary of defense— or the Joint Chiefs, if they come on board." The family was quite surprised.

"The president stays here? There's not even a shower in that little bathroom," Laurie, Jon's sister, replied.

"There's no room for luxury on the E-4B, not even for the president of the United States," Jon stated. "Our mission is too crucial, and we need to use every square foot of this plane to the max."

"How many square feet are there anyway?" Mike asked his uncle.

"Nearly 5,000. And we use it all. You'll see. Let's turn around and see the rest of the plane."

The next space, directly behind the spiral staircase, was a typical airline galley.

"You bake many cakes on board, Jon?" joked Laurie, remembering Jon's sweet tooth.

"I wish," Jon smiled. "They don't let me do any baking. My work is done farther back."

The next two spaces were a conference room and a larger briefing room with rows of high-backed seats, complete with tables, lectern, projection screens, and multiple phones.

"You put on any talent shows in here?" Barb asked, knowing Jon's jovial personality and love of practical jokes.

"I'll plead the fifth on that one," Jon smiled, deciding not to tell them about the times when the crew would break the tension by coordinating the wearing of dark sunglasses during a briefing, or when the unmistakable voice of Elmer Fudd would waft over the intercom system. In a high-stress environment with long hours, these professionals found ways to keep the pressure in check.

Jon ushered his family into the next space—a large, open room with multiple working consoles packed with phones, radios, keypads, and screens, along with printers, a copier, and a fax machine in the back.

"This is the Operations Team area, where folks like me, who work on the battle staff, do our jobs. We have seats and desks for 31 people, and from these consoles, we have access to all the communication and data available onboard. Here, Jordyn, let Daddy show you his desk." Jon sat down with baby Jordyn in front of one of the consoles.

"Don't worry, Jon, we aren't going to ask you what you do here," Pat, Jon's sister, added with a grin, remembering Jon's joke with Jim earlier.

"I bet he plays chess!" blurted out Eric, one of Jon's younger nephews.

"Well, not quite, Eric, not quite." Jon smiled, but his nephew wasn't that far off the mark. Jon's job required decisive, strategical thinking and the stakes couldn't be any higher. Jon and his colleagues knew better than most the dangers that America faced daily, as NEACP had its pulse on the status of all branches of the military around the globe and the fluctuating quagmire of international threats.

During the years Jon served with NEACP, the world underwent significant change, as revolutions and democracy swept through the former Eastern Bloc, the Berlin Wall came down, and Germany was reunified. The Cold War was winding down, as Mikhail Gorbachev and President George H. W. Bush met at the Malta Summit, the START treaty was signed, and by the end of 1991, the Soviet Union ceased to exist.

But what if, in the midst of the turmoil, those Soviet nuclear missiles fell into the wrong hands? What if our allies or our national assets came under fire in these volatile environments? Serving in the emergency actions area of the battle staff, Jon and his colleagues would be tasked to retransmit the go ahead to the affected forces, if the president should need to make the difficult decision to launch a nuclear response. And that was a day that all of them hoped to avoid.

Holding his infant daughter in his arms, Jon knew that NEACP's role wasn't to start nuclear war, but to prevent it. Their readiness and vigilance were powerful deterrents for rogue nations tempted to push the nuclear button and resulted in safety and freedom for his daughter and the next generation around the world.

"What's that grid in the glass?" asked Ken, Pat's husband, as they passed by one of the door windows.

"That's to shield us from EMPs," Jon explained.

"EMPs?" questioned Jon's nephew, Matt.

"Yeah, that stands for electromagnetic pulses. They happen when a nuclear device goes off and those EMPs can wipe out all our high-tech equipment. That metal grid you see in the glass will prevent that from happening. Even the plane's paint is designed to protect us from radiation."

In all the excitement of viewing the top-secret plane, it was easy to forget that the Doomsday Plane was named that for a reason. The family became a little more somber, thinking of Jon being on board should the unthinkable ever happen.

Jon continued the tour, through the Communications Control area, the crews' sleeping quarters, and down to the belly of the plane, where he showed them the reel that housed a 5-mile-long, low-frequency antenna. Next, he led them upstairs to what would be the first-class section in a commercial 747. On the E-4B, this was transformed into a rest area for the flight crew with the cockpit itself in the very front.

"You know, it's not only President George H. W. Bush that makes us take off," Jon stated. "Sometimes it's Mother Nature."

"Mother Nature?" asked Joey, one of Jon's younger nephews.

"Let's say there's an approaching thunderstorm that might cause our plane to be grounded for a while. And what if a national emergency happened at the same time and we couldn't respond? We can't let that happen. If a storm heads our way, a Klaxon goes off, and we have to be ready for takeoff in five minutes."

"Five minutes? That's fast!" Sara, Jon's only niece, replied.

With the tour over, Jon led the family out of the plane, and they turned for one last close look at the Flying White House.

"Do you have to search us to make sure we don't sneak out with something?" joked Jim.

Jon grinned and said, "Well, I know for sure the plane is going to be thoroughly searched when this open house is over."

"Why?" asked Pat in surprise.

"We have to make sure that no bugs or listening devices were hidden during the tour. We can't be too careful," Jon explained.

Again, his family had another revelation of the seriousness of Jon's work and that of NEACP. What a privilege to be allowed a glimpse into Jon's top-secret world. His family, especially his parents, couldn't have been prouder.

Nebraska Family

As a Joint Services tour member, Jon had the honor of serving alongside service members from other branches of the military: the Army, Air Force, and Marines. The camaraderie built between the members of the crew was deep and would last a lifetime. Many said the best relationships they developed in their military career were those forged at NEACP. The longs hours spent together being on call far from home, the stresses of the overwhelming responsibility, the cooperation, trust, and professionalism required to accomplish the mission forged a special bond among these crew mates.

And that bond translated to their families as well. I was the youngest officer's wife with a baby, and I loved spending time with these more experienced military moms and grew very close to them. We shared dinners and cookouts together, including special gatherings at a double-wide trailer near the base, which was placed there so that we could spend time with our husbands when they were on call.

This was especially meaningful if Jon was on call on Christmas or other special days so that we didn't have to spend so many holidays apart. Of course, if a thunderstorm or other emergency interrupted our meal with a Klaxon siren call, the guys would jump up, run out the door, and hightail it back through the gate.

As meaningful as spending time with the NEACP families was, what really made our tour in Nebraska so special was the time we were able to spend with Jon's family. Jon's hometown was only a 90-minute drive away, and we'd often travel through miles of prairie and cornfields to his parent's humble two-bedroom home in Stromsburg for birthdays and anniversaries or simply to visit.

One of our favorite times to visit was during The Swedish Festival, an annual summertime event, where the town of Stromsburg celebrated their Scandinavian roots. The quaint town square was festooned with blue-and-gold Swedish flags around a stage that featured music, dancers in traditional customs, and the Skjaldborg Vikings. The streets were filled with vendors selling crafts and authentic cuisine, including my personal favorite, ostkaka—a scrumptious Swedish cheesecake. Jordyn loved the excitement of the hometown parade and Jon loved the chicken, barbecued pork chops, and Swedish pancakes. We always felt "välkommen" in Jon's hometown.

Whenever we visited my in-laws, within minutes of arriving, I'd be in the kitchen with Jon's mom, while "Jonny" and his father would be outside working on some project. His dad had retired from farming years ago, but he still looked the part in his overalls and flannel shirts. Mervin loved having Jon working by his side in the garden or in the yard, while I cherished my time with Jo in the kitchen. Jon's siblings and their families often joined us at his parents' home, and many special memories were made together.

How rare it was for a Navy officer to be stationed in Nebraska, near his hometown and his family, with an assignment that gave him so much time with the people he loved. Life was easy, and even though Jon's responsibilities were considerable, we weren't at war. We were still newlyweds in many ways, and the lack of stress allowed us a unique season of enjoying each other and our family. Jon excelled at his job and won his highest-ranking medal to date, the Joint Services Commendation Medal. As for me, once Jordyn was a toddler, I found a way to work part time as an adjunct professor at the University of Nebraska Omaha, where I taught advertising classes.

But this tour couldn't go on forever, and as 1990 ended, the time had come for Jon to receive his new orders. Once again, we had options.

But whatever he chose, we knew the next tour would be sea duty. To move forward in his career as a senior officer, Jon's next billet needed to be a VAW department head if he ever wanted a chance to command his own squadron in the future.

We could have returned to San Diego, but now that we had a daughter, we wanted to avoid the high cost of living and hectic lifestyle of California, and we also wanted to be closer to my parents in West Virginia. In the end, we chose to return to Norfolk where both Jon and I had roots. It would be like going back home.

In August 1991, we packed up our belongings, said tearful goodbyes to our new friends and family, and headed east for our next adventure. After completing his four-month mandatory refresher training (RAG), Jon would join the Bear Aces of VAW-124 and later deploy on the carrier USS Theodore Roosevelt. The Navy-wife life was starting its next chapter, and I wasn't privy to what would be written on its pages.

Jon and Kris' Seagrass Reach home under construction.

CHAPTER 15

Seagrass Reach

When we returned to Norfolk, I was by far a different woman than the one who left five years earlier. I still had my competitive nature, but I loved the "mom life," and I was much more relaxed and experienced in my Navy-wife role.

Our decision to keep and rent out our duplex in San Diego while we lived in Nebraska turned out to be a wise one. Thanks to California's booming real estate market, we had a nice chunk of equity when it came time to sell. Compared to California, land prices were so much cheaper in Chesapeake, a growing area south of Norfolk where many military families found affordable housing. That meant we could build the home of our dreams without me being forced to work. We picked out a lot lined with tall pine trees in a developing neighborhood called "Riverwalk on the Elizabeth," where our dollars would go farther, though that meant Jon's commute to Norfolk was a little longer. Even the name of our street sounded like a fairytale forest: Seagrass Reach.

We planned all the details of our custom home together. We chose a gorgeous, two-story, Georgian-style facade in a tasteful, light brick, with curved brick steps leading up to two beautiful, glass-front double doors. The peach-tiled vaulted entry displayed a grand white-spindled staircase that led to the upper-floor bedrooms, including a playroom over our double garage. The downstairs living area included a lovely formal dining room off the generous kitchen.

Some couples say they want to divorce after enduring the stress of a house-building project, but not us. We had no fights or arguments. We wanted to make each other happy. The way we handled this massive task reflected the trust, honor, and space we willingly gave each other. Jon visited the construction site every day to make sure that everything was done according to his high standards. Jon planned to personally do some of the outside jobs, like the fencing, sprinkler system, and landscaping later.

As we prepared to move into our dream home in December 1991, we found that we had another reason to be thankful: I was expecting again! Somehow getting pregnant and moving seemed to go hand in hand for us, but we couldn't have been more excited, and our new home would be perfect for our growing family.

Checking Off Boxes

Once again, I was unpacking boxes. It seemed the Navy life was all about boxes—constantly packing boxes to move out and unpacking boxes to move in. As I mentally checked off my own "boxes," life could not have been more perfect. Perfect home? Yes, and more than I could have imagined. Perfect marriage? Oh, yes, and only getting better with time. Perfect family? Of course, especially with our second child due in August, and now living closer to my parents in West Virginia.

Perfect church? After living across the country, Jon and I were thrilled to return to our roots and chose First Baptist Church Norfolk as our home church. We tried churches that were closer to us, but none of them seemed to be the right fit. The quality of the staff, the solid teaching of our new pastor, Dr. Bob Reccord, and the warm congregation of more than 6,000 members made the long drive to First Baptist well worth it. Right away, Jon and I joined the choir and a couples' Sunday

School class. We began teaching youngsters in Mission Friends and enrolled our daughter Jordyn in the church preschool.

Perfect friends? Reuniting with our old friends, as well as meeting new ones from Jon's new squadron, our new neighborhood, and our church family provided numerous opportunities for relationship. Everywhere we lived, Jon and I dove head-first into community, and our Norfolk move was no different. Besides our church activities, we cooked out with Jon's squadron and got to know our neighbors. One special friend was Jennifer who was often alone because her husband, a Navy officer, served on a submarine. She lived down the street, and she and Jon enjoyed talking about yard work.

Perfect finances? We had a solid foundation, though I always seemed to be stressed about it. Perfect job? Jon was very secure in his Navy career, and with our return to the Norfolk area, I was ready to prepare myself for the future. Regent University, formerly CBN University, graciously allowed me to rejoin their master's program and complete my thesis. Jon finished his RAG training and joined the Bear Aces in January. I knew he would be following his new squadron

to Panama in the spring for drug-interdiction missions, but I figured I could effectively manage being the pregnant mom of a preschooler, completing my master's thesis, plus getting settled into a new home all by myself. I was still a bit of an overachiever.

The one downer in my life was that my dear, old friend—my beloved Sophie—passed away right after we moved into our new home. I was devastated to lose my sweet companion of more than six years, but at least faithful Max—our Norwegian elkhound fluff ball—was still by our side.

More Shoe Boxes

The next few months were like a blur. I juggled all my responsibilities mostly alone. With Jon away in Panama, we were able to phone each other occasionally, but our daily letter writing resumed. I shared with Jon how Jordyn was dealing with experiencing his long-term absence for the first time.

> Hi Babe,
> Well, this is the beginning of another letter-writing relationship between Kris and Jon. I'm sure this tour will fill up lots of shoe boxes ... On the way home from church, Jordyn asked where you were. When I said at work on the plane, she started crying. So I said you were hunting bad guys and then she was OK!
> Jordyn has been such a good girl—she keeps me laughing with all her antics. She started crying, wanting Daddy today. Every once in a while she'll surprise me with wanting you, just out of the blue.

Even though we were writing letters to each other again, our topics were very different from the lovey-dovey letters of our newlywed days. Many of them centered on parenthood. I tried to keep Jon up to date on the other details of Jordyn's life that he had to miss: a beach trip and Jordyn's growing love of the ocean, the fun times spent with other families and their kids and, of course, her health.

I realized Jordyn felt really HOT, so I took her temp and it was 102°!! Poor thing had a fever! So in the five weeks you've been gone, she has had a stomach virus, a sinus infection and now 102° fever. I hate to see what it is going to be like with two kids while you are at sea for six months!

I'm really concerned about the cruise. Hopefully, the baby will make it go faster and by then I'll be back to choir, Bible study, maybe working out again. Anyway, I've been staying busy, but there is still a void, a loneliness, and I get so tired ... but again, that could also be the pregnancy and still the weight of getting this thesis out of the way. Ugh.

Of course, Jon's Panama duty and workups in preparation for a Mediterranean cruise on USS Theodore Roosevelt meant that we not only had to miss Easter together but also our sixth wedding anniversary. With the TR's six-month 1993 Med cruise set to start the following March and end in September, it would be May 1994 before we had a shot to celebrate an anniversary together again. Who knew, with Jon's unforgiving Navy schedule, whether he would even be home then or not?

As I read Jon's letters, I began to learn about some of his squadron mates. In their off times in Panama, they would go scuba diving, golfing, or hang out at the officers club. I was able to match the men to their wives and kids, as I was getting to know the women of the Bear Aces at our regular meetings. He told me about Shelly Messier's husband, John—also known as "Frenchy"—whom Jon thought was the best stick, or the best pilot, in the squadron. I'd already taken a meal over to Paola Dyer, the wife of another pilot, Billy Ray, after the birth of their baby son. I couldn't match unattached Patrick Ardaiz—called "Aardvark"—with anyone, but Jon genuinely enjoyed working with him and found Pat to be a worthy chess opponent. Then there was Katy Forwalder's husband, Bob, who was training to be a CICO, like Jon.

His Panama duty ended in mid May, but by mid June, workups on USS Theodore Roosevelt began, and Jon was once again at sea. Another "hello-goodbye" period had begun, but we also hoped it would be one of our last. Jon had a good chance of being promoted to the rank of commander when the next promotion board met, soon after the start of Jon's 1993 cruise. But he realized that based on the officer roles available in the squadron, his career path would not include being in a command position of his own squadron. I could tell by his workup letters that his priorities were shifting.

Hi My Love,

Well, another period of being apart, but at the same time I realize that you are kept so busy with Jordyn that the loneliness is not as strong, except at certain times. I pray that you do not get sick and that Jordyn stays healthy for you while I am away. I don't spend a lot of time in my room. I am going to finally finish my book, The Bible in 30 Days. The Bible has 66 books.

Kris, going to sea is not what it once was. I miss you and Jordyn too much and love you like crazy. I just pray that this tour gives us what we want for my career. I know that if it is in my power—I really mean God's power—after this tour, no more sea duty for us. I love you and miss you. Jordyn, give mommy a hug! Love, Jon

Unexpected Phone Call

Summer came and I cherished the days that Jon was home. He worked hard on our yard, installing a fence and working on the landscaping. By now we knew we were having another girl, and my due date was only weeks away. One evening, while Jon and I were getting ready for bed, the phone rang. Jon answered and although I couldn't hear the conversation on the other end, the look on Jon's face told me that something was very, very wrong. After asking a few questions, Jon hung up the phone on our nightstand and sat down on the bed in despair with his head in his hands.

"Jon, what's wrong?" I asked, with my stomach in knots. He sighed, trying to find the words.

"There's been an accident, with an E-2C, not from our squadron." He paused. "All five men were killed."

My heart froze. Killed? Dead? All five of them? Jon gave me the rest of the details. An E-2C from VAW-126, the Sea Hawks, was coming back from a routine training flight near Puerto Rico, off the aircraft carrier USS John F. Kennedy. They were only minutes from landing when a fire broke out in the cockpit, filling the plane with thick smoke. They sent out a distress call, but only four miles from the ship, the plane tumbled out of the sky and into the water. One body was recovered, but the remains of the other four men were never found, and they were declared lost at sea.

The VAW community was a tight-knit one, and even though these men weren't in Jon's squadron, they were considered brothers all the same. The crash of the Sea Hawk's 602 sent a jolt through the entire VAW community. And it sent a jolt through me too.

Jon had told me that E-2Cs never crash. Obviously, that was not the case. The plane hadn't gone down in bad weather or because the pilots made a fatal error. The problem was with the plane itself, and those poor men didn't have time to bail out. I could only imagine what the wives and children of those men were going through. It was all I could do to keep the memory of the front-page picture of a Navy widow holding her husband's folded flag—the one I'd seen in San Diego years before—from taking over my mind.

Our Chesapeake Baby

Two other incidents happened during that time, foreshadowing the stresses yet to come. The first was a false-labor scare while Jon was training at sea, when I thought I was going into labor early and I was rushed to the hospital. Jon was sent a Red Cross message but, thankfully, it was a false alarm and I was fine. But the thought of giving birth without Jon by my side was more than I could stand.

My fears were dismissed when, later in August, Taylor Windham Rystrom was born and my biggest fan and best birth coach was there beside me. Even at birth, it was obvious that Taylor looked like her father which made her daddy extremely proud.

But my health scares weren't over. Jon returned to USS Theodore Roosevelt for workups and I added caring for a newborn to my list of duties. When Taylor was about six weeks old, she became very fussy and I took her temperature. Her fever was 103°, and I instantly took her to the doctors. They couldn't determine the cause of her fever and admitted her to the hospital. I tried to stay calm, but as more tests were run and the doctors couldn't give me any answers, I became hysterical.

I was able to contact Jon where they were operating near Puerto Rico. But as much as he wanted to come home, he wasn't allowed to leave. I was devastated. This was my first true crisis without Jon there to calm and reassure me and to balance my intense emotions with his cool-headed personality. Our church rallied around me and our girls, and I stayed by Taylor's side, feeling helpless and afraid. As I lay next to her in that hospital room seeing all the tubes in her, the fear of parenting alone was overwhelming. This experience took the stresses of the Navy-wife life to a completely new level. Thankfully, Taylor fully recovered.

Significant Events

Summer turned to fall. Bill Clinton defeated George H. W. Bush in the November presidential elections, and though I wasn't into politics or world affairs, the military wondered what effect his policies would have on them when he took office in January. The Navy had already experienced budget cuts, but at least they increased one benefit, which allowed Jon to double the amount of his Servicemen's Group Life Insurance policy. Because of the dangers of their jobs, Navy aviators, unlike civilians, found it difficult to buy traditional life insurance, so this benefit was sorely needed.

"If I die, you'll be well taken care of," he joked with me one day. I was not amused.

"Don't talk like that, Jon! Stop!" Maybe it was all the stress of this workup period getting to me, but at times I would look at Jon's hands, his face, his skin, memorizing his scars in case I needed to identify his body one day. That old, dreadful feeling was coming back—the same one I'd felt years ago when I saw the widow's picture on the newspaper in San Diego. And Jon talking about life insurance policies certainly didn't help.

Workups continued off and on into November and December. When he was home, Jon would join me in all our church activities, like singing in the choir together and attending our couples' Sunday School class. And Jon even taught the 3-year-olds' class in Mission Friends, a preschool Bible and missionary class held each Wednesday evening after the family fellowship meal. But even when he was on the ship, spiritual matters were still important to him.

Hey Good Looking,

Are Jordyn and Taylor being good girls? No more hospital trips, I hope ... It was interesting yesterday. I was doing the flight schedule, and it being Sunday's schedule, I didn't schedule anything 'till the afternoon. The CO asked me why no training in the morning and I said it was Sunday and I didn't plan to schedule anything, because there were people who wanted to go to church in the ship's chapel. And he said, "Who would go?" I looked him square in the eye and said that I planned to and I was sure there were others. At that point the XO basically agreed with me, so the CO said OK. I feel good about that—I stood my ground, even though it is a small point ... Well honey, time to go teach and more training. I love you, Jon

Tell Jordyn that Daddy wants to watch "Beauty and the Beast" with her, and Taylor is to wait to roll over 'till I am home.

This Navy wife was tiring of waiting until he was home, and even when he was around, we rarely had the luxury to relax and enjoy it. In my letters, I wondered if our lives would ever be "normal" or not.

Jon, I really hate being alone so much. I know there is nothing you can do, and you've built this beautiful house for me, but it is so hard going day and night, knowing it is still days and weeks before you are home and, basically, just for a visit. It doesn't even feel like I'm married sometimes, and when you are home, all your time is devoted to Jordyn, getting stuff done around the house, and work, again. Sounds like a lonely housewife having a pity party...

I'll just say, after this tour—you will get a shore tour with no separation. We've never had any length of time when you aren't gone for long periods of time for over six years. It is time that you start being a full-time husband. OK?

Jon missed Thanksgiving with us, but he was home for Christmas. We carried out our Rystrom tradition and decorated our Christmas tree together, along with Jordyn's help, who was now 3 years old.

Five days before Christmas, Dr. Bob Reccord performed Taylor's baby dedication service at First Baptist Church Norfolk.

Like we had with Jordyn, Jon and I promised before God, our church family, and each other that we would raise Taylor in a Christian home connected to the body of Christ, with a respect and love for God's Word, and encourage her to have a relationship with God. With our year-old home decked out in holiday cheer, our growing family getting to celebrate the season together, and our meaningful connection to our church family and other friends, that Christmas was a special one.

With the New Year, we began our final push to prepare for Jon's six-month cruise, set to begin in March. One thing that helped us emotionally was to look beyond the cruise, so we planned our family's first trip to Disney World once Jon returned in September. We'd met another Navy family in the neighborhood, the Purcells. Mike was deploying on USS Theodore Roosevelt too, though he wasn't a part of the air wing. He and Jon hit it off right away, and they made plans to share some hobbies together when they got back home.

Jon and I talked a lot about his career after this cruise was over, and his detailer had been helping Jon investigate possible tours. One option included moving to London, but we weren't sure we wanted to uproot our family, sell the dream home we'd lovingly built together, and move overseas. But what if that was the only way to continue his naval career? He'd hoped to retire from the Navy and become a financial advisor, and with the O-5 promotion board set to meet in March, Jon would gain a very good idea of where he stood with the Navy. So many questions—so few answers.

Jon's parents celebrated their 50th wedding anniversary in February, and we took time out of our hectic schedule to travel to Stromsburg with our girls to celebrate this milestone event with Jon's family. Before we left, we went to Olin Mills Portrait Studio to have a formal family portrait made—the first since Taylor was born—to display alongside photos from everyone in Jon's extended family. As an anniversary gift, we even bought each of Jon's parents a nice outfit for the occasion. After our NEACP years, Nebraska held even more fond memories for me, and we were so happy to introduce everyone to our newest member of the Rystrom family.

There are times we don't recognize the significance of events until later.

Once we were home from our trip, my world became very small. All I could focus on was my own family and Jon's upcoming deployment. My Navy-wife hat was about to be worn full time and, to be honest, I was ready for this cruise to get started so that we could be done with it. As far as what our president was doing or what was going on in the rest of the world, I had no idea.

CHAPTER 16

Rosebushes and Goodbyes

Iron Grip

02 MAR 1993
2143 CENTRAL EUROPE TIME, UTC+1
CERSKA, HERZEGOVINA
44.15.18 N, 19.01.34 E

The thin, plastic sheeting stretched over the broken window glass did little to keep out the icy chill that penetrated the remote mountain enclave. In the dark interior of the shell-damaged cottage, a despairing Bosniak Muslim mother and her three young children huddled together in a vain attempt to keep warm. Her desperate husband, most likely shot or captured by the attacking Serbs, had disappeared weeks ago while foraging for whatever food could be scoured from the surrounding snow-covered forests. Random gunfire punctuated the gloomy night as the few remaining village defenders, with their feeble light weapons, endeavored to hold back the far-superior

Serb forces who had encircled the village with an iron grip.

Life hadn't always been like this in the rugged, scenic region of Eastern Bosnia, where the Muslim majority had once lived in relative harmony beside their Serb neighbors. But all that changed when the collapse of the former Eastern Bloc and the splitting of Yugoslavia fanned regional and ethnic divisions and aspirations into full flame. The Serbs, the second-largest ethnic group in the area, wanted Bosnia-Herzegovina to be a part of a greater Serbia, but the more numerous Bosniak Muslims stood in their way.

Backed by the Yugoslav army, Serb forces began a strategy of ethnic cleansing by surrounding and shelling Muslim communities, slowly starving them, and eventually forcing them out of homes that had been in their families for generations. Men and boys who weren't executed and left in mass graves and women and girls who weren't rounded up and raped went on foot by the thousands as refugees in search of safe areas many miles away. To be fair, no ethnic group was innocent of wrongdoing during this convoluted conflict, but the complicated nature of the Bosnian War was irrelevant to a besieged mother in Cerska trying to help her forsaken children live to see another day.

A small number of United Nation convoys had reached her village early in the conflict, but the few medicines, food supplies, and plastic to cover broken windows that they provided was like putting a Band-Aid on a severed limb. The villagers knew it was only a matter of time before the Serbs moved in and their fate was sealed.

The UN had proven incapable of ending the conflict, and the humanitarian airlift called "Operation Provide Promise," which began in July 1992, couldn't erase the effects of the hostilities. Cerska's only hope was a report from a nearby shortwave radio operator who heard that the president of the United States had authorized airdrops of food rations to their area. While the multinational coalition forces running Operation Provide Promise had been airlifting food and medical supplies into Sarejevo for months, this would be the first time that food rations would be delivered to the beleaguered and isolated Muslim areas of Eastern Bosnia.

Large C-130 transport planes flying out of air bases in Europe would drop their loads from high altitudes to avoid being hit by enemy fire. This also meant the accuracy of airdrops would be inconsistent, but the Pentagon felt that even if some shipments missed their mark, the rations that made it through would be worth the effort. Perhaps with the Americans getting involved, Bosniak Muslims hoped they could hold out long enough for a diplomatic solution to end the fighting. And while they were waiting, maybe they could at least receive some rations to ease the gnawing in their stomachs.

The thin night air was interrupted by an unfamiliar sound: the low drones of C-130 transport planes. The mother gasped and her children clasped their hands in hope. Perhaps they would live to see another day after all.

Show and Tell

March arrived and we had only 11 days until Jon deployed to the Med. Somehow in the middle of our crazy schedule, Jon and I managed to squeeze in one final date night. He also wanted to continue our church activities up to the very end and that included showing up at Jordyn's 3-year-old preschool class for career day.

I watched Jon as he put on his flight suit and packed up his other gear, along with a model of the E-2C plane, and we all went in together for Jordyn's show-and-tell at First Baptist Church Norfolk. I was proud and thankful that Jon placed a high value on spending meaningful time with our children, but I didn't know the significant facts that I would learn that day.

Jordyn looked so proud holding her daddy's hand as they entered the classroom. Several parents had come to share, and after several presentations, it was Jon's turn. Some of the kids already knew Mr. Jon from the Mission Friends class he taught at church, but they'd never seen him in his flight suit before.

"Good morning, boys and girls!" Jon began his presentation, as he sat down in a little preschool chair with a wide grin on his face and a twinkle in his eyes. Jon's natural connection with children and his enthusiasm for his job were obvious, as he clearly explained his role in the Navy in ways that a 3-year-old could understand.

"I fly planes in the Navy to keep America safe—in a plane that looks like it has a big pancake on top," Jon illustrated by pointing to his model. "That pancake lets me look at the other planes in the sky, and then I can see the bad guys coming and tell the good guys where to go." The children were fascinated with his explanations and were hanging on his every word.

"Let me show you my flight suit and my survival gear," Jon continued. "My dark-green flight suit covers my whole body, and it's made of fabric that can't burn. And my shoes," Jon demonstrated as he hit the end of them with his hand, "are steel-toed so that my feet can't get hurt. I also wear these gloves and this helmet with a visor that I lock down to keep my head and face safe."

"What's that part wrapped around your legs?" asked one little boy.

"That's a good question," Jon replied. "I have this special webbing that I step into, and it's not only around my legs but also around my waist, my shoulders, and chest too. See?" Jon stood up and slowly turned completely around so that the children could get a better look.

"And I have to make sure it's really snug and tight, because if something happens, this webbing is what holds me to my parachute. And it can really hurt if the webbing is loose when the parachute comes out."

"What's all that stuff stuck on it?" another little girl asked.

"Well, it's all part of my survival gear. Let me show you. Around my neck and waist, I have things I can inflate with air—like one of your pool floaties. That helps keep my head above the water if I have to leave my plane over the ocean. Here's my flashlight, and I've got lots of pockets. Does anyone want to see what's in my pockets?"

They were really getting into Jon's talk, and the children yelled "Yes!" and raised their hands.

"OK, let's see what's in my pockets. Here I have things that I can use if I'm out on my own for a while, like fishing line and hooks, a signal flare, and something that makes smoke and a mirror so that I can let other planes know where I am. I always like to carry a Swiss-army knife with me, and I keep it in this pocket. And all of us on the plane have one of these."

Jon took out a small canister that had what looked like a scuba-diver's breathing device on one end.

"This is a bottle of oxygen—a bottle of air—and that way if our plane goes down into the water, I can pull this out and breathe in here," Jon explained as he put the device up to his face. "That will give me time to find my way out of the plane."

As the eager children asked more questions, Jon patiently answered them all. The kids were clearly entranced by Jon's captivating presentation. When he finished and sat down next to Jordyn, the smile on her face was priceless.

I knew the basics of Jon's job, but I didn't know the details about his survival gear. Getting out of the tight confines of the E-2C in an emergency would be difficult, and being a scuba diver, to know that he had a bottle of oxygen with him brought me some comfort. Not that I ever wanted him to have to use it.

Our last Sunday before cruise, we followed our usual routine and attended church as a family. Jon and I usually went to our Sunday School class together, where he was always so sweet to bring me a cup of coffee, but that Sunday I took my turn helping in the church nursery instead. The friendships that Jon and I had developed in that weekly class were very meaningful to both of us. Several military people went to our church, and everyone there understood the demands that deployment put on military families. I was thankful for that group of people who would help support me during Jon's cruise.

Promise Me

07 MAR 1993
0900 EASTERN STANDARD TIME, UTC-4
FIRST BAPTIST CHURCH, NORFOLK, VIRGINIA, USA
36.50.41 N, 76.11.24 W

The hubbub of conversation slowly faded as the last couples filed into the meeting room and took their seats. Jon smiled and greeted his fellow Sunday School classmates but kept his eye on the class leader, waiting to get his attention. Once the room got quiet, Jon motioned to him and got permission to address the class. With a somber smile on his face, he walked to the front and faced his friends.

Jon had presented briefs, projects, and lectures countless times over the years in front of powerful civilian contractors, Pentagon brass, and all ranks of the military. But what he was about to share made all those times seem insignificant in comparison. He took a deep breath, clasped his hands behind his back, and began his remarks.

"As most of you know, I'm going on a cruise to the Mediterranean for six months, starting this Thursday."

Everyone shook their heads in understanding, as they were familiar with Jon's upcoming deployment.

"I want you to promise me something: I want you to promise that you will take care of Kris and the girls."

"Oh, Jon, of course," laughed one lady softly, familiar with Jon's antics and jokes in class. Others in the room giggled slightly.

"No, I'm serious," Jon said firmly with a solemn look and tone that instantly changed the mood in the room from casual to grave. He paused slightly before continuing. "I want you to promise me that you will take care of my family when I'm gone."

No one had ever addressed the class like that before. Walking alongside military families when a father was deployed wasn't a new idea to the class. Another member, named Dave, was currently deployed on USS John F. Kennedy. Many of them, including Jon and Kris, had been looking after his wife and kids and including them in their family activities. Jon's friends were less surprised by his request than by the soberness in which he delivered it.

"I promise, Jon," answered one husband on the front row. "I'll help Kris and the girls in any way I can."

"We both will," his wife joined in.

"Me too, Jon. You can count on me." And in moments, everyone in the class gave Jon the promise he'd asked for. Jon thanked the class and took his seat, satisfied that Kris and the girls had the support of his classmates. This wasn't Jon's first cruise by any means, but it was his first with children, and that made all the difference. He would do everything in his power to provide for them and leave the rest in God's hands.

Storm of the Century

The final days before Jon's Thursday departure were a whirlwind of activity. Jon put on his Nebraska overalls and completed every last household task that he could, including planting rosebushes along the side of the house. He still wasn't a snappy dresser at times and liked to hang onto other "useful" clothing, like his old, brown, terry-cloth bathrobe. Neither the overalls nor the bathrobe would be making the cruise on USS Theodore Roosevelt.

The TR itself was preparing not only for the cruise but also for a very special visitor. The newly elected President Bill Clinton planned to deliver his first military-themed speech onboard USS Theodore Roosevelt on Friday, the TR's first full day at sea. He would be accompanied by other high-ranking officials and members of the national media, making this a significant and widely-covered event.

As powerful as the president was, even he couldn't control the weather. I didn't usually keep an eye on the forecast, but I couldn't help but hear about a crazy weather system headed our way later that week. Being hailed as the "Storm of the Century," meteorologists described it as a hurricane with snow and potentially lots of it. It would impact most of the Eastern United States, but exactly how it would affect us in the Norfolk area was still unclear.

Wednesday came—the final full day before the cruise. That evening at church, Jordyn enjoyed one more fun evening with her daddy teaching his last Mission Friends class for a while. When we got home, Jon put on his overalls and completed the finishing touches on our new rosebushes and also made sure that our house was buckled down for the approaching storm due to hit that weekend.

Changing Priorities

I joined him on the front steps when he finished, and we talked about our future. In a few weeks, we'd know whether or not he'd be promoted to O-5 commander. His detailer told him that he might not be able to find a shore duty in the Norfolk area and possibly would have to move to London after all. As my hands rested on the bricks of our curved porch steps, I wondered if we would have to sell our custom-built home before we had a chance to raise our family in it. Jon suddenly became very solemn, which wasn't like him.

"Do I still want to do this?" Jon asked, thinking of his 15 years of service in the Navy. That was a good question. We talked about whether or not we wanted to spend the next five years having to uproot our lives and move away so that he could retire after 20 years and receive his pension. Now that we had children, our priorities were changing. Jon adored his girls and wanted to be there for them and not to be gone for weeks and months at a time.

> *... THE LORD WILL PROVIDE; AS IT IS SAID TO THIS DAY, ON THE MOUNT OF THE LORD IT SHALL BE PROVIDED. (GENESIS 22:14 ESV)*

Jon made some phone calls to say goodbye to family and friends. As we put the girls to bed and the house grew quiet on our final evening together, we both took comfort in knowing that this should be one of Jon's last cruises. If we could make it through the next six months, we should have a long break before Jon had another extended deployment. At least that was our hope.

The next morning started out with a bang, literally. Overnight, the time for Jon's squadron to depart was moved up, but we didn't know that, because our phone was accidently off the hook. Someone had to come from the squadron and bang on our door to get Jon out of bed.

Jon ran into the bathroom for a quick shave and shower while I woke up our sleepy girls and frantically got them ready for the van ride to the base. Jon threw on his old, brown bathrobe as he hurriedly finished his last-minute packing. He dressed in record time, and I met him in the garage as we jumped into the van and rushed to the base.

We were all business and there was no time for emotions or sentimentalities. We pulled into the parking lot with a jerk, and Jon grabbed his bags. A quick hug and kiss for me and the girls, along with a "Miss you!" and he was off.

As I watched him run across the parking lot and into the hangar, I actually felt relieved. The cruise was finally beginning, and I simply wanted to get it over with. Workups had been so stressful and, like Jon, I had my orders. The time had come to assume my duties and power through one of the last cruises of Jon's Navy career.

Jon had prepared me well. With my Navy-wife hat firmly in place, I drove home and jumped into being a single mother and handling all the other details of our lives. The first task at hand was to make Daddy's countdown chart. I decided it would be more fun for the girls if we made a paper chain instead. Jordyn and I diligently worked crafting a paper chain out of her colored construction paper. We had so much fun cutting and taping each brightly colored link. Jordyn picked out special stickers to put on each holiday, birthday, and other special occasions, while I wrote the numbers to help us all count the days until Daddy came back home. Each night I planned for us to remove one link together as we prayed for Jon's safe return. Cutting the last of the 183 links couldn't come fast enough for us.

CHAPTER 17

Paper-Chain Prayers

A Salute From the Commander in Chief

12 MAR 1993
1100 EASTERN STANDARD TIME, UTC-4
USS THEODORE ROOSEVELT
EAST COAST WATERS, USA
36.57.50 N, 74.20.50 W

The unmistakable sound of a Sikorsky Sea King filled the air as Marine One prepared to land on the flight deck of aircraft carrier USS Theodore Roosevelt. The sunny skies and calm seas gave no hint of the massive storms to come, as the TR welcomed its commander in chief. President Bill Clinton, dressed in a green flight jacket and brown khakis, accompanied by his secretary of defense, exited the helicopter. He returned the salutes of the multi-colored flight deck crew arrayed to honor him, as he strolled across the tarmac to meet the assembled Navy brass. Warm handshakes, eager smiles, and polite banter ensued before the president was led to the edge of the deck to view USS Arleigh Burke as she paraded by.

The tour continued as the president went below deck and through the enlisted mess line to share a meal with the Sailors. Secret Service officers blended discreetly in the background as a few Sailors with cameras took snapshots of the smiling president who posed for picture after picture. After viewing various aircraft and chatting with the aviators who flew them, the president and other dignitaries gathered on a platform in front of the thousands of Sailors and aviators packed into the massive hangar bay to hear the president's speech. Wearing his new USS Theodore Roosevelt dark-blue ball cap, he stepped up to the podium adorned with the presidential seal and addressed the crowd.

I am honored to be here. As many of you know, it is a great blessing and a great honor to be elected president of the United States. But there is no greater honor in the office than being the commander in chief of the finest armed forces in the world today and the finest that America has ever known.

Our Armed Forces are more than the backbone of our security. You are the shining model of our American values: dedication, responsibility, a willingness to sacrifice for the common good and for the interests and the very existence of this country.

This carrier can extend our reach. These planes can deliver our might. They are truly extraordinary tools, but only because they are in the hands of you. It is your skill, your professionalism, your courage, and your dedication to our country and to service that gives the muscle, sinew, and the soul of our strength. And today, I'm proud to be here to salute you.

This world remains a very dangerous place. Saddam Hussein confirmed that. The tragic violence in Bosnia today reminds us of that every day ... today, there are different security challenges into which we must march. And at times you who serve our nation in uniform may be called upon to answer not only the sound of guns but also a call of distress, a summons to keep the peace, even a cry of starving children.

I know this has been a difficult day for many of you. It can't be easy to leave family and friends for six months at sea, especially when the challenges before us seem unclear and when you wonder whether world events may or may not place you in harm's way. But I hope you understand that your work is vitally important to the United States and to the commander in chief.

This is a new and hopeful world but one full of danger. I am convinced that your country, through you, has a historic role in trying to make sure that there is, after all, a new world order, rooted in peace, dedicated to prosperity and opportunity.

The American people have placed their faith in you, and you have placed your life at the service of your country. The faith is well placed, and I thank you.

As the crowd politely applauded and the president shook hands with the dignitaries on the stage, the rest of the ships in Battle Group 8 were already steaming east to escape the hurricane-force winds to come. USS Arleigh Burke, a guided missile destroyer on her maiden deployment, had been left behind to accompany the TR as she stayed near the coast to accommodate the president's visit. But dark storm clouds were gathering that would soon envelop more than ships, as the president's recent policies to expand the mission of Operation Provide Promise would have far-reaching consequences at home and abroad.

Life as Usual

The weather reports kept calling for severe weather that weekend, but you would have never guessed it the days before. The weather was nice enough on Thursday that I even tried to pick up where Jon had left off and planted a few shrubs around the yard. Jordyn enjoyed being outside playing in the dirt, and we both relished the fresh air. The weather turned colder on Friday, with the major brunt of the "Storm of the Century" due to come late Saturday afternoon.

On Friday, the first full day of Jon's cruise, I resumed my letter writing ritual, but now that I was a mom, it was a little different from past cruises. After dinner and some play time, I'd get the girls ready for bed, and we'd pray for Daddy as we cut off a link in our paper chain. I hoped that Jon liked my idea of helping the girls count down the days. Jordyn loved the long, multicolored chain being in her playroom, and it became a fun waiting-for-Daddy game. Once they were tucked into bed, sometimes I'd chat on the phone with some of my friends before writing my letter to Jon, and then I called it a night.

As I wrote my first letter, I thought about one thing I hadn't done since Jon had left—cry. What a contrast to the buckets of tears that I shed when I dropped Jon off at the San Diego airport for our first mini cruise. And I didn't plan on self-destructing when letters from Jon were delayed, which was inevitable. To help this cruise fly by, I already had a list of projects I hoped to complete and outings to attend with friends.

I kept wondering how bad this anticipated storm would be and how it might affect Jon and the ships at sea. By tomorrow afternoon, the actual impact of the storm on all of us would no longer be a mystery.

Rocking and Rolling

13 MAR 1993
2308 EASTERN STANDARD TIME, UTC-4
USS THEODORE ROOSEVELT
OFF EASTERN SEABOARD OF USA
37.21.25 N 69.21.46 W

Jon felt like he was back on USS Texas as the mighty USS Theodore Roosevelt rocked and rolled in the massive waves. As huge 17-foot swells crashed into the TR's steel hull, waves rose more than 80 feet, and the frigid saltwater spray repeatedly covered the 4.5-acre flight deck and the multiple planes chained to it. Not all of Jon's shipmates were blessed like him with a steel stomach. Men who had spent years serving on carriers and who were unaccustomed to feeling the swaying of the ship were getting seasick by the hundreds.

USS Arleigh Burke had it worst of all. While the rest of the smaller ships in the battle group had escaped the teeth of the storm, she was caught in the thick of it, looking more like a rubber ducky in a bathtub than a 500-foot-long, 9,000-ton vessel with a 300-person crew. At one point, she was completely underwater as a monstrous wave crashed over her mast. Cracks developed in her bulkhead and some compartments started taking on water, earning this new vessel the dubious moniker, "Already Broke."

One rogue wave that slammed the TR caused a section with a massive steel I-beam to buckle like it was made of Play-Doh. The wind and waves were so severe that no one was allowed onto the flight deck for five days. But when the storm finally subsided and the damage was surveyed, they discovered that every plane on the flight deck was encased in a quarter-inch layer of salt. Corrosion control teams would have their work cut out for them.

Jon used the downtime to stay on top of numerous reports and to get settled into his stateroom. He'd already heard of more than one television falling over from the tossing seas, so he and his roommate made sure everything in their cabin was secure. He had to keep an eye on his shifting coffee mug as he sat down that evening to write his first letter of the cruise to Kris.

Jon's letter made it to the mailroom, but the mail couldn't leave the ship until the weather cleared. But the TR wasn't the only place with mail delays. Back in the United States, much of the East had suffered significantly from the "Storm of the Century," all the way from the deep South to the Canadian border. Dubbed a "snowicane," the historical weather system caused everything from tornadoes, thundersnow, flooding, storm surges, damaging winds, and snowfalls measuring in feet instead of inches. The storm back home in CONUS was on everyone's mind as the TR spent another night being rocked by rough seas.

Keep Daddy Safe

The wind started howling like crazy on Saturday afternoon and continued well into the night, rattling the window screens, bending the trees, and causing poor Max to act very distraught. But when I woke up Sunday morning, I was encouraged to find that the storm had passed us by without any major damage. Other than the pilot light going out in the gas fireplace and a few branches down in the yard, all was well. Almost all. The girls were both starting to show signs of a cold, which had nothing to do with the storm. I decided to stay home from church and have a rest day instead.

Over the next few days as the girls' colds ran their course, Jordyn wasn't sleeping well and kept coming to my room at night for comfort. To keep my focus off Jon's absence, I started my cruise strategy of staying busy by starting some sewing and kitchen projects. In the evenings, the girls and I kept cutting off the links of the paper chain and we prayed our nightly prayer, just perfect for a 3-year-old: "Dear Jesus, please keep Daddy safe in his airplane. Amen."

No-Fly Days

18 MAR 1993 THURSDAY
1014 AZOT (AZORES TIME) UTC-1
USS THEODORE ROOSEVELT
NEAR AZORES
38.47.06 N 36.34.19 W

"Sir, if you have a moment, I need your signature on something," said the chief yeoman as Jon walked into the Bear Aces' ready room.

"What is it?" asked Jon, who had just returned from stateroom inspection duty and was getting ready for a brief on the rules of engagement (ROE) for their upcoming mission.

"It's about your life insurance policy, sir."

"I thought I took care of that back in December," Jon responded with a quizzical look on his face.

"That's right, sir, you increased it to the new maximum, but somehow your signature was missed. If you could just verify this form is correct and sign at the bottom, please."

Jon looked it over, made sure his information was correct, and double-checked the beneficiaries. As he prepared to sign it, the stitches on his right arm caught his eye. The small incision where the flight surgeon had removed an annoying cyst a few days earlier was healing nicely, and the hair in the 3-by-2-inch portion that had been shaved should grow back in a few weeks.

Jon smiled politely as he handed the form back to the chief yeoman and took his seat with the other Bear Aces. If they couldn't fly, they could at least prepare in other ways for what was to come, which included briefs and various training. But the no-fly days needed to end, and soon.

Hopes for leaving the bad weather behind as the ship headed east were futile as one storm after another slowed their PIM, or plan of intended movement. The days of no-fly conditions combined with the ship's need to hightail it to the Med meant that pilots and crews were behind on completing the number of day and night landings (called traps) required to clear them for flight operations. Jon and others like him who were responsible for keeping crews "qualed" or qualified were feeling the pressure.

So far, despite the harsh weather, Jon was enjoying the cruise. But not every day on the ship was pleasant, especially when Jon's operation department had a mix-up with an important secret message. Jon became even more depressed when he heard that his beloved Nebraska Cornhuskers had lost their first-round basketball game in the NCAA tournament. Jon hoped that this would be the last time he'd miss watching his favorite sports live because of a cruise.

Saturday was a much better day for the most part. Training was productive but still no flying. The admiral and commander of Carrier Strike Group 8 gave them a 30-minute brief and explained that they were heading straight to the Adriatic with their first possible port of call around 12 April, but that was something he couldn't promise.

The big downer for the day was when news came of an F-14 jet that had gone down after a routine training flight near the North Carolina coast. The RIO on board, Lt. Cmdr. Fred Dillingham, was a former member of VF-84, the F-14 Squadron currently deployed on USS Theodore Roosevelt. A memorial service for Dillingham was planned for the next day in the ship's fo'c'sle, or forecastle, where the massive anchor chains were located. This large open room at the bow, under the flight deck, was a convenient place to hold large gatherings, such as weekly religious services and, less often, memorial services.

When Jon heard that Lt. Cmdr. Dillingham was a husband and father of two kids, his death hit a little too close to home. Jon was suddenly very thankful that the chief yeoman had caught his missing signature.

That evening, Jon sat down at his desk and thought about what to tell Kris. This letter would be No.

8. With the CODs being grounded due to weather, mail both ways was obviously delayed. He would keep writing anyway. He could tell her about the admiral's talk or about how he got locked out of his room earlier that evening, which might give her a good laugh.

His eyes rested on a framed picture of Kris and the girls that he kept on his desk. He couldn't help but smile as he gazed at their precious faces and a little lump formed in his throat. Oh, how he missed them. He felt so blessed to have such a beautiful wife, inside and out, and two amazing daughters.

In his most recent letter, No. 7, written very early that morning, he'd shared more about his day on the ship, and he chuckled to himself, wondering what Kris would think about the item he'd asked her to ship to him. But for this letter, he wanted it to be different. Maybe it was because of hearing the news about Lt. Cmdr. Dillingham's death, but he wanted to take the time to let Kris know how much she and the girls meant to him.

The next day, Sunday, Jon attended the lieutenant commander's memorial service. The somber affair had a great turnout, even from those who never knew the lieutenant commander personally. Naval aviators were a tight-knit bunch.

Finally, the weather was clearing, and for Jon that meant a couple of things. For one, pilots and crews could start to be qualed, which was long overdue. It also meant that if planes could fly off, then CODs carrying mail could fly in. Jon wasn't the only one listening for the sound of a COD landing on the deck, as everyone on board was anxious to get news from home.

As night fell, everyone got their wish as the first COD delivering mail arrived. Jon shot off a brief note to Kris, asking her to send him some statements and papers from home, and then waited for what seemed like hours before he heard those magic words: "Mail Call!"

Jon felt like it was Christmas morning when he ran to the Bear Ace ready room and found three letters from Kris waiting for him, along with some other mail. He knew any letters he'd written were either still on the ship or would fly out with the COD that had just landed. It would be several more days before Kris would hear from him, but he couldn't wait to hear from her. He stayed in the ready room, where he was dressed in his flight gear waiting around for his turn to fly. He tore open the letters and savored every word. By now, it was after midnight, but he couldn't wait to respond now that the letter drought had ended.

He found paper and pen and wrote a letter to tell her about his day: the sorties—or flying missions— scheduled for that night, and their first full day of flying planned for tomorrow. His pen ran out of ink and he grabbed another. But he only had time to wrap up letter No. 9 before he had to fly.

As he prepared to leave the ready room, he hoped that tomorrow he would get even more letters now that the CODs were flying again. Maybe his next "letter" should be his first tape of the cruise with a special part just for Jordyn. But he had to put all of that out of his mind for now and focus on the task at hand, especially after so many days of not being able to fly. However, there was an extra spring in his step as he crossed the flight deck and climbed aboard his E-2C.

CHAPTER 18

Operation Provide Promise

22 MAR 1993

MONDAY

2200 WET WESTERN EUROPEAN TIME, UTC+0

USS THEODORE ROOSEVELT

APPROACHING ROCK OF GIBRALTAR

35.30.42 N 9.56.42 W

Jon had everything ready to make his first recording of the cruise for Kris: his all-important list with every point numbered and notated, Kris' letters and other mail, his microcassette recorder with fresh batteries, and a quiet room (his roommate was away). Jon made sure the tape was rewound all the way and he hit the record button. He was very relaxed, slightly drowsy, and almost talking to Kris as if he were home and it was time for bed.

"Well, honey, I love you very much, and it's 2200 or 10:00 on a Monday night, the 22nd of March. I was going to do the tape yesterday, but I never really got a time to be alone. So my roommate is flying right now, and I decided to take a break. It's been a really quiet day. I wrote ya, I think, letter No. 9 yesterday, so this will be 10.

"And the big thing is that I love you." And the sound in Jon's voice noticeably changed as the pain of being an ocean apart from his soulmate was clearly expressed in those few words. He quickly recovered himself, glanced at his notes, and went on to his next point.

"And no mail today, so I'm still looking at the last letters. Before anything else, I don't want to forget," and Jon started to sound more animated and playful, "to make sure—and, hopefully, it's been nine days—that whoever helps you with the gas fireplace shows you how to shut off the gas. 'Cause with your nose I'm sure you smelled it, but I was a little worried. I haven't heard anything, so I'm assuming—no Red Cross message or anything else—that you didn't have an explosion or anything after the pilot light went off from the storm and that somebody was able to help you shut everything down, OK."

Jon could just imagine Kris' nose wrinkling at the rotten-egg smell of natural gas, so surely she'd had the pilot light fixed by now. Taking care of Kris by handling the little jobs around the house was one thing he truly missed.

"This side of the tape will be for you, Kris, and the other side will be for my wonderful daughter. And if she's listening now, Jordyn, Daddy misses you very much and he's going to come back, as you whittle down your chain—one for every day that I'm gone—you can see that it's going to get closer and closer. It's going to be kind of hard to do, but I'm going to get there."

Jon told Kris about how he'd been involved in handling the aggressive flight schedule for his

226

squadron after not flying for 10 days and what the upcoming mission would be.

"All indications are showing that we're doing this escort. It's called 'Operation Provide Promise.' I don't know if it makes the paper or not. We're calling it 'Provide Promise,' and that's the dropping of MREs or those "meals ready to eat" to the Muslims who are being attacked by the Serbs. I learned quite a bit about where everything is and what's happening, and it sounds like from the paper that they're going to start what's called 'enforcing the no-fly zone.'"

In recent briefings, the air wing had been informed of the atrocities occurring in the Bosnian region. The ethnic cleansing, countless refugees, starving children, mass graves, and raping of women had put a sick feeling in Jon's steel stomach. Helping to deliver much-needed food to those suffering wouldn't fix the situation, but it was something.

"How long we're going to be here, no one, including the admiral, has a clue. I just really don't know." Jon looked at his list before moving on to lighter matters.

"I got a letter from the Sunday School class—it's very nice—really appreciated it. Lots of people wrote comments on it. Nobody knows how to spell my name or your name," Jon grinned, "but the intent is there." Jon and Kris often introduced themselves as Jon without an "h" and Kris with a "K," but it didn't seem to make much difference.

A loud bang in the background from one of the ship's steam catapults interrupted the recording, a sign that planes were being launched. "Well, maybe you can hear that. They're still doin' nights. I'm getting ready to go up in a few minutes to the ready room myself. We're going to go through the Rock of Gibraltar tomorrow, the 23rd, and enter the Med. On the 25th we're going to do the turnover with JFK, so maybe I'll see our friend Dave from Sunday School and say 'hi' to him, if I get half a chance."

A number of officers, including Jon, would be heading over by helo to USS John F. Kennedy, where Jon's friend was serving, as she officially passed the baton over to USS Theodore Roosevelt.

"We're starting to get schooled up on this upcoming Provide Promise mission, real-world stuff, you know, high viz, so Ops (or Operations) are keeping real busy." The high-visibility of this humanitarian operation meant that their actions would make international news.

"Hope you find all this interesting, same way I can listen to you talk all day about Jordyn and Taylor and what you've done, because I'm missing you so much." Jon referred to his notes, and then noticed the small scar on his arm where the flight surgeon had removed a cyst a week earlier.

"Oh, that was the other big thing I was going to tell you. I got my stitches out today on my arm. I've got a 3-by-2-inch shaved patch and it looks really good. There's no infection and it's closing together really well. So by the time you see me, I'll have hair on my arm and nothin' will be wrong.

"I'm lookin' at your letter No. 2, and I'm glad you stayed home from church and took naps. And how long was your nap? I hope you got one. Is Taylor sitting up? Does she grab things? Take those pictures—I'm ready! Have fun at your jewelry party, which I guess is Wednesday." Jon looked at his clock and yawned. "It's 1:30 in the morning on Tuesday the 23rd, so I'll finish up the rest of this tape later."

Long-Distance Dad

The next evening, around 20:30, Jon had time to finish his recording. The CODs kept flying, and Jon received two more letters from Kris, Nos. 4 and 5. He decided to wait until he wrote his next letter to answer her questions from those so that he'd have something to say. For now, at least the details of his upcoming mission were more certain.

"After we turn over with the Kennedy on the 25th, we actually start taking over the missions for Provide Promise that evening. Wish us luck here. Pray for us that everything goes OK.

"And tell Jordyn, and if you're listening, Jordyn, I am definitely coming back as soon as we do our job over here. I have to fly airplanes for a while, and I should be back around the time of your birthday or when your chain gets done. But who knows? Yeah, and I plan to rent a camcorder from special services and take a video soon.

"Talking on the tape makes me feel disjointed. It's hard to talk for a half hour. I'll flip the tape over for a story for Jordyn. I love you, Kris, and you just take care. I hope everything is fine, and I pray for you and love you very much, honey. Give my wonderful little children hugs. I love you, bye-bye."

Jon pushed the stop button and sighed. He knew how much hearing his voice meant to Kris, but he sure liked writing letters better. Now for Jordyn's story. He wished he'd brought some simple bedtime storybooks to read to Jordyn on tape, but he hadn't. He'd have to make up a story, and he'd been thinking about one all day, remembering the names of Jordyn's little friends and all her favorite things. Hopefully he wouldn't make a mess of it. He flipped the microcassette over and took a deep breath before hitting the record button.

"Hi, Jordyn, this is Daddy," he said in the gentle, lilting voice he used with his daughter. "I want to first tell you that I love you. Are you getting ready for bed? Have you brushed your teeth? Are you being a big girl for Mommy?

"Well, I know you are and Daddy is very, very proud of you. I think you and Taylor are the best things that ever happened to me and I love you very much and I wish—I really wish—that I could be with you, but I just can't right now because of having to be on a big boat and fly. But I'm thinking of you all the time and I know Mommy is taking care of you, and we'll try and keep letting you know how everything is going. I know you have a chain for when I come back, and I'll be back around your birthday, OK? Now you either sit with Mommy or I guess you're in bed and you can listen to this story I'm going to tell you, OK?"

As Jon paused, the bang of a catapult launching a plane could be heard in the background, and Jon went into his made-up story. It was about Princess Jordyn and all her best friends who were playing in the forest and making up songs until the skies became very dark and cloudy and one friend disappeared altogether.

"'I know what happened,' called out Princess Jordyn. 'The bad witch has come and got her.' The friends knew if they went together in force to the bad witch's black castle, they could conquer the bad witch by being good. They knocked on the witch's door, but it was unlocked and they went in. They heard their friend crying out, and they found her, untied her, and walked out of the castle." Jon paused for dramatic effect.

"They knew if they stuck together, the bad witch couldn't hurt them, for she only attacked one at a time. Her bad powers could never conquer good people who believed in God. So the friends kept saying, 'We believe in God,' and they knew they could always conquer the bad witch.

"So Jordyn, just remember to always be a good little girl, love God and love your parents, and nothing bad can ever happen to you. OK? So have fun playing, or maybe it's time to go to bed now. Daddy loves you very much. I'll tell you another story on the next tape, OK? I love you. Bye-bye."

Jon wiped his forehead and sank into his pillow. That was harder to do than he expected. He really must ask Kris to send him some books that he could read to Jordyn instead. Making up stories was hard to do, but not nearly as hard as trying to be a long-distance dad.

Cruise Mustache

That Tuesday evening, when I wrote Jon my letter, I was thankful for the updates I'd received about his progress. During a cruise, especially when there were mail delays, the XO would contact his wife and give her updates on the men. In turn, she would get the information to the phone-tree list so that the wives could get the latest news. I knew that everyone was doing fine, that they'd made it through the storm OK, and that they'd arrived in the Med. I also knew they'd had their first mail drop so, hopefully, letters would start coming soon. But there was so much more I wanted to know, and I had so many things to tell Jon, including the unique perspective of our 3-year-old daughter.

Jordyn prayed tonight that Daddy won't grow a mustache because she'll be scared. We were talking and I asked her if she wanted you to grow one and that is what she said. I thought you might want to know. I love you! Kris and the girls.

With mail on its way, maybe I'd find out if Jon had started growing his traditional "cruise mustache" or not. Either way, I'd give anything to just see his face one time before the end of the cruise.

Cool Guy

24 MAR 1993
WEDNESDAY
1910 CET CENTRAL EUROPEAN TIME UTC+1
USS THEODORE ROOSEVELT
MEDITERRANEAN SEA
38.21.39 N, 10.56.54 E

Jon looked over the TR patch freshly sewn onto his friend's flight jacket. It looked good, and he set off, walking past Air Ops, the department that controls the air traffic 10 miles out from the ship, and went next door to Combat, the ones who control the air traffic beyond 10 miles. Jon was hoping to see if Mike, his neighbor from Chesapeake, was there. Mike was an air resource element coordinator who worked with the air wing squadrons. Though they didn't cross paths in their regular duties, Jon and Mike had managed to meet up a couple of times on ship. Mike had shared some helpful information with Jon from his experience in combat, talking about missions and what was going on in the Adriatic region.

But Mike always felt that he received more than he gave in his relationship with Jon. Jon's enthusiasm washed off onto everyone he encountered, and Mike was looking forward to gaining a close friend. Jon, who was jokingly nicknamed "Rooster" by the Bear Aces because of the way he gave out orders, was one of those "cool" guys you just wanted to be around. When Mike told Rooster that he'd been on the TR for months but didn't have anybody to sew a TR patch onto his flight jacket, Jon told him he'd have his people take care of it.

Mike looked forward to returning the favor, maybe with a special dinner out when they got home. Since Mike and his wife had been living in the area longer than the Rystroms, he and Jon had already been talking about new restaurants to visit together with their wives when the cruise was over. Until then, Pizza Night would have to suffice.

My Navy Earrings

On Wednesday afternoon, I'd been invited to a jewelry party hosted by a good friend, and I didn't need to get a babysitter. Other stay-at-home moms would be there too, and our kids could have fun together while the moms got to enjoy looking at the latest accessories.

When I arrived and walked into my friend's den, I knew right away that I'd never been to a home party like this before. Cheryl Reccord, our new pastor's wife, had her own business representing Premier Designs Jewelry, and this was her first show in our area. She was dressed so cute and stylish and had a beautiful display of lovely necklaces, rings, bracelets, and earrings in all the current styles. I was impressed not only with Cheryl's professional, yet charming, manner but also the gorgeous jewelry she was sharing.

After the moms introduced ourselves, Cheryl showed us how to accessorize our outfits in various ways that were both practical and fun. I decided to order a set of gold and navy-blue earrings with a gold anchor dangle charm, perfect to wear to the military functions that Jon and I attended. I was mesmerized by it all, especially when I saw how much free jewelry my friend, the hostess, received. When Jon was on cruise, money was always tight, but I was excited to learn that I could host a party and earn the jewelry instead of buying it. I was already dreaming about the pieces that I could "earn."

Even though I'd had a busy afternoon, I still went to church that evening. Wednesdays always made for late nights for me, but it was well worth it. My friends at First Baptist Church Norfolk were like a second family to me. Wednesday nights included a shared evening meal, then teaching the 2-year-old's Missions Friends class, followed by rehearsal with our more than 150-member choir. Wednesday church activities were always a highlight of my week. My girls were tired and ready for bed, but we still managed to pray for Daddy and cut off another link of his chain before I settled down to write my letter to Jon.

Hi,

Of course, it is late tonight because of choir (11:20 pm) so I won't make this letter long, but I always feel that my day isn't complete without talking to my honey. I had a flash tonight when I was in choir—what would happen if one night on Wednesday when I'm in choir, you come walking in to surprise me (obviously this is after you get ranked #1 or you get picked up for O-5 and they send you home early). What an awesome thought! Just wishful thinking—I know I'm not even thinking such positive thoughts but, you know, it could be possible …

The chaplain's wife from the TR that goes to our church said she got her first letter on Monday, so it is starting! I love you and can't wait for my 1st letter. Love, Kris & girls.

Ready to Launch

25 MAR 1993
THURSDAY
0700 CET CENTRAL EUROPEAN TIME UTC+1
USS THEODORE ROOSEVELT
IONIAN SEA, NEAR THE BOOT OF ITALY
38.31.45 N 17.36.55 E

Jon rolled over in his rack and turned off his alarm. He'd been up super late the evening before, getting a brief together for that night's first Provide Promise mission. Now he had to get ready to take a helo over to the JFK for the turnover. On his first cruise, when he was a younger man, getting by on less than four hours of sleep was a piece of cake but not anymore.

A shave and shower helped him wake up before he headed to the officer's mess for a quick breakfast. The table talk was about the latest O-5 promotion board that had just ended. Jon wasn't the only lieutenant commander waiting to see if he'd been promoted to commander. But it would be at least a month, maybe two, before the official list was released. The waiting was always the hardest part.

Jon had even more waiting to do, as he found out that the helo that he was slated to ride wouldn't launch for another hour. If only he could have had that extra hour to sleep. Until the turnover was completed, there was little else to do, so he returned to his stateroom. He looked at his messy rack and decided to make his bed for a change, something his roommate would probably appreciate.

With housekeeping done, he sat down at his desk and found himself staring at the pictures of Kris and the girls. He might as well go ahead and write Kris a letter. He usually wrote his letters at night after the day's work was done.

But Jon had a lot on his mind, like the O-5 board. He remembered how upset he'd been when he missed his O-4 promotion back when he was with the Hormel Hawgs. But he wasn't the same Jon Rystrom that he was back then. He had changed. Of course, he wanted the promotion, but through the uncertainty, God had given him a peace that Jon couldn't quite explain. He gazed again at his family's pictures and smiled. He knew what was truly important, and the rank of commander had nothing to do with that.

He thought about that night's Provide Promise mission and how the Germans and the French were flying with them as well. He would have sat out on this mission, except the XO was away on assignment for a few days. As the next senior CICO, the CO had assigned Jon to fly in the secondary E-2C, 603, while the CO himself would be CICO in the primary plane, 602. Jon's plane would be piloted by Frenchy Messier with Billy Ray Dyer as copilot, and sitting ACO and RO next to Jon would be Aardvark Ardaiz and Bob Forwalder. Jon was pleased with his crew. Due to the difficulty of the mission—night flying in dark, hazy conditions, the first time flying in the Adriatic, and the high-viz nature of the mission—the higher-ups decided that this was a varsity evolution and wanted only their best aviators in the air.

After staying up to 0300 putting the brief together, Jon knew the details by heart: They would brief the crews at 1730, launch at 2100, and land at 0100 on Friday, the 26th. The aircraft from the TR would direct traffic and provide an escort, along with the French and Germans, for the large, C-130 cargo planes flying out of Ramstein Air Base in Germany that would drop much-needed food into Eastern Bosnia and the besieged capital of Sarajevo. USS John F. Kennedy had flown these missions for the past few weeks, but after the turnover, TR would take her place. During the day, the Air Force provided control and escort for the airdrops, while the Navy did those duties at night.

Jon looked at his clock. It was 0830. If he was going to write Kris a letter before he left on the helo for the JFK, he'd better get to it. He found her last two letters and made sure to answer any of her questions and ask his own in return. Three pages later, he was finished. As he sealed the envelope and left his stateroom, he really hoped he could find his good friend Dave on the JFK. Too bad they couldn't trade places and Jon could be the one heading back to CONUS instead. Jon had just enough time to get his letter in the mail before his helo was ready to launch.

USS Theodore Roosevelt

CHAPTER 19

No Horizon

25 MAR 1993
THURSDAY
1700 CET CENTRAL EUROPEAN TIME UTC+1
USS THEODORE ROOSEVELT
IONIAN SEA, NEAR THE BOOT OF ITALY
38.50.72 N 17.60.58 E

The aircrews of both 602 and 603 gathered in the Bear Aces' ready room for their pre-brief. Crew assignments were confirmed and the mission parameters defined. At 1730, the entire mission was briefed to all the participating air wing crews, via the onboard closed-circuit televisions found in each squadron's ready room.

The ship's meteorologist confirmed everyone's suspicions: The nearly moonless night—coupled with the haze in the "Mediterranean Milk Bowl," which made it a challenge to pick out the ship from the water—meant that aircrews would most likely be flying all night by instruments, called IFR conditions.

Below the 1,500-foot ceiling, the complete and total darkness meant that no horizon would be visible during the approach phase of the carrier landing. Not the greatest conditions but certainly well within everyone's limits. The E-2C crews concluded with an additional briefing of their own and grabbed some dinner before their launch.

THURSDAY, NOON, EASTERN STANDARD TIME

The girls and I slept in Thursday morning after our late night, but we were all ready to eat when lunchtime came around. I put Taylor in her highchair and let her entertain herself with her favorite snack, Cheerios, while I prepared a simple meal for Jordyn and me. I kept looking out the window for the mail carrier to drive by. Maybe today would be the day I'd finally get a letter from Jon.

I heard a familiar sound from outside and smiled. It was a hummer, an E-2C, probably flying off for a routine exercise. Living so near Norfolk Naval Air Base, aircraft of all kinds often flew overhead, but the daily sound of the hummer always put a smile on my face. It reminded me of my Jon and how proud I was of him and the important job he did. One day, quite a few paper-chain links from now, I'd hear the sound of Jon's hummer coming back home at the September Fly-In. What a sweet sound that would be!

2114 CENTRAL EUROPEAN TIME, 3:14 PM EASTERN TIME

Flight ops for Operation Provide Promise began. The flight deck of USS Theodore Roosevelt was buzzing with activity as the various aircraft prepared to launch. As was customary, the "Plane Guard" helo launched first to provide an airborne safety net should any planes experience difficulties around the ship. The Bear Ace E-2Cs launched next, with 602 taking the lead, followed by Jon's 603. One by one, the jets launched in quick succession, their bright-blue afterburners piercing the pitch-black night. All told, nine fixed-wing aircraft left the flight deck of the TR, including pairs of F-14 Tomcats, FA-18 Hornets, A6-E Intruders, and one EA-6B Prowler. This was a fairly small and straight-forward mission, nonetheless an important one.

One thing that each pilot noticed as he sped away from the ship and climbed through the 1,500-foot ceiling was that the haze conditions didn't let up. IFR conditions were almost immediate after launch, although not a surprise. The meteorologist's forecast was right on the money, and each plane headed to their assigned stations.

Soon after launch, it was time for the NFOs in Bear Ace 603 to "turn and burn," rotating their seats and switching their radar from standby to operate. But there was a problem. The radar wasn't working. Over a secure radio, 603 notified the primary E-2C of the issue.

"Uh, 602, our radar is not working. IFF is functional. Do we RTB?"

The Bear Ace CO and CICO in 602 thought a moment. He didn't want 603 to RTB (return to base) if their IFF antenna that identified friend or foe was still functioning.

241

"Negative, 603. Go to tanker duty, and we'll cover the Control."

"Affirmative, 602. Moving to tanker duty."

Unfortunately, keeping the complicated equipment in top-working order was a challenge, especially with the budget cuts that the Navy was experiencing. Nothing on the $60-million-dollar E-2C was cheap to fix, and maintenance crews worked hard to keep all the systems operating. This wouldn't be an exciting hop for 603, as guiding the various jets to a tanker plane to get more fuel was a very basic job, but it was an essential one. There weren't many aircraft to control, even including the French and Germans, so 602 would be able to handle that job just fine. As the C-130s approached their drop zones, hopefully, their loads of relief supplies would land accurately.

4:00 PM EASTERN STANDARD TIME

Finally, the mail carrier came. I rushed out to the mailbox, pulled open the door, and there it was: Jon's first letter! I was so excited that I jumped up and down like a little girl. It had been so long since I'd had contact with Jon, and I was desperate to find out how he was doing.

"Look, girls, a letter from Daddy!" I exclaimed, as I ran into the house, waving his letter in the air.

"Yay!" yelled Jordyn, as we sat down together and I ripped the envelope open. The back had the number "5" on it, so that meant there were four letters before this one. My hands were almost shaking as I read aloud the first words I'd heard from Jon in two weeks.

Midnight, 18th

Dear Kris,
A fairly uneventful day today, still no flying because of ...x and being behind PIM.

I frowned slightly, as I couldn't make out his scribble in front of the "x," and I had no idea what "PIM" meant.

We had a major jane inspection today. I had to hide my VCR since it doesn't have a tag, cuz I don't want the recording function clipped.

That part I understood. Electronics brought on board had to be approved, and that sounded like Jon, not wanting his VCR to be messed with. He went on to describe where he did his inspection, the training he had, and something about "ROE Exercise MSG #2." This part of his letter wasn't packed with "meat," but I cherished any word that came from Jon at this point.

My roommate sawed logs like you wouldn't believe.

I had to laugh at that. I knew Jon could learn to sleep through most anything, but I wondered if he took any earplugs along.

Well we are now up to dinner. I had dinner with the flight surgeon and the chaplain from our church choir. Had a good conversation. It's nice being able to talk to somebody different than just Bear Aces. I know quite a few other O-4s of other squadrons. I am glad—it is a nice change of pace.

Jon was such a social guy, and I was glad to see that he was enjoying making the rounds.

Well, good-looking, how was that for a day? Then the squadron watched a movie called Sneakers. I'd never heard of it. Excellent movie, not real serious about computer hackers. Very enjoyable. Still no mail, so I hope everything is OK. I love you and miss the girls. Love, Jon.

"Mommy, where's my name?" Jordyn asked, when I finished, with a puzzled look on her sweet little face.

"What do you mean?" I asked, looking again at the letter. "Oh, I see. Daddy said he misses the girls, and that would be you and Taylor, wouldn't it?" Her face told me she was hoping for something more than that.

> HE WILL COVER YOU WITH
> HIS PINIONS, AND UNDER
> HIS WINGS YOU WILL FIND
> REFUGE; HIS FAITHFULNESS
> IS A SHIELD AND BUCKLER.
> (PSALMS 91:4 ESV)

I read through the letter again and again. Just holding it made me feel closer to him, knowing his hands had touched it. I smiled as I put the letter away, and I was already thinking about what I would write to him that evening. I'd start by asking him the meaning of some of the abbreviations that he used.

2228 CENTRAL EUROPEAN TIME, 4:28 PM EASTERN TIME

"Wave-off, low approach," radioed an LSO from USS Theodore Roosevelt as some of the first planes from Operation Provide Promise began to return to mother.

That's not what 512 wanted to hear, as the A6-E Prowler ascended past the ship to make a second pass. The pilot had the sensation that he had over-rotated. A quick glance at the instruments in his cockpit told another story. He hadn't rotated enough. Such was the phenomenon called vertigo, the bane of every pilot.

Flying on instruments for extended periods of time, when there was no visual reference point, tricked the body into thinking that up was down and down was up or anywhere in between. In more modern terms, it is referred to as spatial awareness or spatial orientation. Pilots trained specifically to trust their instruments and not their own internal "gyros," which could be misleading when flying in dark, hazy conditions. Assigned as a tanker that evening, 512 would have to wait for other planes to land before making his second attempt, but he wouldn't be the only pilot to suffer the effects of vertigo that night. The captain of the carrier, watching from the bridge, hoped the rest of the recovery went smoothly.

The F-18 Hornets were the next to land. The primary Hornet, 301, had been keenly aware of the zero horizon and super-dark conditions from the start. The altitudes they were supposed to meet at had to be elevated so that they could get above the clouds—up to 27,000 feet. Coming back to the ship wasn't any better, with the final descent requiring a high degree of focus. This was definitely not a night for nuggets. Next to land, 301 had no trouble. But later, his wingman in 304, feeling like he was extremely nose-high when, in fact, his nose was barely angled, boltered and had to go to the tanker for more fuel before he could have another pass.

6 PM EASTERN TIME

I was so happy at dinner that night, and my girls picked up on their mommy's chipper mood. Hearing from Jon was like a breath of fresh spring air, one that I greatly needed after enduring weeks of full-time parenting alone.

From experience, I knew that once the letters started coming, they would keep coming. Sure, there would be delays now and then, but the first letter of the cruise was always a milestone to celebrate. Surely he had received at least one of my letters by now. I had noticed the postmark on his letter No. 5, and it didn't take that long to reach me. Hopefully, my letters would get to him as quickly now that the mail drops were happening.

0042 CENTRAL EUROPEAN TIME, 6:42 EASTERN TIME

An F-14 Tomcat, 202, broke out of the haze bubble at 1,500 feet and found himself in a totally black pit. The pilot of 202 was the CO of the F-14 squadron and had been designated as one of the primary leaders in this first night of Operation Provide Promise. An exceptional pilot, he'd anticipated experiencing vertigo after flying 3.5 hours in the cloudy clag, and he was right. As he leveled off at 1,200 feet, he began experiencing difficulty in maintaining a straight approach and turned down the intensity of his cockpit lights to compensate for the intensity of the darkness after leaving the clouds. No horizon was visible, and he felt like he was doing a barrel roll around the ship as he prepared for final approach. He made a quick decision.

"Ah, Approach, 202's going to wave it off. I got a severe case of vertigo. I need to get up under control."

"Roger," responded Approach, pausing for just a moment. "Take angels one point two."

"202," he responded, as he ascended toward 1,200 feet.

"202, update state."

"Five point five," 202 responded, letting Approach know he had enough gas for another pass without going to the tanker or a bingo field, which was a land-based airfield with fuel available. After flying an elongated box pattern at 1,200 feet, the vertigo sensation subsided. When he made his second pass, the vertigo was still there but not nearly as bad as before, and he was able to trap, or land, without issue.

0045 CENTRAL EUROPEAN TIME, 6:45 EASTERN TIME

E-2Cs were the first fixed-wing aircraft to take off on a mission and usually the last ones to land. Tonight, 304, the F18 that had boltered, was returning from the tanker but behind both the E-2Cs. The primary E-2C, Bear Ace 602, landed and proceeded out of the wires and to its parking place. Bear Ace 603 was just minutes behind 602 on their final approach.

"603, left one six zero," radioed Approach, giving 603 its proper heading.

"603," the copilot acknowledged.

"603, dirty up," Approach instructed, telling them to drop their landing gear and flaps, which would also slow down the plane. 603 acknowledged and continued on course.

"603, fly the final bearing one eight zero." Once again, 603 acknowledged Approach's instructions. Watching the radar, the guys in Approach kept a close eye on 603's progress.

"He's not chasing his line at all," one operator said to another.

"You're right," the other agreed. "He's got the straightest approach of anyone tonight."

As 603 got closer to the ship, the Final controller took over Approach's job and continued to give 603 the guidance it needed to stay on the glideslope.

0051:40 CENTRAL EUROPEAN TIME, 6:51:40 EASTERN TIME

"603, at three-quarter mile, call the ball." Final prepared 603 to enter the groove and to notify them when they had a visual of the ball.

"603 Hawkeye ball, four point one," 603 responded, with 4,100 pounds of fuel in her tanks. Now the LSO gave 603 the flight deck wind conditions.

"Roger ball 28 knots axial."

Twenty seconds later, the gear petty officer contacted Pri-Fly on his radio.

"There's a problem with the No. 4 wire supports," he shouted quickly. 603 was just seconds from landing, but a faulty arresting cable was a dangerous situation that had to be avoided.

"Foul deck," called the air boss over the flight deck's 5MC intercom system. The arresting gear officer immediately released the "dead man" pickle switch, fouling the deck and causing the Fresnel lens light system to flash red.

"Wave-off foul deck," instructed the LSO to 603, as the pilot began to ascend over the deck.

"603, Approach, take angels one point two, when level cleared downwind, report abeam heading three six zero," said Approach.

"603," the plane acknowledged.

The captain on the bridge watched Bear Ace 603 carefully and saw it perform a normal wave-off. The pilot of 301, the F-18 CO and lead pilot of the mission, had just parked his plane and saw the foul deck lights, then watched 603 abruptly pull up and over the ship, as expected, until he went out of sight.

"It must be nice to have a second pilot to back you up on a night like this," he thought to himself, as he completed his plane's shutdown.

Mike, Jon's friend, was on watch in Combat observing that night's plane recovery, along with the rest of the guys, on the video ILARTS system that recorded every trap and fly out. He saw the Hawkeye climb out well early at a good rate of climb. Mike walked over to his desk to check on some paperwork.

The operator of the ILARTS camera on the island trained the camera on Bear Ace 603 to follow the wave-off. He was ready to turn the camera back around in preparation for the next plane to land, but something caught his eye. The E-2C seemed lower and slower than usual, so he kept the camera pointing toward 603 instead. The plane was now almost a mile off the ship's port side. It looked to him like the plane was going into the water.

TR's captain, sitting at his station on the bridge, looked to see what the foul deck was all about. He then wondered where was 304, the F-18 that had boltered. He glanced back at his monitor above the front bridge window. Something in his peripheral vision didn't feel right. He looked out in front of the ship, on the port side, and saw a red, blinking, twirling light that was too low, and it was going lower.

Then it disappeared.

CHAPTER 20

Bear Ace 603

26 MAR 1993 FRIDAY 0052:47 CENTRAL EUROPE TIME
25 MAR 1993 THURSDAY 6:52:47 EASTERN TIME
SEAGRASS REACH
CHESAPEAKE, VIRGINIA, USA
36.44.14 N 76.16.19 W

Dinner dishes didn't take long to clean up these days. I was looking forward to some "me" time once the girls were put to bed, especially since I finally had a letter from Jon to respond to. I could hear Jordyn playing with her Barbie dolls in the den. I wish I had half her energy, especially since I was living like a single parent.

"Hey girls," I called out. "It's time to go cut off another link from Daddy's chain and get ready for bed."

"And pray for Daddy," Jordyn called back.

"That's right, honey, it's time to pray for Daddy."

0052:47 CENTRAL EUROPE TIME 6:52:47 EASTERN TIME
USS THEODORE ROOSEVELT
IONIAN SEA
39.07.5 N 18.25.8 E

"Did you see that?" said a flight deck petty officer to one of his green-shirt mechanics. "That blue flash!"

"Yeah, like a camera bulb going off. Was it lightning far away?"

"I don't think so. Do you think the plane hit the water?" the petty officer asked anxiously.

"I don't know. It's weird."

One of the operators in Combat was still watching the video of 603.

"Hey, do you see that? Something doesn't look right," he exclaimed. Mike turned from his desk and walked toward the video monitor. At the same time, the captain was calling Air Ops next door.

"Are you talking to 603?" the ship's captain asked hurriedly. The commander was taken aback. He didn't receive calls from the captain very often.

"I think so, sir," he answered unconvincingly.

"Are you talking to him now?" the captain yelled. He'd already gotten the run around from the air boss in Pri-Fly who couldn't say whether they had a visual on 603 or if they'd seen it fly into the water. The captain demanded answers, and he wanted them now.

"Sir, let me check," said the commander nervously, realizing something was seriously wrong. The last transmission from 603 was at 0052:37. It was now 0053:52, well over a minute later.

"603, Approach, radio check," came the call out to the missing Bear Ace. There was no response.

"603, Approach." Still no response. The Commander immediately called the ship's captain.

"Sir, no, we've called twice with no answer, and there's no radar squawk either."

The captain took in a quick breath and clenched his fists. His worst fears were confirmed.

"Call a plane in the water!" urgently ordered the captain, in a brusque voice to the officer of the deck. Immediately, a blaring Klaxon alarm went out over the 1 MC intercom system that covered every part of the carrier, along with these words:

"Plane in the water! Plane in the water, port side! This is not a drill. I repeat—this is not a drill. Plane in the water, port side! Man all search and recovery stations."

Within seconds, waves of people began rushing onto the flight deck. Down below, every Sailor, cook, janitor, nurse, brown shoe, black shoe, enlisted man, and commissioned officer knew that one of their own was in peril. What affected one, affected them all.

Approach continued to call out to 603 but no response. In desperation, Approach tried the guard frequency but to no avail.

"603, Approach on guard check in 15. Approach on guard out."

Silence.

"603, Approach on guard, acknowledge." Even the LSO made one last futile attempt.

"603, Paddles."

No response. Nine times the call went out to Bear Ace 603 and nine times the result was the same.

Silence.

Bear Ace 603 was missing.

The helicopter that was always operating to assist in these situations was vectored over the ship to search for 603. But they still had one more plane to recover, 304, the Hornet that had boltered earlier. As 603 had gone down off the port side, the ship continued on her forward heading. There was no danger of running over the downed plane or its crew. Once the Hornet landed, two more helos were launched to search for Bear Ace 603, and another warship in the battle group—the USS Hue City—joined the SAR effort.

Up on flight deck, the Bear Aces' CO scrambled to the edge of the ship when he heard that 603 was down. He frantically shined his flashlight into the water, but it was no good. The night was as black as he had ever experienced, and his beam didn't even reach the watery depths below. It was a useless attempt, but what else could he do?

He had a knot in his stomach as he rushed down to the ready room. He knew the cold temperature of the water. He knew all too well how difficult it was to navigate the tight, confined spaces of the Hawkeye's interior in good conditions let alone in a plane that might be upside down and underwater with an injured crew. And that was the best-case scenario. His men were highly skilled, but no amount of training could overcome basic physics.

The ship's three chaplains sprang into action with one reporting to the Bear Aces' ready room, one with the leadership of the air wing, and the other down below at the deck house to wait with the men anxiously standing ready at the whaleboat eager to go retrieve the missing crew as soon as they were found.

Within an hour of the disappearance of Bear Ace 603, USS Theodore Roosevelt transmitted a confidential notification through the official Navy channels:

"603 E-2C BUNO 161549 CRASHED INTO IONIAN SEA APPROX 1NM AHEAD OF CVN-71 AFTER FOUL DECK WAVE-OFF. FIVE SOULS ON BOARD. SAR IN PROGRESS. COMMANDERS ESTIMATE: ABLE TO CONTINUE PRESENT MISSION, PRESS

INTEREST LIKELY, FIRST REPORT THIS INCIDENT, AMPLYFYING INFORMATION TO FOLLOW."

0200 CENTRAL EUROPE TIME, 8:00 PM EASTERN TIME

Jordyn, freshly bathed and dressed in her pink pajamas, danced around the long colorful paper chain as we prepared to cut off another link. At 7 months old, baby Taylor was still too little to be much help, but her 3-year-old big sister absolutely loved this nightly

ritual. I wish I shared Jordyn's upbeat perspective on how many days were left in this cruise. After 14 days, I didn't even have to prompt Jordyn on what to pray: "Dear Jesus, please keep Daddy safe in his airplane. Amen."

0218 CENTRAL EUROPE TIME, 8:18 PM EASTERN TIME

SAR efforts were aggressive as the search for 603 intensified and more helos were launched. Searchlights from the surrounding ships scanned the water, but the only items found were a few floating charts and pieces of paper. The dark, hazy conditions worsened to the point that the helo crews' NVGs (night vision goggles) were useless. Until sunrise, visibility would be severely limited. Mike, along with many others, was still in Combat keeping up with the latest news.

By this time, the video of 603's crash could be replayed, and everybody viewed it carefully and solemnly, looking for clues as to what went wrong. To Mike, it appeared the aircraft climbed out normally and then began to lose lift and settled into the water off the port bow about a mile ahead of the ship.

The left wingtip caught the water first, which caused the aircraft to spin around. The plane's lights lit up the massive splash made on impact, explaining the bright-blue flash that some on the deck had observed. After viewing the tape, hopes for finding the crew alive grew very dim.

SAR had been going on for about an hour at this point, but little more was being said officially. Mike thought that surely Jon knew more than he did since the plane came from his squadron. He got on the phone and called the Bear Aces' ready room to talk to the squadron duty officer.

"Hey, this is Purcell down in Combat. Is Lt. Cmdr. Rystrom around?" Mike asked gently, understanding that VAW-124 had lost one of their planes. There was a long pause on the other end.

"Uh, don't you know?" he said, in a hesitating voice.

"Know what?" Mike replied, with a growing sense of unease.

"Rooster was on 603." Mike's heart stopped and he caught his breath.

"I, uh, I didn't know. Sorry," and he hung up the phone in disbelief. He sat numbly in his chair, soaking the sad truth in, then overcome with shock, jumped up and left Combat and stumbled down to his own stateroom. He sat at his desk and dropped his head into his hands in despair. He tried to choke back the tears, but he couldn't do it. A hot mix of pain and anger cut him in two. His mind flashed to Kris and the girls in front of their beautiful, new home without Jon by their side.

"Dear God, why? How can this be!"

Mike was a man of faith, but he felt shaken to the core. His mind went to his wife back home. She would hear the news long before a letter from him could reach her, but she'd have to sort through the same emotions that he was feeling. The Rystroms weren't just another Navy family—they were friends.

Mike got out pen and paper and let his fury out in an emotional letter. He saw his flight jacket hanging up in the corner, and he reached out to touch the TR patch. Tears filled his eyes again. It would take more than a patch to heal his broken heart. He couldn't even begin to imagine what it would take to heal Kris'.

0400 CENTRAL EUROPE TIME 10:00 PM EASTERN TIME

The girls were sound asleep and I'd been busy on the phone catching up with friends and family and planning different things, like the Sunday School potluck coming up on Sunday and, of course, my jewelry party. Now it was time for me to relax and write my favorite person in the whole world. Writing letters was so much more fun when you could respond to one another.

Thur. 3/25

Hurray! My 1st letter came today!

It only took 6 days! It was so great to get it. The funny thing is it was #5, so half the stuff you told me didn't make sense.

No flying because of "... *" and "being behind PIM"? "Sawed logs"—is that sleeping? I've never heard you say that before. "MSG #2"?

When I showed Jordyn your letter, she was looking for her name in it (all you said was "the girls"). So I would suggest writing her name in every letter even if it isn't one specifically for her and print it, because she can recognize it if it is printed. Yesterday, she pointed out a little "r" to me—amazing!

We are still cutting a link off every night, but it doesn't seem to make a dent yet. But Jordyn has such a positive attitude. I'm not sure she can really relate the length to how long it really is. She just loves this big, long chain in the playroom. Hopefully, close to the end, Taylor can help take some links off. That will be the biggest change—she won't be much of a baby anymore.

I gave Jon a rundown of all the people whom I had called and the plans that I had made. Keeping busy was one cruise strategy that I had learned worked for me.

So you can see, between these calls, giving both girls a bath, and fixing dinner, I've been busy. Of course, Jordyn's 4-hour nap this afternoon helped. Even I took a good 2-hour one (I only had 5 hours of sleep last night thanks to "Munchkin").

Taylor is getting more and more vocal. She is starting to use the syllables "ba-ba." So I figure the "da-da" will be coming. I'll show her your picture when she starts.

Well, babe, that wraps things up today. I'm glad you are doing well and especially glad that the mail has started. I love you! Kris, Jordyn and Taylor.

I made sure to print "JORDYN" in nice block letters to remind Jon to include her name in his next letters. Tomorrow would be a busy day with us needing to be out the door by 7:30 so that I could get Jordyn to preschool. And, hopefully, another letter or two would be waiting for me in my mailbox. I looked at the clock. It was getting close to 11:00. Even with a nap that day, I needed to get some rest.

Tough Assignment

25 MAR 1993
2300 EASTERN TIME
VAW-124 BASE
NORFOLK NAVAL AIR STATION
36.56.23 N 76.17.31 W

When Lt. Cmdr. Rick Vanden Heuvel reported to the headquarters of Airborne Early Warning Wing, Atlantic, he knew something major had happened. Four other casualty assistance calls officers (CACOs) were there, along with several chaplains, the staff officers, senior officers' wives, and other personnel—about 40 people in all. No one knew what was going on, but they'd all been called to the wing just before midnight, and that was never a good sign.

Finally, the commodore, responsible for the training and maintenance of all the Atlantic Fleet E-2C Squadrons, called everyone into the conference room. The mood was somber as he broke the news about Bear Ace 603 going down off USS Theodore Roosevelt. The SAR effort was officially continuing, but everyone there knew that the chances of the men being found alive were practically zero. The commodore identified the crew members and made the notification assignments as to which one of the CACOs would lead the teams to notify the next of kin. Rick and the other four CACOs sat down with the commodore and developed a plan.

At that hour, the Navy had a policy that prohibited waking up the next of kin before morning. One of the families had to be contacted in Baltimore while the rest were in the Norfolk area. The important thing was that all the families were notified at roughly the same time. Rick was very familiar with the "wife-net" where word would spread like wildfire before they could deliver their official notifications. Waiting a few hours would give time for all of them to be in place by morning.

The other consideration was that the loss of 603 was certain to make international news, because it concerned Operation Provide Promise and the growing conflict in Bosnia. The press wouldn't want to be kept waiting to break the story, and no one wanted a family member to discover their loved one was lost by hearing it on the news. Being a "Navy Town," the Norfolk local media would be all over the story.

> .... *WHEN YOU PASS THROUGH THE WATERS, I WILL BE WITH YOU; AND THROUGH THE RIVERS, THEY SHALL NOT OVERWHELM YOU; WHEN YOU WALK THROUGH FIRE YOU SHALL NOT BE BURNED, AND THE FLAME SHALL NOT CONSUME YOU. FOR I AM THE LORD YOUR GOD .... BECAUSE YOU ARE PRECIOUS IN MY EYES, AND HONORED, AND I LOVE YOU .... (ISAIAH 43:2-4 ESV)*

For Rick, this was the first time he'd had to carry out his CACO duties. He'd been trained on the protocol and how to guide the survivors through all the unavoidable red tape. But for Rick, it went a step further, as it did for most CACOs. Rick was making a personal commitment to walk by the side of the affected family, not only for the next few days or weeks but for life. He considered it his duty to assist them in any dealings they had with the military now and into the future.

The commodore looked at Rick and said his assignment was to notify Kris Rystrom, Lt. Cmdr. Jon Rystrom's wife, of Chesapeake. He sighed when he saw that she had two little girls. This was going to be one of the hardest assignments he ever had.

Cheated

26 MAR 1993
0540 CENTRAL EUROPE TIME, 11:40 PM EASTERN TIME, 25 MAR 93
USS THEODORE ROOSEVELT
39.24.5 N 18.56.2 E

The early morning sun that rose over the chilly Ionian Sea couldn't penetrate the thick fog bank that hung in the sky above the TR or the grim mood that dominated the ship. Mike made his way to the bridge, high up on the ship's island, and found a pair of unused handheld binoculars. Someone else was already using "Big Eyes," the massive high-power binoculars mounted to the ship, and Mike joined him in scanning the vast, gray ocean for any signs of life.

Mike had been up for more than 24 hours at this point, but there was no way he could sleep. He felt so helpless, and he had to do something, even if there was little likelihood that the crew of 603 was floating in a life raft somewhere waiting to be picked up.

As his eyes strained for any speck on the horizon, Mike could honestly say that everything that could be done was being done to find the crew of 603. And after watching the replay of 603's final moments, he felt that Jon's death would have been sudden and, therefore, painless. That was a small consolation considering the loss, but it was something.

Mike felt cheated. Cheated out of a good friend. Cheated out of all the fun hobbies and experiences they'd planned on sharing together after the cruise. Cheated out of getting to become close to one of the coolest people he'd ever met.

Mike was still scanning the ocean when the call came in from a helo that wreckage had been spotted not far from the original site of the mishap. Not surprisingly, it was the lightweight radome that was first seen or at least what was left of it. Other smaller pieces of wreckage were floating nearby. But only wreckage was seen—no bodies and certainly no survivors. Whaleboats were launched to begin the salvage process. Mike tried in vain to choke back the tears as he sat the binoculars down in their place. Looking further was futile now. His friend and the other four crewmen were gone.

He thought about the letter he'd written earlier that morning to his wife and decided it was best if he didn't send it. His emotions had been so raw, and he didn't want his wife to have to process such volatile feelings. But if he couldn't find Jon, dead or alive, the least he could do was recount the events in detail so that Kris would have some knowledge of the night's events. He'd give anything to be able to wake up and find out this nightmare had only been a bad dream.

As the few remaining pieces of shattered Bear Ace 603 were being plucked from the Ionian Sea, the chaplains of the TR were planning a memorial service for the five men to be held the next day. The crew of USS Theodore Roosevelt did not have the luxury of extended time to mourn the loss of their friends and crewmates. The chaplains knew the ship needed an opportunity to grieve together before returning to their duties.

The thousands of people serving on the carrier were like one, large, extended family. Even enlisted men working below deck felt the pain of 603's loss. But the crew of the air wing felt it even deeper.

And the Bear Aces felt it most of all. Five of their close friends were gone. Suddenly. Forever. That's even tougher when the show must go on. The Bear Ace Squadron would be able to take a few days to deal with their grief. But then the responsibilities of Jon and his lost crewmates had to be assigned to others, and the next mission had to be planned and executed.

More Boxes

Even more difficult to bear was that the personal belongings of the lost airmen would have to be carefully collected from their bunkrooms and other shared places and sent back to their grieving families. As boxes were packed with the guys' clothing, pictures, flight suits, and personal items, the mourning squad mates who had to carry out the grim task were also packing up other boxes of their own.

Naval aviators and flight officers are trained to box up and compartmentalize their emotions. When the mission planning started and the flight suit went on, everything else had to be left behind. Marriage trouble, financial stress, grief, loss, anger—it was all put in a box, closed with a lid, and left untouched until one had time to open up the box and deal with what was inside. During a mission, that box had to stay closed, because if you weren't totally present in the moment, your distraction could be deadly.

The loss of 603 would require a very large box. Operation Provide Promise had to go on. Jon and his fellow crewmates on Bear Ace 603 would have expected nothing less.

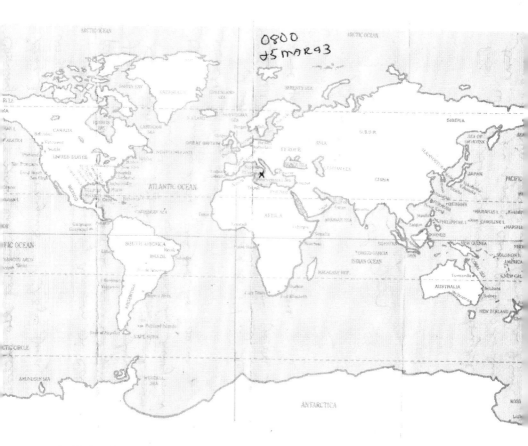

In his last letter, Jon hand-marked the location of the Ionian Sea, near the boot of Italy 38.50.72 N 17.60.58 E, not knowing this would be the final resting place for him and the crew of Bear Ace 603.

CHAPTER 21

Lost at Sea

My alarm went off, and I rolled over in bed and squinted at my clock: 6:30 a.m. I groaned as I struggled to find the energy to get up and face our Friday morning routine of breakfast, packing Jordyn's lunch, feeding Max, and buckling up the girls in our minivan for the 25-minute ride to Jordyn's preschool. Before we left the house, I smiled as I ran outside, opened our mailbox, and put in my letter to Jon. As I closed the lid, I could just imagine finding more letters from Jon that afternoon.

On my drive into Norfolk, I planned the rest of my day: Once I got home, I would catch up on chores, put Taylor down for a nap—maybe grab one for myself, if I was lucky—drive back to preschool to pick up Jordyn, do our nightly routine, and cut another link off Daddy's chain. Just another ordinary day in the life of a Navy wife.

The White Car of Dress Blues

26 MAR 1993
0730 EASTERN TIME
SEAGRASS REACH
CHESAPEAKE, VIRGINIA, USA
36.44.14 N 76.16.19 W

Lt. Cmdr. Rick Vanden Heuvel sighed as he pulled into the driveway of the Rystrom home and turned off the engine. With him in the white, four-door, official Navy car was the rest of his notification team: the XO's wife and a Navy chaplain. The officers were wearing their Navy dress blues and the mood was quiet and somber. As the CACO, Rick's responsibility at the moment was to follow protocol and lead his team as they notified the next of kin. His team's duties would be over in a few hours or maybe days. For him, his job was just beginning.

Rick knew that coming to the Rystrom home before 7:30 a.m. would be too early, but the pressure to notify all the families and release the media to break news of the tragedy meant that they needed to move quickly. Hopefully, Mrs. Rystrom wouldn't still be in bed.

"Any last questions before we go?" Rick asked his team. But everyone knew what to do, though no one wanted to do it. As they exited the car, the men put on their Navy covers, or hats, as they all walked down the sidewalk, climbed up the curved, brick steps, and stood together in front of the large, double doors. Rick took a deep breath and rang the doorbell.

No answer.

Rick rang the bell again, but no one came. As he was peering through the glass inserts to see if anyone was inside, he heard a woman's voice calling out behind him.

"Hello, excuse me?"

Rick and the others turned around to find a woman running across the Rystroms' front yard with a look of concern on her face.

"Are you Mrs. Rystrom?" Rick asked, as the woman reached the bottom of the stairs.

"Oh no, I'm Jennifer, a friend of hers from down the street. My husband is a Navy officer," she explained nervously. "Please, sir, tell me why you're here."

This Navy wife obviously knew why they were there, but Rick couldn't divulge any details.

"We need to find Mrs. Rystrom, ma'am. Do you know where she is?"

"She left to take her daughter to preschool, but she should be home soon. Please, tell me, what's wrong? Has something happened to Jon?"

Rick could see the tears forming in her worried eyes, and there was no way to hide the grim truth that showed on their faces. Rick tried to give her a polite smile.

"I'm sorry, ma'am, but we really need to speak to Mrs. Rystrom first, before anyone else." Rick hoped that she understood his double meaning and wouldn't start the "wife net" before they had a chance to deliver the news.

"I understand," she replied solemnly, as she walked briskly away.

"Well," said Rick, as he turned to go back down the brick steps, "I guess we need to pull around the corner and wait for Mrs. Rystrom to come home. We certainly don't want her to find our car in the driveway when she returns."

Going through a trial run didn't help to settle anyone's nerves, because they all knew the next time they stood before those double front doors, there would be no turning back.

Rick and his team had a clear view of the Rystrom house from the side street less than a block away, but there was no sign of Mrs. Rystrom. Eventually, a minivan approached the home and pulled into the garage.

"Let's give her a little time to get settled," Rick said, and the rest agreed. After they waited a few minutes, the CACO team knew the dreaded time had finally come. Rick drove the car back to the Rystrom home and pulled into the driveway.

This time, Rick didn't say a word.

Stripes By My Windows

As I carried Taylor into the kitchen from the garage, I wasn't sure which chores to tackle first, but maybe I would start with picking up Jordyn's toy clutter downstairs. Taylor's fussiness interrupted my plans, and I knew I wouldn't get anything done until I gave her a mid morning snack. Our nursing days were almost over, and with her enjoying more solid foods, I loved the freedom her new eating routine gave me. A sprinkle of her beloved Cheerios would keep her happy, and I sat her in the highchair and took the box from the pantry. Max was waiting nearby, probably hoping for a treat of his own. As I leaned over the highchair to pour out some cereal on Taylor's tray, I heard Max begin to stir. I glanced up to see what could be bothering him, and I saw something unusual.

I saw stripes going by my dining room windows.

Naval stripes.

Stripes sewn on the sleeves of naval officers.

Stripes on dress blues.

Stripes just like the ones sewn on Jon's naval uniforms hanging in his closet upstairs.

My first reaction was, "Why are naval officers coming to my house on a Friday morning while Jon is at sea?"

In an instant, time stopped.

The doorbell rang.

I couldn't move.

I tried to walk toward the front door, but my mind was frantically spinning and my body was frozen. Through the glass inserts of our front double doors, I could see the naval officers. There seemed to be so many of them. As if in slow motion, I staggered through the dining room and toward my front door.

Jon had told me about this day. He had frequently joked with me that if I ever saw a group of naval officers wearing dress blues walking up to my door, they were coming to tell me that he was gone. I knew. They didn't have to say a word. Jon had prepared me. God had prepared me.

I found myself in the front foyer and saw my shaking hand reach out to turn the knob and open the door.

I saw faces. Faces of strangers—strangers in their dress blues—faces with tears streaming down their cheeks. There were no greetings. There were no introductions. There was nothing but silence and tears. Nothing was said—their faces said it all. They didn't have to speak. I already knew.

My eyes swept over these men in stripes until I found a familiar face. There stood my friend, the XO's wife. Her hands were covering her mouth while she wept.

My knees buckling, I stumbled back to the bottom step on our foyer stairway, my knuckles turning white as I grabbed onto the white spindles of our banister, gripping them for support so that I wouldn't fall. Gripping them to steady my shaking body. Gripping them as I threw back my head and wailed in disbelief and despair. Wailing for my Jon, my beloved. This wasn't happening.

The mournful screaming. Deep, raw, wailings of a wounded animal erupted from the bottom of my being. The kind of screaming that comes from the depths of your soul. The wails of despair that you don't know are there—those hidden deep within you. The screams of loss, of unbelief.

My Jon, my precious love, my life—our life, our girls, our home—my Jon. The perfect life shattering before me—shattering before these men in stripes. Shattering on our beautiful floor—the peach tile we picked out together. My life being ripped from me. My life as a Navy wife and a stay-at-home mom was now suddenly thrown into the dark abyss of being a Navy widow and a single mother.

Jon always told me that he flew the safest plane in the Navy. That thought shocked itself into my mind. Suddenly I turned from my own tragedy. Instantly my mind became clear, like coming out of a coma.

I hadn't noticed that these strangers had stepped into my foyer and closed the front door behind them. I lifted my head and once again found my friend's face.

"Who else was on the plane?" I asked, in words that came out slowly but clearly. I knew there were four other men from Jon's squadron who had lost their lives as well. I dreaded hearing their names. My mind went immediately to their wives—my dear friends. Our squadron wives' group had become very close recently. I wasn't the only one having men in stripes come to the door today. The XO's wife took a deep breath and stammered as she began.

"Frenchy," she whispered.

Oh no, not Shelly! She and John "Frenchy" Messier were newlyweds. Jon would always brag on Frenchy, a top-notch pilot. "He is the best stick in the Aces," I would hear him state many times with pride.

"Billy Ray," she continued slowly, as I began to sob again.

I thought of Paola Dyer and their 11-month-old baby, Christopher. My tears and gasps were becoming more uncontrollable. But the dreaded list of names went on.

"Aardvark," she spoke softly.

Jon loved Pat Ardaiz. Patrick was Jon's chess buddy. Thankfully he didn't have a wife or children, but the loss was still deep.

I couldn't stop the sobs. These sobs were now for my friends. Jon's friends. Our Navy family.

One name remained. I shrank back, anticipating the horror of hearing it.

"Bobby," she finished, as she wept from the weight of delivering the tragic news. This name shocked me most of all.

"Bobby Forwalder?" I gasped aloud. My mind couldn't comprehend this one. Not Bobby. Of all our guys, not Bobby. Bobby and Katie were expecting their first baby any day.

"What about Katie?" I cried. "Does she know yet? What about the baby?" My own loss was temporarily pushed out of my mind. I could only think of Katie—Katie and her unborn baby.

There were no answers to my questions, as my mind struggled to take it all in.

Jon. Frenchy. Billy Ray. Aardvark. Bobby. What went wrong?

"What happened?" I heard myself ask.

One man stepped forward and explained the situation. I couldn't process all he said, but the phrases "Operation Provide Promise mission last night," "foul deck wave-off," "went into the water," "plane crash," "missing plane," and "Ionian Sea" came through. I had never heard of the Ionian Sea.

"Where is my Jon?" I questioned back.

"They've been searching with helos for hours now and the search and rescue operation is ongoing, but so far no survivors have been found," was the solemn reply.

My mind exploded with a thousand questions.

What do you mean you can't find them?

How do you lose an E-2C Hawkeye? How do you lose five men?

What do you mean you don't know what happened?

Who are you? Aren't you the Navy? Aren't you skilled and trained for anything?

But I didn't ask any of these questions out loud. These questions had no answers.

They were telling me that he was missing—not that he was dead. But I knew. I knew that they didn't send out these men in their stripes to tell me he was missing. That would give me hope. My hope was gone. My hope was lost at sea. Jon's plane had gone down, and my perfect life had gone down with it.

A little squeal interrupted my thoughts as I was jolted back to the present. Taylor! My sweet baby was still sitting happily in her highchair snacking on her Cheerios and completely unaware that her little life was changed forever. One of the men, a chaplain, walked toward the kitchen to check on the baby.

My eyes drifted over to our den floor, scattered with Barbie dolls where Jordyn had been happily playing the night before. In my fog of shock, something told me that more uninvited guests would arrive. They couldn't find our home looking like this. I walked over to the den, bent down, and started to pick up the toys. The XO's wife knelt beside me to help. I turned to her and our eyes met.

"What am I going to do?" I whispered hoarsely. Her tear-stained eyes told me that she didn't have an answer. I looked back at the Barbies. In Jordyn's innocent world of make-believe, there was no sadness or tragedy. My girls were going to experience what little girls should never know. They were fatherless. No, it was more than fatherless.

That term now seemed so cold, so heartless, and so impersonal. No, my girls were left without their daddy.

I was still picking up the dolls when the doorbell rang again. One of the men in stripes opened the door and Jennifer, my neighbor, came running in.

"Kris!" she screamed in a desperate cry. I stood up and turned to face her.

"Jen, he's dead!" I cried out and ran to her open arms. "He's dead, he's dead, Jon's dead," and she held me close as I shuddered in her arms. I was saying these words for the first time. With each phrase, it was as if knives were slicing my throat. We clung to each other and we both wept uncontrollably.

"I am here for you, Kris," she kept saying over and over. "I will take care of Taylor—don't worry about her," she assured me. And she did. She went to the kitchen, relieved the kind chaplain, lifted Taylor out of her highchair, and held her closely. Jennifer stayed next to me the entire day, making sure that tasks were being carried out, phone calls were made, and Taylor was cared for.

At this point, the man in charge introduced himself and the other man with him. But I didn't want to know their names or who they were. I didn't want these strangers in my home—the home that Jon and I had built together. Their news wasn't welcomed and neither were they. I wanted them to leave and leave now!

My mind was screaming these thoughts to these men in dress blues, but my words were polite and respectful of their stripes. I knew what their stripes meant. I knew that they didn't want to be there. To be given the orders to deliver the news that would destroy my life must have been horrific. So I was polite to these strangers in my home—to the one in charge who told me to call him "Rick." What I didn't know was that this man would become my lifeline over the next days and months—a friend who would help me navigate my new life as a Navy widow.

The next minutes and hours were a whirlwind. I don't remember much of anything in any certain order, other than my mind was racing with details on how to tell my parents, Jon's parents, and most importantly, Jordyn.

All the years of taking care of our home and family while Jon was at sea suddenly took over. I wasn't processing anything as a woman who had just learned of her husband's tragic death. On the contrary, I was thinking as a Navy wife. There was a task at hand and I was the one to do it. I could hear Jon's words that he wrote to me in hundreds of letters, "You can do it, Kris. I have faith in you!" "I always had the utmost confidence in you, Kris"

Next of Kin

Immediately, I knew that I needed to get word to Jordyn's preschool. I didn't want her coming home. Not yet. The last thing I needed was my sweet 3-year-old walking into a confusing group of strangers and complete upheaval in her normally quiet home. Arrangements were quickly made for her to spend the night with a preschool friend.

Once I was certain Jordyn was in a safe place for the next 24 hours, I knew that my next task was to inform our closest family. Oh, how I dreaded them hearing the heart-wrenching news! But I had to push these emotional thoughts aside and focus on the job in front of me. Rick, the one in charge, explained that we had to make the phone calls quickly. The media had already heard the news and they were waiting. They were on standby—waiting ... waiting for those words that have been heard over the airwaves countless times—waiting "until the next-of-kin has been notified."

Our family was now part of their news story. My Jon was getting ready to have his name and picture shown on news stations and printed in newspapers around the country. I had watched these tragedies over time—a pilot lost here, a policeman killed in the line of duty, a family that perished in a fire—but now it was me. It was my husband on the news. It was our family that was being labeled "next-of-kin."

I started the painful notification with my parents. Oh, how my heart ached for my dad. He loved his son-in-law so dearly, but Jon was more than that. Jon was his friend. I called my dad at work and when I heard my father's voice, an overwhelming wave of despair came over me. I burst into tears as I tried to say the dreaded words.

"Dad, something terrible has happened ..." I fought to find my breath through my uncontrollable sobs.

"It's Jon," I struggled to continue. "His plane is missing. They can't find his plane. Oh Dad, please hurry ..."

"Krissy, are you alone? Is anyone with you?" My father's first thoughts were to take care of me.

I told him the Navy was with me and handed the phone over to Rick who gave him the pertinent details. After Dad's call was completed, there was a short sense of relief. My parents were on their way and though they had a long drive to reach me, they should arrive that evening.

> FATHER OF THE FATHERLESS AND PROTECTOR OF WIDOWS IS GOD IN HIS HOLY HABITATION. (PSALMS 68:5 ESV)

The next difficult call was to inform Jon's parents. But given their age and more delicate health, I didn't want to shock them with an unexpected phone call. I had Rick phone Pat, Jon's sister, instead. After he broke the news to her, Pat and I cried together over the phone. I told her not to give Mervin and Jo any hope. I knew the search and rescue operation would be futile, and there was no way that Jon or the other men had survived the crash. My suggestion was for Pat to go to a nearby town and find a reservist officer so that she didn't have to give her parents the tragic news alone.

With the most important phone calls made, I got out my address book and gave orders about whom else to contact and how. Like most homes, we only had one land line for making phone calls and before other notifications were made, I asked Rick to call my pastor, Dr. Bob Reccord. He and his dear wife Cheryl came over right away.

The men in stripes went into action and were respectful and efficient as they carried out their duties with military precision. As the hours passed, I learned that they weren't there to simply deliver the news. They were there for me. They were the Navy, and they were there to take care of their own. I was one of them.

Life suddenly became very chaotic—very demanding—as word of the tragedy broke and my home began to fill with people. Faces were everywhere. Faces from church, our Sunday School class, and choir. Faces from the neighborhood. Faces from the Navy. So many faces. Faces of people I had never met.

Women were in my kitchen making coffee. Our coffee maker. Women were putting food in the refrigerator. Our refrigerator. People were opening the front door. Our door. The phone wouldn't stop ringing. Ringing and ringing. People were answering the phone. Our phone. Who were these faces? I wanted to be nice. It felt like I was supposed to be happy with all these people in our home. The people were sad but so very busy.

My mind was so foggy as I sat at my kitchen island and watched them work. I just sat. Numb. As each new person walked into my kitchen the sobs would come again. All this food. All the pound cake. I wanted to visit with each of the faces. I wanted to thank them. Receiving all this attention was embarrassing. My desire was to let loose and scream and give full vent to my sorrow, but I couldn't. I didn't want to lose it in front of all these people. Sometimes I would run upstairs to my bedroom, close the door, and grieve alone for a few minutes. I would dry my tears and put on a brave Navy-wife face before presenting myself again. All I could think about was Jon. My Jon.

Then a call came—the call that the men in stripes were waiting for. I already knew. Rick hung up the phone and sighed. As he slowly walked over to where I was sitting, the people filling my house grew quiet so that they could hear the news. Rick knelt down before me and stared me straight in the eye, making sure that I would hear what he was about to say. His face was grim and his words were measured and clear.

"Kris, the Navy has recovered a few pieces of wreckage from the plane. They've discontinued the search-and-rescue operation, and the air crew has been officially declared 'lost at sea.'" Rick paused, and added plainly, "There are no survivors. Jon is dead." My Jon was gone. My Jon was lost at sea.

5 fallen naval aviators mourned

Top: An honor guard performs a 21-gun salute at Norfolk Naval Base near the end of a memorial service held Tuesday for the five naval aviators who died Friday when their surveillance plane crashed in the Ionian Sea, east of Italy. The five were members of Norfolk-based Carrier Airborne Early Warning Squadron 124, operating from the USS Theodore Roosevelt. **Above:** The wife and child of a deceased aviator leave service.   Photos by **Craig Moran**/Daily Press

CHAPTER 22

Love Letters From the Grave

A World-Wide Stage

The magnitude of the tragedy still did not register in my mind. I couldn't understand anything. How did the safest plane in the Navy disappear off a carrier? Did Jon try to get out? Did he know that the plane was going down? Did he drown? Was he trying to help the other guys escape? Jon was the senior officer on board and the mission commander, and I knew that he would have done everything he could to save the other four crewmen over himself.

All these questions and the men in stripes couldn't tell me what my mind was screaming to know. Neither could the growing crowd of people in my home on Seagrass Reach. There were so many tears everywhere I turned. This wasn't happening to me, to my girls, to my Jon.

The continued blur of faces and tears and numbness was briefly broken that afternoon when President Bill Clinton came on television for a previously scheduled news conference with German Chancellor Helmut Kohl. The strangers in my home anticipated that the tragedy of Bear Ace 603 would make the national news, and so they had the television on. I was never one to pay much attention to the news, but this time the broadcast had my full attention. I didn't have to wait long to see if the president would acknowledge our loss.

Good afternoon, ladies and gentlemen, President Clinton began. *Before we begin the press conference, I have a sad announcement to make. I have just been informed that five United States servicemen on a routine training flight with the United States ship Theodore Roosevelt have crashed at sea within a mile of the carrier. I want to express my deep concern over the accident.*

Just two weeks ago, I visited USS Theodore Roosevelt and met the fine Sailors and Marines serving their nation at sea there. I was profoundly impressed by their commitment, their dedication, and their professionalism. They made America proud. And I want to say that my thoughts and prayers are with the relatives and the shipmates of those five servicemen who are missing at sea.

While I appreciated the president's sentiments, not even he had the power to bring Jon and the other men back to life. The German chancellor shared similar condolences when his turn came to address the press.

Mr. President, ladies, and gentlemen, Helmut Kohl started, in his thick German accent. *First, Mr. President, allow me to express my heartfelt sympathy on the loss and the fear, because we don't have any detailed information about the loss of life of five American officers. I hope very much that these soldiers may be able to return to their families safe and sound, because they serve the freedom and the security of their country, the United States of America. And without that service, there would be no freedom and peace and no reunification for Germany. And this is why I am very sad about the things that you have just had to present to us. And I should like to ask you to convey to the families of the people concerned my feelings of sympathy.*

Of course, we knew that Jon and the others had been declared lost at sea, and there was no chance of them returning to us "safe and sound." The logical part of me understood that with notifications ongoing, these officials couldn't tell the whole truth of what was known about the mishap to the international news outlets. But these leaders' words reminded me that Jon and his Navy brothers had died doing something noble: They died in service to their country. I couldn't help but wonder if Jon knew that his story was on the world stage and how he would feel about that.

The Rystrom Promise

The initial wave of shock had subsided, and I began to interact more with all the faces in my home. Friends encouraged me to eat something, and I went to the kitchen and politely attempted to comply, but the few bites I managed to swallow were like sawdust in my mouth. My appetite disappeared completely. On the surface, as I sat at my kitchen island, picking at my food, I was calm and controlled. Underneath I was frozen in a suspended animation of grief.

Until the mail came.

My friend, Jennifer, sat down beside me and handed me some envelopes. She whispered quietly, "Kris, I got your mail. There are some letters here—letters from Jon."

One glance at Jon's familiar scribbling of our address on the envelope of the carrier's official stationery and my frozen grief instantly erupted into red-hot tears and guttural wails of anguish. Everyone in the house could hear my cries. I couldn't control my spontaneous outburst of despair. The letters. The letters that had once nourished my soul. That had filled me with such joy. That had sustained me through lonely months when Jon was out at sea. Now that he was lost at sea, those same letters pierced my soul and left me shaking and screaming like a wounded animal again.

And yet, as I grasped the letters in my trembling hands, I clung to them as though they were the only remaining remnants of Jon's tender love and devotion for me. These were his last words—some of the final messages that I would ever receive from my beloved Jon. Painful, yet precious. Wounding, yet healing. I rushed from the table, ran up the stairs, and retreated to the solitude of my bedroom so that I could open them, alone.

I fell onto my bed and after taking a few moments to allow my sobbing to subside, I turned my attention to Jon's latest letters. They were marked with numbers "7" and "8." I opened No. 7 and pulled out a single page. He had written "Saturday night" but didn't give the date. It must have been written a couple of days after the No. 5 letter that I'd received yesterday.

Dear Kris,
A lot better day...

I wish I could have said the same. He went on and described some training and a brief he'd attended, and how he'd enjoyed Pizza Night. What he wrote next both cut and comforted me at the same time.

But most of all, I realized how much I love you and miss family life. I have been writing the letters in bed usually but a few have been at my desk. And as I write this letter, I look at your pictures and realize just how beautiful you are and how lucky I am to have you as my wife. Kris, never forget how important you are to me and how important you are to our children.

Jordyn is so cute; I look at her and all these memories just flow through me.

We just heard that an ex F-14 RIO from VF-84 never returned from a hop at Oceania. Did that make the papers? Lt. Cmdr. Fred Dillingham. A memorial service will be held tomorrow sometime. He left a wife and two kids. It makes one think.

He went on to ask about Jordyn's preschool and how they were heading straight for the Adriatic. The poor thing even managed to lock himself out of his room that night. He closed his letter with these words:

Well kiddo, hug Jordyn and Taylor for me. Love you, Jon.

Tears kept streaming down my face, knowing that Jon would never hug his sweet girls again. I hadn't heard about Lt. Cmdr. Dillingham's death, but it was clear that the wives of 603 weren't the only new Navy widows in our area. How chilling to think that Jon received this news just days before his own tragic accident. Maybe God had been preparing him for what was to come.

I opened letter No. 8, but it was simply a brief note he'd written before the first COD of the cruise departed, asking me to mail him some paperwork. I was hit with the harsh fact that Jon—responsible, organized, detailed Jon—would no longer be handling the details of our family's finances and household. My grief was so raw that, in that moment, I couldn't begin to process all the troublesome ramifications of Jon's death.

It was clear that when Jon wrote these letters, he'd yet to receive a letter from me. Had he received any of my letters before he died? I'd written faithfully, everyday. But what if none of my letters ever got to him? What if the last words he heard from me were that rushed goodbye on the morning of his departure? I desperately hoped that was not the case.

The daily mail would become a bittersweet ritual. For the mail would keep coming. The Rystrom promise had been kept and now it meant more to me than ever. I read the letters again, and this one phrase stood out to me:

Kris, never forget how important you are to me and how important you are to our children.

Jon, as if from the grave, was asking me to make another promise. As I closed my bedroom door and slowly descended the stairs to rejoin the waiting crowd below, I hung onto Jon's words of encouragement to help me survive his being lost at sea.

Navy Proud

Surviving the upheaval in my home was my more immediate problem, as my house continued to fill with a never-ending stream of people. As hard as Jennifer and Rick tried to protect me, well-meaning friends kept asking me questions, wanting a piece of me that needed their attention. There was a constant pulling at me from all directions as my mind screamed silently in despair. The chaos revolving around me shoved every thought of Jon into an ever-spinning painful void that I couldn't outwardly express.

As the hours ticked off one by one, I found myself gathering a strength that I didn't know I possessed. Unplanned and clearly unscripted, I kept my presence calm and controlled for the people around me. I couldn't, and I wouldn't, lose it. I now had to be strong, like my Jon. I could not give into my spiraling emotions. I was a Rystrom. I had carried his name for seven years, and now I had to hold that name firmly in my grasp, being steady, level-headed, and methodical in every step. The people around me would not watch me crumble. That was for later, in the silence of my own place—our place. Not on public display. I was an officer's wife and everything I did in the hours to come would make my husband proud—would make the Navy proud. I was and always would be the U.S. Navy, and this would not break me.

Little did I know that through the years of Jon's constant words of encouragement, there had been a deep reserve that God was preparing within my soul—a well I would draw from for many years to come. This was His well of grace that my Lord had prepared specifically for me so that I could stand strong as my world came crashing down.

Afternoon turned into evening and people started leaving, going back home to their perfect worlds, to their normal lives, to their families where death had not come to visit. The few friends who remained were waiting for the arrival of my parents, who had a long drive from West Virginia.

Baby's Comfort

The one thing in that day of hell that gave me a smile was my sweet baby girl, Taylor. She smiled and cooed at every person who held her, loving the extra attention, hugs, and snuggles that she received. My innocent baby was oblivious to what had just occurred. She couldn't understand that her loving daddy was never going to hold her again. He wouldn't be able to tell her he loved her, laugh at her cute giggles, or read her bedtime stories. Seven-month-old Taylor would never know her amazing father.

These thoughts started to overwhelm me as I realized I needed my baby girl to comfort me. She was the closest thing I had to her daddy— to my beloved Jon. I took my baby from a friend's arms, as Taylor rubbed her little eyes in exhaustion from the chaotic day. I carried her upstairs and slowly walked into the nursery, gripping her tighter as I softly began to weep. I breathed in the baby smell on her little neck while my tears slid down my cheeks and landed on her precious face. I quietly closed the door and sat down in the rocker that Jon and I had painted just for her, gently rocking her back and forth, singing softly to my baby girl. Her life and mine had made an unexpected and violent shift. With the chaos to come, I made a difficult decision. As I rocked in the nursery that Jon and I had planned and decorated together, I nursed baby Taylor for the last time.

Once Taylor was sound asleep in her crib, I was in no hurry to leave the solitude of the darkened nursery. I continued rocking in the chair, as my mind swung back and forth with so many unanswered questions. The basic facts of Jon's mishap were still cloudy to me, but I knew for certain that Jon's body wasn't found. I prayed that somehow the Navy was wrong and that Jon and the rest of the guys had miraculously survived and that they'd be spotted in a life raft once daylight broke over the ocean. But then Rick's plain words came back to my mind: "There are no survivors. Jon is dead." My heart was tossed to and fro like the waves of the Ionian Sea that now covered the final resting place of my beloved husband.

My mind kept thinking of the love of the ocean that Jon and I shared. A picture of Jon giving two thumbs up while deep underwater reminded me how much Jon enjoyed scuba diving. He never got enough of visiting the wonders of the underwater world. Now the depths of the ocean were his graveyard and his beloved E-2C Hawkeye, his coffin. I remembered the little bottle of oxygen that Jon showed Jordyn's preschool class. Did he have time to use it? Did he panic when the cabin filled with icy water? Did he drown? Was he scared? Or did he even survive the impact long enough to know he was in trouble? Did he have time to think of us, wish us one last kiss, give us a hug and a "miss you" before he stepped into eternity? He was always at home in the ocean and now it was his forever home. Or was it? Wasn't Jon in heaven now?

> REMEMBER YOUR WORD TO YOUR SERVANT, IN WHICH YOU HAVE MADE ME HOPE. THIS IS MY COMFORT IN MY AFFLICTION, THAT YOUR PROMISE GIVES ME LIFE. (PSALMS 119:49-50 ESV)

That thought turned my mind to much darker questions. Didn't God hear our prayers to take care of Jon? Didn't He hear Jordyn's prayers to "please keep Daddy safe in his plane"? Why would He allow this horrific tragedy to happen to us? Was God angry at us? It wasn't fair! Jon and I had gone to church for years, read our Bible, given faithfully of our time and money to our church. We were honest, God-fearing people. I had always believed the Bible and God's promises. What good were His promises now? I was questioning everything that I had ever known.

I prayed alone in the darkness and pleaded with the God whom I had loved and served my entire life. What have You done to my Jon? Why have You taken him? You told me You'd never leave me or forsake me! Where are You now? I believed that God had turned His back on us, and I felt the ice-cold withdrawal of His protection. This sort of thing wasn't supposed to happen to good people like Jon, and certainly not to me. I had all my boxes checked, and now my boxes weren't just empty—they were demolished.

Into Loving Arms

I heard a commotion downstairs and I realized that my parents had arrived. All day long I had been grieving with friends, but this was the first time I could grieve with my family. I hurried from the nursery and rushed into my parents' loving arms. Any lid I'd managed to seal over my soul was completely removed and the shock of Jon's death hit me afresh as we poured out our grief together.

My parents and I spent the late hours of that fateful Friday talking through all the details Rick had told me about Jon's mishap. My family was in total shock. I was still my daddy's little girl, and I knew he would do all that he could to help me navigate this nightmare. But he was grieving too. He had lost his best friend. My mom was crushed, but there was no question that she would comfort and care for her granddaughters and stand by me through it all. I wanted to assure my parents that the girls and I would be fine, but I didn't know if we would be. My dad was so much like Jon with his analytic, discerning mind, and he would do his best to fill Jon's shoes.

But now was not the time to dig into the harsh realities to come—my body was completely exhausted. With my parents' arrival, the brave Navy-wife face melted away and my energy came crashing down. Like it or not, I had to sleep, for tomorrow would be another day filled with more visitors, more phone calls, more questions, and few answers.

My parents would sleep in our playroom, where the girls' paper chain was still hung in its place. Another wave of sobbing hit me, as I realized no link would be cut off the chain tonight. There would be no prayers for Daddy's safety in the airplane. But the worst part was yet to come. Tomorrow my little Jordyn, Jon's Jordyn, needed to be told that her daddy wasn't coming home.

With tears in her eyes, Mom asked if I wanted her to stay with me in my room that night. But I knew I had to face my bedroom alone, without my beloved Jon. As much as I was accustomed to sleeping alone through Jon's many deployments, I always knew he would be coming home. Now I knew he would never be coming back.

As I opened the bedroom door, a rush of emotions overwhelmed me. Loss. Darkness. Hopelessness. I ran to his closet and clutched the closest thing that I knew would bring me comfort: his brown, worn, terrycloth bathrobe. The robe he wore when he would get up with one of the girls in the middle of the night. The robe he wore when he would bring me coffee in the morning. The robe he wore the morning he rushed to get ready to leave for the ship—the day I said goodbye to my husband for the last time. I could still smell his cologne lingering on his robe. I fell to the floor inside his closet. I couldn't stop the screaming. I muffled my screams with his robe. I finally could mourn for my husband. My Jon, my love, how will I live without you? I screamed and sobbed until I had nothing left. The same questions I'd asked myself in the nursery kept repeating like a macabre carousel that I couldn't stop.

Time stood still as I cried mournfully in the closet. At last my fatigue overwhelmed my grief, and I lay down in my cold, empty bed and drifted into a fitful sleep.

Kris, Jon, and Jordyn at a Bear Ace Squadron picnic.

CHAPTER 23

Is My Daddy Happy?

Fo'c'sle Farewell

27 MAR 1993
1100 CET CENTRAL EUROPEAN TIME UTC+1
USS THEODORE ROOSEVELT
IONIAN SEA
38.31.45 N 17.36.55 E

Nearly 36 hours had passed since the mishap, and the time had come for the crew of USS Theodore Roosevelt to mourn the loss of Bear Ace 603. The fo'c'sle was packed as service members of every rank gathered together, from the rear admiral commanding the carrier battle group to the lowest-ranking enlisted man. To honor the men, a candlelit table was set up at the front. In the middle of the table was a folded flag, surrounded by a picture of each man dressed in his flight suit, along with five Navy dress white hats, called covers. The scene was like the one that Jon witnessed six days earlier at the memorial service for Lt. Cmdr. Fred Dillingham.

The three chaplains officiated the "Service of Recognition and Thanksgiving," which included prayers, readings from the Bible, and remarks from the Bear Ace Squadron's commanding officer. Most touching were words of remembrance offered by the Bear Aces who served alongside the lost men. Tears were seen in many eyes as each man was mentioned—Frenchy, Billy Ray, Bobby, Aardvark—and Rooster's eulogy was no exception. Jon was described as a loving and faithful husband, a loving father, and a friend to the entire squadron, "the kind of guy you could count on when the chips were down," who "always tried to do the right thing."

A poem written by an enlisted Marine was read, which put the feelings of everyone in attendance into words.

> It was six in the morning when I first heard,
> VAW-124 had that night lost a bird.
> On its final approach the plane was waved off,
> Did a quick flyby and started to loft.
> As it rose up and banked off to the side,
> For reasons unknown everything died.
>
> The worst part of all was the five men aboard,
> For them and their families our sympathies poured.
> All through the morning we didn't know what to say,
> The whole ship was depressed all of that day.
> For airplanes can be bought with dollars and cents,
> But you can't replace a person no matter how much you've spent.
>
> It must be real hard to tell a man's wife,
> That the plane had crashed taking his life.

Or to see the little kids' tears start to churn,
When they learn that their dad will never return.
Or to tell two parents of the death of their boy,
That they will never see their pride and joy.

Though we're not all Bear Aces we still feel your
pain,
For the whole ships morale was just sucked down the
drain.
Where we used to see laughing and joking around,
People don't say a word and just stare at the ground.
But we must pull together through thick and thin.
So this kind of thing won't happen again.

—by LCpl. Chris Anderson, VMFA-312

As the service concluded with the singing of the "Navy Hymn," a final prayer, and a trumpet playing "Taps," the CO of the Bear Aces knew that, although the service was over, the grieving of his squadron was not. After taking off a few short days to pause and catch their breath, it would be time to get back to the business of flying. In the days and weeks to come, the CO would provide strong, calm, and much-needed leadership to help his squadron move forward and focus on the mission before them.

For the next several days, a palpable sadness permeated the entire ship. An unusual quietness ruled conversations as men struggled to make sense of the loss of their Navy brothers. In the air wing, everyone was thankful to be alive, yet they couldn't understand why a seemingly perfectly operating plane was flown into the water.

For the men serving in the Bear Ace Squadron, the tragedy created a deep sorrow that time would not erase. For decades, the loss of their friends would haunt them, bringing a lump to the throat and tears to the eyes at just the mention of Bear Ace 603. Having to pass by the few scraps of recovered wreckage down in the hangar bay, roped off and guarded by a lone Marine, didn't help.

In less than a week, a representative from the Judge Advocate General, or JAG, would come aboard USS Theodore Roosevelt and commence a thorough investigation into the mishap, including taking sworn statements, analyzing all the records and video footage from the evening, and carefully examining the wreckage. While such an inquiry was necessary, none believed it would bring any lasting resolution to affected families and friends.

Lt. Cmdr. Rick Vanden Heuvel had a different mission of his own to perform, and while he was thankful the

294

first difficult day was behind him, he knew that many more painful days were ahead. Rick watched in admiration as Kris' church family rallied around her, keeping her home running like a well-oiled machine. He was amazed that her pastor, Dr. Reccord, even took time to personally minister to him. Reflecting on the love and generosity that he'd witnessed from Kris' church family, Rick told his wife, "Honey, if anything ever happens to me, call the Baptists."

Fog of Grief

The sun came up. Another day began. My mind started to awaken from the fog of sleep. Suddenly, my thoughts from what had happened the day before hit like a shotgun blasting a hole into my soul. Jon was gone. The stripes, the plane, the people, the news—it all came rushing back into my memory. It sucked the air out of me. My body went into spasmodic sobs as I grabbed my pillow to smother the sounds of my screams. A deep, sick, eroding ache in my stomach set in, as the nightmare of my new reality took over from where it had left off the day before. I didn't want to come out of my lonely bedroom to live out this horror—to face the faces.

My rational mind took over. Taylor. I needed to check on Baby Taylor. I threw open my bedroom door and ran into her nursery. She was still sleeping in her crib. Quiet. Innocent. Peaceful. This child would become my newly found source of serenity. She would help me breathe again. She would help me face today.

But I still wasn't ready to face Jordyn. I wanted to keep her innocent of the news about her daddy as long as possible. My parents and I agreed to arrange for Jordyn to come home later in the afternoon. Let her keep playing with her friend was my thought. But that reminded me of something Jordyn loved playing with: the paper chain hanging in the playroom. Jordyn and I had carefully cut out each strip from colorful construction paper and taped each link together, putting stickers on the special days we'd celebrate while Daddy was gone. What was once a symbol of hope and anticipation was now a taunting reminder of loss.

I walked into the playroom and sighed as I held the paper chain in my hands. So fragile, so light, yet so very heavy. Here were all the special days we'd never celebrate together again. No more links would be removed—the uncut links now stretching into eternity. Life ... fragile as a paper chain. Hope ... torn apart and thrown away, piece by piece. I shuddered as I placed the cursed chain in a black, plastic garbage bag and asked my dad to hide it in the attic.

By now, the news of the mishap had hit everywhere. As the morning hours passed, the phone resumed its incessant ringing and more people began to arrive in my home. But unlike yesterday, my parents were by my side. They provided a much-needed buffer for me, handling many details and decisions so that I didn't have to, especially the arrangements for our relatives who were arriving from far away.

> JORDYN'S VERSE: AND AFTER YOU HAVE SUFFERED A LITTLE WHILE, THE GOD OF ALL GRACE, WHO HAS CALLED YOU TO HIS ETERNAL GLORY IN CHRIST, WILL HIMSELF RESTORE, CONFIRM, STRENGTHEN, AND ESTABLISH YOU. (1 PETER 5:10 ESV)

Through the efforts of so many, I saw God's people come to my rescue. Like a warm blanket, God was covering my cold, chilled soul with His love, through His children. Wonderful women from my church became my lifeline, keeping everyone fed, washing the dishes, answering the phone, recording sympathies, and maintaining household order. Multiple casseroles, plates of sandwiches, and an assortment of desserts kept appearing out of nowhere. Thoughtful friends brought paper products to make feeding the onslaught of family and friends easier. Jon would have been thrilled to have attended the party that was being thrown for him.

My CACO, Rick, was always there, and I was learning to trust him and his calm, reassuring nature. Rick informed me that the Navy had decided to honor Jon and the other lost crew of Bear Ace 603 on the following Tuesday in David Adams Memorial Chapel at Norfolk Naval Base. This service would follow Navy tradition and would require very little input from me, unlike Jon's personal memorial service, which our family decided to have the day after, on Wednesday, at First Baptist Church Norfolk. This was all new for me. Even though I'd been to many funerals, I didn't realize there was a funeral when there was no body to bury. Dr. Reccord was so gentle and kind, helping me plan a touching service that would have made Jon proud.

As the fog of grief loomed into another day, I was able to have more time alone, thanks to my parents taking over my roles. Throughout the day I would slip up to the solitude of my bedroom and weep in my "Cry Room," mourning for my beloved Jon. The gut-wrenching questions, the disturbing images, the overwhelming fears, and the relentless sorrow were no less present than the day before.

During one of these moments, I heard my mom gently tapping on my bedroom door, and I opened it to see what she wanted. She held our cordless phone in her hand, but the look on my face plainly told her that I didn't want to talk to anyone.

"Kris, I think you need to take this one. It's Olga Plautz. She lost her husband in the E-2C crash last summer."

I gasped in shock. She knew. This woman on the other end of the phone understood exactly what I was going through. I grabbed the phone from my mother's hand as if I were grabbing onto a line to hope.

"Hello, Olga?" A soft, woman's voice was on the other end.

"Kris. Yes, I'm Olga, and I am here for you."

The two of us wept on the phone. This woman whom I had never met was reaching out to me in my grief. Nine months earlier she had stood where I was standing now. I remembered how shocked Jon was when he received the call about the fiery E2C crash that took the lives of five men. I remembered feeling sorry for the men's families, never knowing we'd suffer a similar fate. In Olga, I found a new friend—a Navy widow and a single mother of a baby boy. I was now a member of a new squadron: The Navy squadron of the wives left behind.

Later that morning, my good friend and neighbor, Jennifer, asked me quietly what she and our neighbors could do to bless me. I knew that Jennifer and Jon shared a love of landscaping, a honey-do that Jon had not had time to complete, except for the planting of his precious rosebushes. With so many friends and family arriving, he'd be embarrassed to show off our gorgeous new home surrounded by a bare yard with mounds of dirt. We needed flowers and we needed mulch. Jennifer understood completely and she reassured me that this was a mission she and our neighbors would be honored to accomplish.

I was a little better prepared when the mail ran that Saturday afternoon, but the sight of Jon's handwriting on another envelope was still painful to bear and reduced me to sobbing once again. I retreated to the quiet of my bedroom to process his latest letter, alone. It was No.6, written one week earlier on March 20.

Good morning sweetheart,
I hope today is better than yesterday. Yesterday sucked...

I couldn't get past those first few words without breaking down. What an understatement, yet Jon never knew the circumstances under which I would read his words. Obviously, the day before he wrote the letter had been a hard one for him, with some important message that didn't go right. The next paragraph was completely unexpected.

Guess what I need? My battery-operated squirt gun. Send it when you send my 1st care package. No hurry. I just need it in a few weeks. It appears the new XO is into it and blatantly told everyone he brought his, and where's ours?

I couldn't help but smile through my tears. Oh, Jon, always the jokester. I could imagine him in a spirited water-gun fight with his squadron mates after a long day of flying.

I heard Nebraska lost, the turkeys, but Wake won, so it is Nebraska in football and WFU in basketball.

I wasn't up to date on college sports, but I remembered Jon writing me once that he had two great loves: me and college football—and in that order. I managed another weak smile.

Still no mail. The COD had to turn back cuz of wx. I think you will hear me talk or mention wx a lot.

"Wx." I remembered writing Jon about what that abbreviation meant. I would have to figure it out on my own. Perhaps it meant weather? That would make sense. And still no mail. Surely he'd received a letter from me at some point.

The admiral is briefing us today at 1300. I bet it's about our role in the Adriatic.

Love you, Jon.
Kiss my little sweeties, OK?

The Adriatic must have been close to the Ionian Sea. No one would have guessed the consequences of Jon's role in that region and in Operation Provide Promise. What about my role? Now that Jon was gone, what role would I have to play?

"Kiss my little sweeties, OK?" Jon was asking me to make another promise. Yes, Jon, I'll kiss your little sweeties. I could do that much today. As for the rest, I'd have to take it one day at a time.

A Little Girl's Heart

Jon's request reminded me that there was one task I had to face—the one I dreaded the most. That afternoon, Jordyn would come home, and I wouldn't be able to shelter her any longer from the cold, hard truth. My parents and I discussed how best to break the news, and we agreed that we would tell her together. How do you tell a 3-year-old that her daddy is dead? I only hoped I could find the right words.

When Jordyn walked through the door, she was thrilled with excitement to see all the people there, including several church families with children. In her innocent eyes, it was a party. She was especially excited to see her grandparents from West Virginia. After a few minutes of Jordyn getting settled, I asked her if she would come upstairs to the playroom. Her grandparents and I had something very important to tell her. Without hesitation, her little legs ran up the stairs. She wanted to return as fast as she could to play with the kids who were visiting.

Mom, Dad, and I sat down together on the bed in the playroom, and Jordyn stood in front of me. There was a solemn stillness in the room. Jordyn didn't notice that the paper chain that she had so proudly hung around the room was missing. I took her little hands in mine, and I stared into her big, beautiful, hazel eyes.

"Jordyn, Mommy has something very sad to tell you." Jordyn got very quiet.

"What is it, Mommy?"

I started very slowly and calmly. I spoke with no tears. Unscripted, I simply said, "When Daddy was flying in his plane last night, his plane broke and it crashed into the water. Jordyn, Daddy died last night."

As much as I wanted to protect Jordyn's little heart from the reality of our tragedy, I couldn't soften the news. I didn't know how else to say it. As if she was trying to comprehend the words that I had just spoken to her, her worried eyes met mine and she asked, "Is my daddy ever coming home?"

The tears started creeping down my cheeks, and I said to my daughter for the first time, "No, honey, Daddy isn't coming home again."

She looked at me and then to my weeping parents and burst into tears. The wails from my sweet, innocent child on that day will never be erased from my soul. I was watching my daughter's life be torn in two, just like a link torn from her beloved paper chain. I held her close as we all mourned together. Suddenly, Jordyn stopped crying. There was a quiet pause. She looked at me with a profound question that I will never forget: "Mommy, is my daddy happy?"

In amazement at the words spoken from the innocence of a child's heart, I was able to smile. Perhaps my first smile since I'd seen the stripes pass by my window. A calmness came over the room. With a sober confidence, I answered her, "Yes, Jordyn, your daddy is happy because he is with Jesus."

Jordyn smiled, wiped away her tears, and politely asked if she could go outside and play. To our amazement, Jordyn left her playroom with the satisfaction of knowing that her daddy was with Jesus. God brought the reality of eternal life into a little girl's heart that day.

CHAPTER 24

My Folded Flag

All Wrong

On Sunday, my CACO Rick drove me to the memorial service for Bobby Forwalder, the first Bear Ace to have his funeral. Getting together for the first time with Katie, Bobby's wife, and the other widows, Paola and Shelly, was intensely emotional for all of us. Naturally, we were concerned for Katie, since she was due to have her baby any day. I couldn't imagine how distraught she must have been, preparing for her firstborn under those trying circumstances. Bobby's service was a wonderful celebration of his life, but it was challenging for me to process the sudden death of five men, along with my personal loss. The fog of grief was only growing thicker, and Bobby's service was merely a warm-up for the much larger Navy memorial service to come.

On Tuesday, Rick drove my sweet girls and me to the Navy's tribute to Bear Ace 603. Everything about that service seemed wrong to me. I deeply appreciated the Navy honoring my husband and the other men, but I walked through the events of the memorial as if they were scenes in a distorted nightmare.

Pulling up to the gate at Norfolk Naval Base was wrong. Jon wasn't by my side, and he wasn't the one being saluted. We had prepared that day as though we were going to church on a normal Sunday morning—the girls and I dressed in pinks. But this was wrong. Wrong that my family was going to a church on a naval base on a Tuesday. Wrong that we were going to a memorial service for my husband. Wrong that we were going to sit with three other widows. Wrong that four children were never going to see their fathers again.

As we made our way into the crowded David Adams Chapel, I realized that hundreds of people had already taken their seats. I carried Taylor and held Jordyn's hand as Rick escorted us down the center aisle between the rows of sorrow-filled faces. This was an aisle meant for joy, perhaps for a new bride or a parishioner going to the altar for prayer, not for a widow and her children walking down an aisle of grief.

Familiar, friendly faces of my choir friends, who had come to sing for the service at my request, greeted me from behind the pulpit as I got closer to the front. Dressed in robes and sitting in rows, the choir had left one chair empty, save for a single white pillow in remembrance of Jon. What I wouldn't have given to see him wearing his choir robe and winking at me from the tenor section.

From their warm smiles, my eyes fell onto the somber stares from the pictures of five Navy aviators' faces, framed and displayed on a wooden table in front of the pulpit: Frenchy, Billy Ray, Bobby, Pat, and Jon. My Jon. Smiling. In his flight suit. I took strength from Jon's beaming face and sensed my heart steadying as I met his photo gaze.

Now on view in a chapel packed with mourning friends, the crew of Bear Ace 603 had not known that they were posing for their obituaries when these portraits were taken. Behind each picture was a folded American flag, one for each man that had given his life for a country that he would never see again. A single ceremonial Navy sword lay on the table. "Welcome to the Navy, Mrs. Rystrom," flashed in my mind as the smack of the saber at our wedding welcomed me. The sword that had cut my wedding cake now proclaimed that I was a widow. Everything was wrong.

As I turned to find our seats, I looked at all the people sitting in the pews behind me, but every seat was taken. I frantically looked around, realizing that no one had saved a seat for my girls and me. In front of the packed crowd, I started to sob hysterically. I turned to Rick and cried out, "There isn't a seat for us!"

This strong officer's wife, who was going to make Jon proud—make the Navy proud—had a meltdown in front of hundreds of people. Rick jumped into action, and front-row seats were quickly cleared, and my girls and I sat down in silence. It was wrong.

The Navy memorial service honored Jon and the crew of Bear Ace 603 well. Stripes were everywhere as hundreds of naval officers had come to pay their respects. I quietly sang along as our choir performed familiar songs, ones that Jon and I had once rehearsed together. As a Navy chaplain spoke his words of comfort, my eyes were glued to Jon's framed photograph. Even through the tears of loss, I was still being comforted by him from the grave. Our love was so deep that even death could not win. Death could not destroy what God had gifted to us.

As the service drew to a close, a sobering military tradition began. I watched as one naval officer walked to the memorial table and picked up one of the five folded American flags. He stepped over to Pat "Aardvark" Ardaiz's mom, Sheila, and whispered something softly to her. With reverence, his white-gloved hands gently placed the folded flag in her frail arms. Next was Katie, then Shelly, then Paola. I watched each of my friends receive their flags one by one as each naval officer continued in silent procession. Then it was my turn.

One of Jon's closest friends and a fellow Navy officer picked up the flag, neatly folded into a triangle, behind Jon's picture. He turned from the table and bent down to me and whispered in my ear as he wept.

"Kris, on behalf of the president of the United States and the chief of naval operations, please accept this flag as a symbol of our appreciation for your loved one's service to this country and a grateful Navy."

He gently placed the flag in my hands. I clutched the folded fabric and pressed it close to my chest as I sobbed in my friend's arms. With no body to bury, the flag had now taken the place of my Jon.

The service concluded with a silent procession to a courtyard outside in front of the chapel. I held Jordyn's hand as we gathered around our family. Throughout the service, Mom had held Taylor and she was content to stay with her. While we waited, I noticed an army of camera crews and reporters from the local news stations. This was a national news item, and they didn't want to miss the chance to tell the world their story of another fallen hero. As we waited for the rest of the mourners to collect outside, Jordyn's preschool teacher knelt down and presented my daughter with a pink peony. During such a somber moment, my daughter was being nurtured through the tender gift of a flower, something Jon loved dearly.

A single trumpet filled the air with the familiar sound of "Taps," followed by a 21-gun salute—seven rifles shot three volleys into the air. Each blast shook me to the core. Then, in the distance, I could hear them coming. The familiar and distinct hum that I heard every day over my house: the hum of an E-2C Hawkeye. But this hum was different, much louder than I'd heard before. People all around me started scanning the sky.

What happened next was a moment I will never forget. I looked up and saw five E-2C Hawkeye planes flying toward us in a single V formation, their hums growing louder and louder, the deafening buzz taking over my mind as they flew closer. Suddenly, one E-2C banked hard to the outside and flew up and out of formation, a reflection of the lost crew. The remaining planes continued flying overhead in a missing man formation. As the one plane flew out of the pattern and the others continued on, I frantically ran to the open grass. Wails erupted from my soul as I dashed toward the planes. Running for my Jon.

In the solitude of my bedroom, I had painfully imagined Jon's terrible plane crash many times. But as I watched in horror as the missing man formation flew over my head, it was as though the terrifying crash was happening before my eyes. I clung to my flag, to my Jon, as he was lost forever in front of me. My friends, my family, and my daughters watched in anguish as I screamed in despair. I didn't care that hundreds of people were watching me lose control. I didn't care that the camera crews were taking videos and pictures of this officer's wife lamenting the loss of her husband. I didn't care anymore. I couldn't stop the screams. That was the day I said goodbye to my Jon forever.

All those years ago in San Diego, the disturbing image of the young Navy widow from the front page of the local paper had clenched my heart in an icy grip of fear. Now I was that woman. I was the young, Navy widow, clutching my flag—my moment of heart-wrenching grief frozen in time on the front page for all to see.

Flight Suit On

Two surprises awaited me when I returned home from the Navy memorial service. While we were gone, our sweet neighbors lovingly transformed our barren yard into a splendidly landscaped lawn, complete with colorful pansies and boxwood hollies. After the emotionally draining service, it was a blessing to be greeted by a vivid reminder of life, beauty, and the kindness of dear friends. Jon would have been proud.

The sweet smell of fresh mulch filled the air as I went to the mailbox and found my second surprise—another letter from Jon. My heart always skipped a beat and that now-familiar internal ache intensified whenever a letter from Jon arrived, yet I held onto each letter as if I were holding a priceless diamond. As I walked past the newly-planted spring flowers, I felt as if my own winter was just beginning.

In the privacy of my bedroom, I opened his latest message. This one was dated Monday, March 22, at 12:11 a.m. I tried to smile at how detail oriented he was and realized he had written this letter just past midnight.

> *My wonderful bride,*
> *Finally, 3 letters, I really should say wonderful feelings and informative pieces of art.*

At last, Jon had received my letters! I was so thankful that he had heard from us before he died and saw his Jordyn's precious pictures one last time. He wrote that he'd enjoyed a letter from our Sunday School class as well. I wish Jon could have seen the way those same people rallied around me in the days after his death.

> *I fully understand what you said about not crying. I fully believe that, because of our faith and our love, our bond is closer than most couples.*

I had shed buckets of tears over the last several days, and it took a moment before I remembered what Jon was referring to. I'd written him about how I hadn't cried this time when he deployed. I'd sure made up for it since then. That close bond built on our faith and love now felt shattered, yet I found myself drawing strength from his words.

> *Do the shrubs look nice? Did Jordyn have fun with playing in the dirt while you planted the shrubs?*

If only Jon could see our yard now with all the new flowers and mulch from the neighbors, enhancing his rosebushes and the shrubs I'd planted before the "Storm of the Century" blew through.

The paper chain is a great idea and, yes, it probably is 183 days in all.

Could Jon see from heaven that the paper chain was discarded in a black garbage bag in the attic?

I pushed the issue of no training on Sundays and the XO and CO bought off on it. I attended a memorial service for Lt. Cmdr. Dillingham. The chaplain from our church presided over the memorial.

Jon had grown greatly in his faith over the years. I cried to think that Jon had attended a memorial service a few short days before his own, conducted by someone from our church. I remembered that this chaplain's wife was one in the army of women who selflessly served our family. This same chaplain would have helped conduct Jon's shipboard memorial as well.

CO and I attended a full ops brief given by the 6th Fleet people about the Med. No new news. We expect our first full day of flying tomorrow. I am writing this in the ready room as I wait for an airplane. It is past midnight. I expect to get to bed about 2.... Well sweetie, the airplane has arrived, so kiss my girls and I miss you,

Love, Jon.

Jon's love of flying was something we didn't share, but I'd always admired that about him. Now his love had cost him his life. His plane had arrived, but there was never a guarantee that it would bring him safely home. But being an aviator, Jon was a member of a tight-knit community. As word spread of the mishap, our military family from coast to coast reached out to express their sympathies, and several flew great distances to attend Jon's personal memorial service.

Kiss my girls. Another promise that I would keep. I knew more letters were to come, but one day the letters would stop. What would I do then?

Exhausted with the emotions of the day and knowing tomorrow was Jon's memorial service at First Baptist Norfolk, I went to bed early that evening and attempted to get some rest. Late that night, I heard voices from down below and knew that Jon's family had arrived from Nebraska. With my heart so heavy and my body so spent, I knew I could not face them just yet. In the morning, our welcomed embraces would be replaced with yet another anguished round of grieving.

> BLESSED BE THE GOD AND FATHER OF OUR LORD JESUS CHRIST, THE FATHER OF MERCIES AND GOD OF ALL COMFORT, WHO COMFORTS US IN OUR ENTIRE AFFLICTION, SO THAT WE MAY BE ABLE TO COMFORT THOSE WHO ARE IN ANY AFFLICTION, WITH THE COMFORT WITH WHICH WE OURSELVES ARE COMFORTED BY GOD. (2 CORINTHIANS 1:3-4 ESV)

Jon, the girls, and I had visited them only a few weeks earlier when we attended Mervin and Jo's 50th wedding anniversary celebration in Nebraska. I was so thankful that we took the time and made the effort to attend, not knowing that it would be the last visit Jon would make to see his family. How would my sweet, elderly in-laws who lived such a simple, Midwest life ever recover from the tragic death of their beloved youngest son, Jonny?

As much as I dreaded grieving with Jon's family, I was relieved that we would be together as we celebrated Jon's life the next day. Every detail of his service had been planned as if Jon were watching me from heaven. In my mind, I kept asking him, "Jon, what do you think of having the choir sing this song? What about having our Sunday School teacher give your eulogy? How about Dad sharing some words?"

I knew this was probably silly, but I kept imagining that Jon was cheering for me as I carried out my newly assigned duties, not as a

Navy wife but as a widow planning his funeral. Although I was still emotionally raw from the Navy's memorial service, tomorrow would be for Jon alone, and I would be strong for him. For my precious love, I would make him proud.

First Baptist Church was overflowing with people. This was more than a church—for Jon and me, this was home. We sang in the choir together, shared Wednesday dinners in the fellowship hall with friends, taught Mission Friends to Jordyn's preschool class, and studied the Bible under Dr. Reccord's teachings each Sunday. Our Sunday School class was our family. A few short months before, Jon and I had dedicated our infant daughter Taylor to the Lord in the same sanctuary where Jon's life was to be remembered.

Living in a military community, stories of Sailors and soldiers dying was not unusual. But this wasn't another face on the news. Jon was one of their own, not a pew-warmer who attended church like a bystander when he wasn't deployed. Jon faithfully served our church family and was cherished for it.

The Rystrom and Windham family, along with the other widows from 603, sat in the front rows as Jon's celebration of life service began. I smiled through tears as we sang songs to our Lord reflecting on our Savior. The death and resurrection of Jesus was now personal. Eternity became part of me, because my Jon was experiencing it himself. Jon was living with Jesus. I was going to see Jon again and as the service continued, I prayed that he and the angels were watching. How many times had we stood in this sanctuary side by side worshipping our King? Now I worshipped alone. But I worshipped with the blessed image of my Jon surrounded in God's welcoming glory.

Our Sunday School teacher shared a warm eulogy, including the reading of several excerpts from Jon's most recent letters. Dr. Reccord gave a heartfelt sermon that comforted my soul. But what touched me most of all was a poem that my dad, and Jon's best friend, wrote for the occasion. Tears were in his eyes as he read it, but his voice was strong and his admiration for Jon was evident.

Jon Alvin Rystrom

Some of us called him Commander;
Others of us called him Jon, some Jonny;
Some affectionately called him Jonathan;
Others—Brother, others—Uncle Jon.
Two of us called him our Son;
One of us called him Daddy,
But I called him My Friend.

He was all of these to each of us,
But first and foremost he was a teacher.
Each and every one of you that knew Jon
Learned something from this Teacher-Man.

He may have taught you guys how to throw and catch a ball;
He may have even taught you a game or two,
Or even an evening prayer.
For us who are Navy, a button or a switch on an E2,
Or lever on the Dog Machine at the Mess Hall.
Some of you, I know he taught you how to
Smile and to laugh.
Two of you I know he taught how to love.
Me, he taught me how to hug another man.

But today he taught each and every one of us
How to die...
You die with your Flight Suit on!

—Chuck Windham, March 31, 1993

312

I know Jon would have been humbled by all the kind thoughts shared, but the words from Jon's "friend" would have impacted him deeply. He would also have been touched by the outpouring of love for his two daughters. In lieu of flowers, an educational fund for Jordyn and Taylor was started, thanks to the generosity of others.

After greeting all the friends and family that came to Jon's service, I breathed a sigh of relief when I could finally go home and put his funeral behind me. The out-of-town friends and family said their sad goodbyes and returned to their lives. But my new nightmare was just beginning.

My CACO Rick helped me begin the process of working through the mountains of red tape that Jon's death caused. With my dad's assistance, several important decisions were made right away. For one, after looking closely at my financial situation, if I made wise choices, finding a job to replace Jon's income right away wouldn't be necessary. As far as where to live, I considered the loving network that surrounded me, especially my church family and sister widows. Along with the access I had to military benefits, I made the decision to remain in the Norfolk area and in the home that Jon and I had built together. My mother decided to stay with me for the next several weeks while I tried to piece my shattered life back together.

Jon's Nebraska family wanted to hold a memorial service in mid April for him in his hometown of Stromsburg, so I would have one final funeral to endure. But I knew that Jon would be moved by their tribute to him, and it would be a crucial step in his family's grieving.

Mixed Emotions

As the days passed by, my mailbox filled with sympathy cards and letters from friends and family, far and wide, including a formal letter of condolence from President Bill Clinton. Sorting through them all was a mixed pleasure, as I enjoyed hearing from old acquaintances, but I wished these were Christmas cards instead. One thoughtful friend gave me a stack of thank you notes and stamps, and I slowly started the process of expressing gratitude to those who had blessed me.

Mixed in with these cards were priceless letters from Jon. Each day the mail ran, I would hunt through the stack of envelopes, anxiously looking for Jon's familiar scribble. One day soon, very soon, my last letter would come. How I dreaded that day.

The next letters I received from Jon were from the first days of his cruise. The horrible weather from the "Storm of the Century" had delayed these letters longer than usual. Jon had kept his promise and written every day, but getting the letters so far out of order meant that I had to piece together his last days like a puzzle.

His No. 1 letter from the cruise was dated March 13, the first full day he was gone.

My dear, wonderful wife, beautiful daughters, and mighty protector, Max. Well, it is finally for real, deployment to the Med ... We are hearing rumors already that the first several port calls are in jeopardy and we are heading directly for the Adriatic Sea, between Italy and Yugoslavia, Bosnia and Serbia ... The weather is really bad. We couldn't fly today cuz the seas were too rough. I heard the majority of the storm missed Norfolk ...

Now to the only part of the letter that really matters. I love you and miss you like crazy. Tell Jordyn that Daddy misses reading stories to her at nite. And give Taylor a big smooch for me. I want to get this in the mail in case a COD flies off tomorrow by chance. I LOVE YOU.

I didn't know where the Adriatic Sea and the Ionian Sea were before, but I did now. Jon missed me like crazy and he'd only been gone 24 hours. There was no way I could put into words how much I missed him.

His next two letters were written while the storms were at their peak. He even included a picture from the Rough Rider, the TR's newspaper, that showed a blast of salt water spray from waves that rose more than 80 feet soaking the parked planes on the flight deck. Had I known how intense the storms were, I would have feared for Jon's safety much sooner.

Jon described in great detail the procedure to remove a cyst in his arm. I'm sure he was fascinated by the minor surgery, but with my mind already filled with images of Jon drowning and sinking to the bottom of the ocean, I didn't enjoy his play-by-play explanation.

For the first time, he mentioned Operation Provide Promise and needing to prepare a brief on the flights where C-130s dropped MREs (Meals Ready to Eat) in Bosnia-Herzegovina. He knew my lack of geography knowledge and marked out the Adriatic Sea for me on the blue map on the back of his official TR stationary. Even in the everyday things he mentioned: whom he ate meals with, reports he had to prepare, moving their clocks ahead as they headed east, or the XO who swore off dog (the ice cream machine) until he lost some weight, I treasured the glimpses into Jon's final days on Earth.

The letter he wrote on St. Patrick's Day, March 17, was filled with little comments that seemed so ironic.

We have onboard a satellite phone called INMARSAT and when we are in satellite range we can call home. It is for anyone. It costs $35 for 5 minutes. So if I call you, and say Kris, this is an INMARSAT call, you will know it is only going to be 5 minutes in length.

I remember in the San Diego days that we would stress over the long-distance phone bills when Jon would call from overseas. I'd give anything to talk to him again.

My arm feels pretty good. It is starting to itch where the four stitches are but I get them out on Monday. I am going to try to get my teeth cleaned in the next several days while it is slow due to no flying.

Here he was, dealing with stitches and a dentist visit, not knowing about the tragedy to come. His closing paragraph brought me to tears.

I pray everything is going OK. I love you, Kris, and really miss our little girls. Is everyone healthy? I guess I worry about that the most. I love you and miss you. Jon.

No, Jon, everything was not OK. And I wasn't sure that it ever would be again.

The next envelope I received from Jon was actually a tape. He labeled it No. 10, and he recorded it over two days, ending the night of Tuesday, March 23—just two days before he died. Hearing Jon's voice was gut-wrenching for me. At least I got a good laugh when Jon asked about the pilot light in the gas fireplace and whether we'd had an explosion as a result. But the rest of the tape was agonizing to listen to.

I wept when he talked about the paper chain and how hard it would be to get to the end of it. He talked more about Operation Provide Promise and how he planned to visit Dave, our friend from church who was serving on USS John F. Kennedy, on March 25. I'd almost forgotten about Dave, who was due to come home any day now. I wondered if he and Jon had met on that fateful day.

When mentioning how his cyst stitches were healing and that "by the time you see me I'll have hair back on my arm and nothin' will be wrong," I completely lost it. The rest of the tape was almost too painful to hear, and I let Jordyn listen to the other side, for her final bedtime story from her daddy. Jon's made-up story had a moral that was hard for me to swallow:

So Jordyn, just remember to always be a good little girl, love God and your parents, and nothing bad can ever happen to you.

Something bad had happened to Jordyn—to all of us. Was it somehow our fault? This tape would not be something that I could listen to over and over again. Jon's voice stirred too many deep emotions in me.

After playing it through and sharing Jon's story with Jordyn, I tucked it away and out of sight with Jon's other letters.

USS Theodore Roosevelt CVN-71

Hey Woman   25 Am

It is 0830 on the 25th I was up to 0300
and planning a brief for C68 (ADR Johnson, Cags
Direct Boss) then it is up at 0700 to get on a
helo for the JFK. I'm getting to old for this
stuff.

Well the dye is cast, the O-5 board
ended yesterday. We should know our future
in 6 to 8 weeks. I keep thinking that I
should have done something differently but then
I realize I need to eliminate I and put my
faith + trust in God, it is hard sometimes but God will take care of me. I have
you, two healthy wonderful children, I am
healthy, when I think of all of this I
realize how insignificant making O-5
really is. I know I would trade making O-5
in an instant if you, Jordyn or Taylor were
not healthy. I just thank God for the great
life he has given me.

We are making history today. The
Germans and French are also flying today. 1ST
time. CO in the 1ST F-2 I in the second.

CHAPTER 25

The Last Letter

I quickly learned that my daughters weren't grieving the way I was. They loved having their grandmother around, and I'm sure their playful personalities did my mother a world of good. Expecting them to be weeping and mournful like me wasn't fair. Little Taylor had no reason to think anything had changed, and Jordyn rarely left her world of pretend and make-believe, but I couldn't hide my sorrow from my intelligent daughter. Rick and I marched through our paperwork, and I quickly grew to depend on his quiet strength. I didn't learn until years later that Rick, also an E-2C aviator, took a one-month break from flying. This was due to how emotional the mishap was for him and also to dedicate himself to assisting me.

Finally, it came. Jon's last letter. I was going through the daily mail as always, and there was letter No. 11, postmarked March 25. I knew there would not be another. I decided to leave the girls with Mom and take a private stroll around our quiet neighborhood to savor Jon's final words to me. Perhaps I was trying to avoid another meltdown, which by now I should have known was something I couldn't always control. But this beautiful neighborhood was an extension of our home—the home that Jon and I had chosen, together. It seemed fitting to carry his words around the familiar streets for a final walk, together. My hands shook slightly as I opened up the envelope and found two sheets of paper and three handwritten pages, dated the morning of Thursday, March 25.

Hey woman,

It is 0830 on the 25th. I was up to 0300 planning a brief for Carrier Group 8 and the admiral. Then it is up at 0700 to get on a helo for the JFK. I'm getting too old for this stuff.

Well, the die is cast. The O-5 board ended yesterday. We should know our future in 6 to 8 weeks. I keep thinking that I should have done something differently, but then I realize I need to eliminate "I" and put my faith and trust in God. It is hard sometimes, but God will take care of me. I have you, two healthy wonderful children, I am healthy. When I think of all of this, I realize how insignificant making O-5 really is. I know I would trade making O-5 in an instant if you, Jordyn or Taylor were not healthy. I just thank God for the great life He has given me.

We are making history today. The Germans and French are also flying today, first time. CO in the first E-2, I in the second. I wonder how long before it makes the news? We launch at 2100 and land at 0100 on the 26th.

I plan to see Dave today if I can. Depends on how busy I get. We are going to the JFK to get a turnover from them. I am in Helo 4 lot 3. They just launched lot 1, so I imagine it will be an hour or so...

When it comes to the girls, Kris, I trust your judgment. Do what you gotta do. How is the blue shelving paper project coming? Are you planning just the kitchen? Have fun with your friends! I hope Jordyn is good for you. I figure she will come in every nite that she wakes up. You are her security while I am away.

I have an appointment to get my teeth cleaned April 10 so life does go on. I love you Krista, and miss you. Kiss my 2 babes! Love, Jon.

P.S. Doing the tape was really tough this time. When you send a care package, include several thin books for Jordyn so I can read them to her. I should have brought some. Jon.

As I made another loop through Seagrass Reach, I read the letter a second time and realized Jon's final words to me were an indescribable gift. I looked at the time he'd written the letter, and remembered he almost never wrote me in the morning. What if he'd waited until he came back from his mission to write me, like he usually did? Was God at work, behind the scenes, to coordinate this last treasured letter I held in my hands?

This was a letter written by a man at peace. At peace with his wife, at peace with his life, and at peace with his God. I couldn't make a satellite phone call to Jon in heaven, but my fingers touched these precious written words that I would recall in the days, weeks, months, and years to come.

"It is hard sometimes, but God will take care of me."
"Kris, I trust your judgment. Do what you gotta do."
"You are her security while I am away."
"So life does go on."
"I love you Krista and miss you. Kiss my 2 babes!"

I shared Jon's letter with my mother when I returned home and we wept together. Getting the mail would never be the same again. But a ray of sunshine soon found its way into my mailbox and it took me completely by surprise. That same week, I found an unexpected envelope in the daily stack of sympathy cards, bills, and junk mail. I was shocked when I saw the address: Kennebunkport, Maine. The name? President George H. W. Bush.

A Little Strength

I ran inside and showed my mother, who was just as surprised as I was. We sat down together, and I ripped open the envelope to find this typed note inside:

April 5, 1993
Dear Kris,

I was so very sorry to get the news about your husband, Jon—a courageous man who gave his life while serving his country in the most honorable of ways. I want to wish you and Jordyn and Taylor well.

One of the great joys of my presidency was seeing, from time to time, the courageous Navy pilots to whom I felt so close. I didn't know Lieutenant Commander Rystrom personally, but what I do know is that he was a wonderful person serving our country with honor.

It must be extremely difficult for you, but perhaps you can get a little strength from knowing that a lot of people are thinking about you. Barbara joins me in conveying to you and yours our most sincere condolences.

Sincerely,
George Bush

I was stunned. While I appreciated the letter from President Clinton, I cherished this letter from former President George H. W. Bush so much more. Though he had never met President Bush, Jon served him during his tour at NEACP in Nebraska, and it was one of our NEACP friends that had written the former president about my husband's death. President Bush was also a naval aviator who survived being shot down and bailing out at sea. He understood Jon's service and sacrifice as few leaders did. Knowing he and his sweet wife were thinking of us meant the world to me.

Just days before the girls and I flew out to Nebraska for Jon's final memorial service, I received another surprise. Dave, our friend who served on USS John F. Kennedy, returned home from his cruise and came to visit me. I was comforted to find out that Jon and Dave had indeed met, and we hugged each other and wept, knowing he was the last friend from home that Jon ever saw. I was thankful that Jon took the time to make the connection happen. Dave told me that Jon basically passed the baton to him, saying he had looked after Dave's wife and kids, and now it was Dave's turn to look after the girls and me. And he did. Dave faithfully helped mow my yard, along with other men from our Sunday School class, and he and his wife included my girls and me in many of their family outings.

Dave's return from his cruise reminded me that USS Theodore Roosevelt was still at sea. I had no contact with anyone from the ship and while the squadron wives were still supportive of me, now that I was a widow, my connection to the Navy was shifting. And I couldn't help but wonder at times what life was like on the ship after the mishap.

Scuttled Wreckage

16 APR 93
0700 CET CENTRAL EUROPEAN TIME UTC+1
USS THEODORE ROOSEVELT
ADRIATIC SEA
42.40.18 N 16.42.89 E

Three weeks had passed since Bear Ace 603 was lost and USS Theodore Roosevelt continued flying daily missions in support of Operation Provide Promise. Four days earlier, on 12 April 1993, Operation Deny Flight began as NATO (North Atlantic Treaty Organization) enforced a no-fly zone over Bosnia and Herzegovina established by the United Nations. Carrier Air Wing 8 would have no problems staying busy.

During the days after the mishap, a Judge Advocate General (JAG) representative came onboard the TR to conduct a formal investigation. The officer in charge was a captain and E-2C pilot with nearly 4,000 flight hours and various command positions under his belt. He carefully reviewed all the records and evidence from the event and conducted numerous interviews with the personnel involved in the mission. Today, he was wrapping up the last of over 30 sworn statements and would soon return to CONUS to complete his exhaustive final report.

While it was too early to make a final determination of the cause of 603's crash, one decision had already been made: the scuttling of the wreckage into the sea. Over 80 pieces of wreckage had been salvaged: multiple pieces of the light-weight radome, shattered sections of the fuselage and wings, two helmets, headrests, a carpet piece, navigation chart, and more, including multiple "possible" pieces that couldn't be accurately identified. Most pieces were only a few feet in width, with the radome pieces making up the bulk of it. Bystanders viewing the wreckage were surprised that so little was recovered from such a large plane.

After close examination by experts, it was determined that all necessary data had been gleaned from the wreckage and, while a few items were kept for research, the leftover fragments should be discarded into the sea, which would also free up much-needed space in the crowded hangar bay.

No one would miss having to walk past the grim reminder. But scuttling the wreckage did not remove the wounds from the hearts of those who knew the men of Bear Ace 603. The ship and her crew had moved on, but they had not recovered.

Hometown Hero

Flying so soon after Jon's mishap was not what I wanted to do, but there was no way that my mom, my girls, and I could drive out to Nebraska for Jon's final memorial service. I called the stewardess over and quietly explained our situation so that she could help make this difficult trip easier for us.

The drive to Stromsburg, through the endless acres of prairie farmland, took me back to happier days when Jon was serving with NEACP and we'd make regular trips from our home in Bellevue to visit his family in his hometown. My Cornhusker Swede had turned in his golden fields of corn for the deep dark waters of the ocean's depths. He was always home in the ocean, and now it would remain his forever home.

As we drove by the old town square, usually festooned with multiple Swedish flags during the annual summer festival, my heart was touched to see an ocean of American flags instead—a beautiful tribute to my husband. Their hometown boy was now a hometown hero, and the entire town proudly displayed their appreciation of his sacrifice.

Jon's family organized a beautiful service, including several personal stories shared by Jon's childhood friends and close relatives. The service was followed by another 21-gun salute, and the sounds of the rifle shots still pierced my soul. His family had a memorial headstone erected and a college scholarship was set up in Jon's honor to benefit graduates of the local high school. While I was still grieving deeply, Jordyn was thrilled to play with her Nebraska cousins. I had to remind myself of some of Jon's final words: "So life does go on."

Yet Another Box

We returned to Seagrass Reach, and I attempted to go on with my life. But unpredictable reminders kept coming that made it challenging to keep my head above water. Jon's letters had stopped, but the mail didn't. I was stunned one day when an envelope arrived with familiar handwriting on it: my own. My stomach twisted inside when I realized what I was holding: the last letter I wrote to Jon, postmarked March 26, 1993.

I knew what was inside, but the outside of the envelope was a revelation. On the back, I found where I had labeled the letter #14, but next to it I saw where the TR had processed it on April 9th. On the front, the envelope was stamped in red with the iconic "Return to Sender" hand and marked "Unclaimed." Then below the address, another red stamp marked the reason for the letter's return: "Moved, Left No Address." The irony cut at my heart.

April showers bring May flowers and while being stuck inside on one of our rainy, gray days, I passed by our double glass doors to look out at the colorful flowers that our neighbors had lovingly planted weeks earlier. But something unexpected caught my eye. There was a package of some sort left on our front steps. Perplexed, I opened the door and stepped out into the rain to find a large, crumpled box addressed to me. It was from USS Theodore Roosevelt.

I struggled to pick up the heavy box and managed to bring it into the house. I closed the door and turned to face the curious package. It had obviously experienced significant wear and tear to reach me. What could possibly be inside?

I tore through the packaging tape and opened the flaps, and I was overcome with a shockwave of despair. For inside this crushed box were all of Jon's personal possessions from his stateroom onboard the ship. Why I thought his things would stay on the ship until the squadron returned home from their cruise in the fall, I don't know.

But I was completely blindsided by this Pandora's Box that landed unannounced on my front steps.

My intense reaction was a complicated mixture of anger, confusion, sorrow, and comfort. Anger, because it appeared that Jon's precious things had been thoughtlessly dumped like leftover trash into a flimsy box. Whoever cleared out Jon's things might have carried out the dreadful task with the greatest of care and respect. But after travelling for thousands of miles and crossing an ocean, it appeared that the tattered box, which should have been labeled "Fragile: Handle With Care," had instead been marked "Fragments: We don't Care."

Confusion, because there had been no warning, no heads up, no instructions to prepare me for its arrival. Why had Jon's things been handled so poorly? Sorrow came with every item I found inside: his extra flight suits, his precious flight jacket with patches covering the back reflecting the ships and squadrons he'd served on over the years, his worn leather Bible, his leftover toiletries, family pictures he'd displayed on his desk, letters from me he'd received, socks, shoes, and so much more. One everyday item touched me in particular. It was a tear-away calendar, filled with sports trivia. It stopped on March 25. Processing one letter at a time was hard enough. Facing a mountain of memories in an instant was overwhelming. I was completely undone.

I also had sorrow about what I knew I would never find in this box: his wedding ring. That had gone down with him into the depths of the Ionian Sea. But I took comfort in the fact that the golden symbol of our marriage would stay with him in that cold, dark, lifeless place. Having the last things that Jon saw with his eyes and touched with his hands back home where they belonged brought me comfort as well. But the painful memory of finding that crushed box on my doorstep haunts me to this day.

THE LAST LETTER

Jordyn and Taylor at their daddy's Arlington National Cemetery marker.

CHAPTER 26

How Do You Get Through?

The memorial services were finally behind me, and I refused to have a fourth when Jon's headstone was placed at Arlington National Cemetery. While I'd had enough of funerals, the grieving had only begun. The time had come to move on, but I felt like a rudderless ship adrift at sea.

When someone hears my story for the first time, they often ask the question, "How did you get through it?" The next two chapters are designed to help answer that question. Everyone grieves uniquely, but many of the emotions and experiences that I endured are common to all who have suffered significant loss. My hope is that, if you are walking through grief, whether it's fresh or something from your past, these topics will help you on your journey. And if you aren't grappling with grief, these pages will give you the understanding to support those around you who are.

Unwanted Companion

I had no idea what grief actually was before Jon's sudden death. Being so young, my friends weren't dealing with grief, and I had never lost anyone close to me before losing Jon. Even after becoming a widow, grief was something that I wanted to escape, deny, and avoid. That, of course, was impossible to do. Grief became an unwelcomed and constant companion, sometimes hiding in the shadows and at other times viciously throwing me down the stairs or repeatedly slapping me in the face.

Grief was more than an emotion. Grief ate away at my soul, kept my mind in a fog, and interrupted my life at the most inconvenient and unexpected moments. As painful as the depths of grief were to experience, it was a necessary part of my healing. To be honest, grief never completely goes away. The journey changes over time as the sun comes out, the flowers bloom, and joy returns. But in the beginning, walking through grief is grueling, demanding work.

Sanctuary

My bathroom became my crucible of grief. I called it my Cry Room, because it was the one place that I could be completely alone, with no distractions and no fear of my sweet girls hearing the release of my intense, gut-wrenching emotions. When planning our dream home, we chose a lot with no neighbors behind us and a beautiful view of pine trees and the wetlands beyond. Jon and I designed the grand bathroom in our second floor master suite to take advantage of this vista, creating an intimate oasis to enjoy together. With a large, palladium window over the Jacuzzi tub, a spacious double vanity, and luxurious, emerald-green and burgundy ornamental wallpaper, our bathroom resembled a model home's showroom display. This private sanctuary that Jon and I had envisioned being our decades-long honeymoon suite took on the morbid atmosphere of a funeral parlor.

Everywhere I looked, I saw Jon. The vanity held his personal toiletries, like his razors and cologne. The view from the large bathroom window not only gave me a glimpse of the tall pine trees lining our backyard but also the fence that Jon had built and the swing set for the girls that he'd installed. Right off the bathroom was his sizeable walk-in closet, filled with clothes that brought back special memories.

The most precious article of his clothing wasn't a Navy uniform or one of his silk suits from our time in Hong Kong—it was his old, brown, terrycloth bathrobe. His robe was such an intimate item—the last thing he had worn on his body that final morning together when he rushed from the shower and put on his uniform. When I hugged it close and buried my face in its soft folds, the fragrance of Jon's favorite cologne lingered still. Sometimes I would enter his closet, turn off the light, close the door, cling to his bathrobe, and lie on the carpeted floor in utter darkness.

During those lonely times in the dark, I would weep: deep, heaving, sobs of sorrow. Surrounded by his clothes, I would ask myself equally dark questions that seemed to have no answers. Did Jon feel the impact of the plane when it hit the icy water? Could he unbuckle from his seat in time? Did he try to swim? How long until he couldn't breathe? Were there screams? Did they even have time to cry out? To pray? The image of Jon lying at the bottom of the ocean wouldn't leave my mind as I replayed the crash—at least how I envisioned it—over and over. I had spent time at the bottom of the ocean myself, though my dive

wasn't even close to the nearly mile-deep water where Bear Ace 603 had crashed. But I knew something about the cold, dark, lifeless places of the deep. My one comfort was that there were no sharks living at those depths to disturb his body.

Being in our bathroom wasn't always torturous. Often, I would go about my daily routine, putting on my makeup or brushing my teeth, and the emotions wouldn't hit me. But at other times, the painful feelings would flood in and I could hardly breathe, or a deep sadness would permeate the room and my soul. These episodes were an amplified version of what I had experienced early in our marriage when Jon was deployed. Living alone in San Diego in an empty house with an empty bed had made me feel as though I were married to a man who was never present. I remembered going through his closet and putting on one of his shirts so that I could feel close to him. And that response was merely from a temporary delay in receiving his daily letters. The heartache I'd felt in San Diego was genuine, but nothing compared to the anguish of knowing my husband would never return.

At the beginning of my grief, I didn't immediately reach out to God. My anger at God caused me to turn to the one thing I had depended on for years—myself. I wasn't reading the Scriptures for solace or hope, and I wasn't praying for guidance and healing. But the difficult questions that I asked God in my first days of grief were questions I continued to ask, not expecting any answers. Why did this happen? Was it my fault? How can God take away the dad of these precious girls? Are You punishing me? If You're such a powerful, loving God, why did You allow this to happen? Don't You care? Do You hear me?

Having a private, safe place to grieve is critical for anyone who has experienced loss. As agonizing as it can be to mourn and face tough questions, healing won't come if grief can't be released. And I quickly learned that grief would find its way out no matter how hard I tried to subdue it.

Crashing In

Grief would hit me out of the blue, crashing in like a rogue tsunami wave. I remember being at the kitchen sink and the girls were sitting at the center island eating dinner. Suddenly, the pain of Jon's death hit me like a freight train out of nowhere. I tried to hide my grief from my girls, but as my shoulders began to heave, they couldn't help but notice. I would turn around and tell them that I was just feeling sad about missing Daddy. At times, I would be having fun playing a game with my daughters when a wave of grief would wash over me, swirling my emotions into a riptide of sorrow.

Sometimes it felt as though I was finally putting one foot in front of the other, making it through the day, then suddenly grief would slap me across the face. I'd shake it off and keep going, but grief would slap me again. I could only take so much before I'd crumble. Other times, grief seemed particularly harsh, like it was throwing me down the stairs. I'd pull myself back up, battered and bruised, but grief would throw me down the stairs again.

I wanted to have a "normal" life and not have to walk out the story of a widow. I found myself living in a land of make-believe with my girls, turning our home into a "Beauty and the Beast" movie set, filling our house with toys and kids' music and tea parties. But the crashing in of grief removed my fantasy and brought me back to my harsh reality.

Almost as suddenly as these waves of loss hit me, they would retreat. Minutes later, I'd be back to doing the dishes, the laundry, or playing with my girls. Over time, the monstrous waves that had tossed me to and fro weakened and grew farther apart, gently rocking my world. In between, I could live somewhat normally and enjoy life to some extent. I also learned to anticipate the crashing in, for instance, when a special holiday was coming up.

Thankfully, I was able to swim out of the surf zone, although in the beginning I felt as though I'd dwell there forever. The day finally came when I realized that I hadn't cried in the last 24 hours. Then a few days went by, then a week, and so on. It takes time. For the sake of my girls, I didn't wait until the waves were rare occurrences before returning to my regular life. I was proactive in making sure that they were playing with other children on a regular basis.

Nighttime

During the day, I focused on my girls and made their joy and happiness my priority. But once they were put to bed and nighttime permeated the house, I would grieve, especially in my Cry Room. Friends encouraged me to journal, but that seemed like a horrible reminder that my nightly routine of pouring out my feelings to Jon in a daily letter was over for good.

One thing that brought me solace was talking on the phone with my widow friends. Olga, the pilot's wife who called me after Jon died, was one of them, along with the other widows from Bear Ace 603: Paola, Shelly, and Katie who was now the mother of a healthy baby boy. Late at night, we knew we could reach out and hold each other up in our times of weakness. Another widow friend told me about Tylenol PM, which she used to help her sleep. But I would take only one so that I could be alert for my girls the next morning.

On the Shelf

As a Navy wife, I'd handled many boxes in my life and grief became one of them. There were times I had to put my grief box on the shelf so that I could focus on the task at hand, be it household chores or dealing with financial matters. When life was less hectic, I could take the grief box off the shelf, open it up, and deal with what was inside. Sometimes, unannounced, my grief box would come tumbling down and spill its painful contents all over the place. No one in mourning needs to feel guilty for setting aside grief for a brief season in order to focus on other things.

To help me deal with my grief box, I would imagine that Jon was watching me, cheering me on, and I wanted to make him proud. He wouldn't want me to wallow in grief and sorrow, yet I often couldn't help it. I had lost so much.

Till Death Do Us Part

When I lost Jon, I felt as though I lost everything. In the seven short years that we knew each other, Jon became my best friend, my lover, my encourager, my biggest fan, my provider, and the father of my daughters. I never stopped being married to him. We made the traditional vows of "till death do us part," but even in death, I was still committed to him. Jon was not my "ex" and I still carried his name. I was mothering his children and carrying on his legacy. My love for Jon will never die. When it comes to love, our hearts truly are without capacity or limits, as in loving more than one child. A heart can learn to love again, and a second marriage does not erase the love built in the first, although it takes a remarkable man to step into a deceased husband's shoes.

Loss of identity was one of my greatest struggles. This point was driven home when my CACO Rick, took me to the naval base to change my military I.D. card to show that I was now a URW: un-remarried widow. I had no desire to embrace my new identity. I felt like I had a large "W" plastered on my forehead, and I tried in vain to hide it. I kept attending the married Sunday School class at church, and it took some time before I moved to the singles class. I didn't fit in there either, as most of the singles in my age group were divorced.

In the first several months after Jon's death, when faced with the fact that I was a widow and a single mom, I told myself that it didn't matter, because Jon would have been at sea anyway. I was just living the Navy-wife life. Nothing had truly changed. I loved being an officer's wife—being saluted when we drove onto the base. That salute still came because of the tag on my car, but I knew that my Jon wasn't there to receive it.

One bright spot after Jon's death was when news came of his promotion. Jon never knew that, days before he died, the promotion board had approved him for the rank of commander. I had the additional stripe added to all of Jon's uniforms and the golden "scrambled eggs" (golden oak-leaf embellishments) were added to Jon's covers (hats).

Losing Jon also meant losing my security and many of my dreams for the future. I was so thankful that Jon had increased his insurance policy, and I didn't have to sell our home. By no means was I set for life—I knew that I would need to reenter the workforce at some point. Jon had always been so adept at handling our finances, and I had never bothered to learn much about how he did it. I wish I had. Dreams of him retiring from the Navy and starting a new career were over. My own dreams of earning a doctoral degree seemed meaningless. Dreams we'd shared of travelling, seeing our girls go to college, and becoming grandparents had all disappeared in one awful moment.

I wasn't the only one suffering loss. My girls had lost their father, though it would be many years before they could comprehend what that truly meant. Some losses were immediate. Jon wouldn't be home by Jordyn's birthday like he'd promised. He wouldn't join her for rides at Disney World in the fall. Daddy wouldn't teach Jordyn's Mission Friends' class again.

Other losses were long term by nature. Jon would never teach his girls how to ride a bike or how to drive a car. He'd never watch them go on their first dates, see them graduate from high school, send them off to college, or walk them down the aisle on their wedding days. Their daddy was gone forever.

I felt this "daddy" loss most acutely at church of all places. There I would watch other fathers with their daughters and feel the pang of knowing that my girls were missing out on their dad's affection and presence. While these families would go home after church to a nice Sunday roast and houses filled with happiness, we had nowhere to go, except to a house filled with silence.

Jealousy of those who weren't suffering like me was a constant temptation. My Jon was a good and honest man, and it didn't seem fair when men of far less character seemed to be living a charmed life. Feeling like a victim was easy. Making the choice to be thankful for what I had and grateful for even the small things was the path to wholeness.

God brought people into my life to help fill the voids in my heart through their love for my girls and me. Many answered the call to be a defender of the widow and to reach out to the brokenhearted. Being a young widow at age 31 was quite different from being an older widow at age 70, and I learned to embrace close relationships and not journey through grief alone.

True Blues

Those close relationships were what I liked to call my "True Blues," my amazing friends and family that walked alongside me. Jon and I had always prioritized relationships and that choice paid off when my world came crashing down. My church family mobilized into a loving army that became the hands and feet of Jesus. They covered practical needs—like mowing my lawn for the first year, doing household repairs, or watching my kids—as well as meeting emotional needs, like making sure I wasn't alone on special days and including me in family gatherings. My network of widow friends was a constant source of mutual support as well.

But nothing compared to the sacrifice that my parents made for me. My sweet mother stayed with me for the first month and, before the first year had passed, my parents retired, sold their home, and took a detour to their beach-house retirement in order to be close to the girls and me. They were on a mission to rescue me and their granddaughters from this horrific tragedy, and their love and support were beyond measure. Now I had a Sunday roast to come home to, and their presence helped fill the void of Jon's death that we all felt.

Beyond my inner circle, other kind people reached out to me to offer their sympathies and concerns, like neighbors, friends from across the country who heard the news of Jon's death, and former college classmates. But another class of people came into my life, and they were not my True Blues.

Pound Cake People

In the days and months after Jon's death, everyone brought me food, including many people who didn't know me very well. But for some of them, once they brought me a casserole or dessert, they felt validated to get into my business and give their opinions on how I should be living my life. Mom and I came up with the term "Pound Cake People" to describe these well-meaning but nosy, pushy individuals.

Their hearts weren't wrong, but these people who barely knew me were pressuring me to live up to their expectations and ideas. I was told when to go through Jon's things, when to take off my wedding ring, when I should or shouldn't date, and how to raise my daughters. They would ask me what I was going to do with the house or with Jon's car. Not only was I told that I should move but also when, to where, and how I should do it! They didn't understand my true situation or the fact that grieving had to be done on my schedule, not theirs.

Some of these Pound Cake People had no clue what I was going through. One situation that I remember, in particular, was when a woman asked me to pray for her, because they were putting a pool in their backyard and they had issues with the company installing it. The workers were late, which was a bother to the family, causing them undue stress. I wanted to grab her by the shoulders and shout, "You're stressed about a pool while my husband is dead at the bottom of the ocean! Do you realize that I'm struggling to keep my head above water, really!?!"

As difficult as it was to receive the Pound Cake People with their desserts and casseroles, I really needed them in the painful days after Jon's death. They helped feed my family, and I appreciated their love and concern. Eventually, they did leave, and a year later when they were gone for good, I did miss them a little. The bottom line is that you can't live your life trying to meet everyone's expectations. Listen closely to your True Blues, and simply smile and say thanks to the Pound Cake People.

Dead Books

Mom and I created another term to describe the stacks of books that I was given after Jon died. We called them "Dead Books." In no time, I accumulated a massive library of books on grief, death, and dying. I couldn't read them at first. These Dead Books made me sad. I wanted joy, encouragement, happy thoughts, and laughter. A part of this revulsion came from my denial of widowhood. I wanted to keep pretending that Jon was still at sea and that this nightmare was temporary. Sometimes Pound Cake People gave me Dead Books, along with their casseroles. Others came from True Blues, and one of those books changed my life. But I'll share more about that later.

Not all widows shared my distaste for Dead Books. One widow friend of mine read all of her Dead Books, and they were an immense help to her. Sometimes it's more a matter of timing. I'm glad that I didn't toss my collection, because as time progressed, I found some of them meaningful in ways that I couldn't have at first. No matter the book, I always wanted to receive the love intended when it was given, and that was a great comfort. I find it ironic that after avoiding Dead Books in the past, I have now written one myself.

The greatest book of all on grieving is not a Dead Book—it's God's Living Word, the Bible. And as the shock of Jon's death softened, I began turning to the Scriptures, looking for answers, guidance, and comfort. What was God telling me in the stories of heroes of old, in the Psalms, and in the words Jesus shared with His followers? I found multiple verses that talked of God's caring for the widows and the fatherless. When I read the Scripture about the sea giving up its dead at the resurrection, I took great comfort in knowing that particular verse applied to Jon. But some people had a twisted view of Scripture, and they weren't hesitant to share their warped theology.

Stupid Things People Say

Sometimes the Pound Cake People were guilty of sharing some real humdingers, and other times it was from people in passing who didn't know me at all. Whether it was distorted opinions or inappropriate questions from strangers, here are some of my infamous favorites:

"God needed another angel in heaven."

"This was God's will. He's in a better place now."

"You're lucky you didn't get his body back after his awful accident."

"You should move back home with your parents."

"Are you going to remarry?"

"What are you going to do with Jon's car? (This really meant I want to buy it, even though it's just been a few weeks since he's died.)

"You got off easy. My marriage is falling apart, our finances are a mess, and I want a divorce."

Some of these statements had elements of truth in them. Jon was in heaven and that is a far better place, but this was not comforting to me with him dying at age 38 and leaving a wife and two little girls behind. As for not recovering Jon's broken body, I had a widow friend who had only her husband's foot to bury or other friends who lost loved ones in violent car wrecks, but there was at least something to bury. Not having anything to bury makes closure hard to come by. When or if I remarried was no one's business and neither were my plans for Jon's car. A failed marriage certainly isn't a cakewalk, but losing the vibrant, loving, and passionate relationship that Jon and I shared was nothing short of devastation.

People will always say stupid, inappropriate things—it is inevitable. What I did with these words was my choice. Letting their careless words run off like water on a duck's back, creating healthy boundaries, and extending grace to the clueless people who said such things kept me in a healthier place.

Routine

Life needs a rhythm and a purpose. For me, caring for my two daughters helped me keep living and moving forward. I couldn't crawl into my bed, hide under the covers, and check out. My daughters needed to be fed, bathed and, more importantly, nurtured and loved. In my situation, once the memorial services were over, my daily routine was not much different than before Jon died. Unfortunately, this enabled me to live in denial of his death.

Daily tasks provided structure and a sense of control and accomplishment. Did I make my bed today? Check. Did I get the garbage out on trash day? Check. Did Max get fed and does he have fresh water? Check. The mundane chores of life kept me sane and propelled me forward.

My church involvement and my goal to make life as fun and normal for my girls as possible got me out of the house and back into community. But the fatigue of grief meant that I couldn't burn the candle at both ends like I had in the past. I had to extend grace to myself and take things one day or, sometimes, one hour at a time. There were days when even my best efforts at keeping a regular routine got derailed by a new enemy—triggers.

Bear Ace 603 "Wids."
L to R: Katie Forwalder, Kris Rystrom, Shelly Messier, and
Paola Dyer. The Bahamas, 1994

CHAPTER 27

From Triggers to Moving On

Red Corvettes

Triggers are sensations or events that instantly, and often unexpectedly, throw you down the stairs and into an unplanned eruption of grief. The best way that I can describe it is to imagine that you live near a Corvette dealership that only sells red cars. People are test driving them all the time, travelling down your road daily. Your spouse loves the sight of these gorgeous, crimson Corvettes and decides to take one for a spin. Unfortunately, your spouse crashes and dies as a result.

But every day the red Corvettes are driven down your street. You can pull the curtains, but you can't shut out the sound of the supercharged V8 engines. You pass the dealership filled with the red sports cars every time you leave your house. Whenever you see or hear one of those Corvettes, you instantly relive the loss of your spouse. Even when you go on vacation, a red Corvette unexpectedly appears in a parking lot, on the interstate, or at a stoplight. Can you see how hard it would be to escape the constant reminder of your grief?

That's what triggers are like. Some are a one-time occurrence, like when I received Jon's personal items in a crumpled, cardboard box on my front steps. But most of them are recurring. The unique humming sound of an E-2C flying over my house every day was one of these triggers. What had once filled my heart with pride and joy, now unleashed a torrent of sorrow, pain, and uncontrollable tears. When I needed to drive onto the Norfolk Naval Base to shop at the commissary, being saluted at the gate was a trigger. Once I walked into the Navy grocery store, triggers were everywhere: aviators in their flight suits, officers in dress blues, and Jon's favorite vanilla sandwich cookies on aisle 4. All these sights brought me to tears.

One embarrassing incident was when my parents and I decided to take the girls to enjoy the public beach at Dam Neck Naval Base. Of course, this was also where we had our wedding, but months had gone by since Jon's death, and I thought I could handle it. However, once on base, my mind was distracted and I didn't pay close attention to my speed. A military police officer pulled me over and asked for my I.D. The sight of his uniform and being in such a memorable place, combined with the stress of getting a speeding ticket, instantly did me in. I completely lost it. I was sobbing and screaming so hysterically that the officer had no idea what to do with me, so he called the paramedics. My parents and my little girls were helpless in managing my meltdown, and what was supposed to be a fun beach day for the girls turned into a torture session from hell. And all because of triggers.

College football, one of Jon's greatest loves, was another trigger. So was anything Nebraska: football, basketball, or a license plate. Our house was perhaps the biggest trigger of all. When I looked out the window over our kitchen sink, the sight of our fence or our sprinklers would bring up the image of Jon in his familiar, worn overalls working in the yard. As we had designed our home together, every tile, every piece of molding, and every door could trigger an episode of grief. Even though reminders of Jon surrounded me, I didn't want to leave the home that we had built together.

Some triggers were smells. Fresh-baked chocolate cake reminded me of when Jon would bake in the kitchen after a hard day at work. The smell of mulch still takes me back to when we returned home from the Navy memorial service, and my neighbors had planted flowers and mulched our yard. Even now, I can recall the smell of Jon's favorite cologne that I always bought for him.

Special days were triggers, such as the day of our first date or our wedding anniversary. Movies were triggers too. After 25 years, I still can't watch "Top Gun" or "An Officer and a Gentleman." The ocean and the beach were places that would send me into a sobbing frenzy. Living so close to the beach and having kids meant this wasn't a place I could avoid. To me, the ocean was Jon's grave and the beach reminded me of special memories like our wedding, living in San Diego, and tropical vacations that we enjoyed together.

Over time, some triggers can take on dual personalities—painful or comforting. Max, Jon's Norwegian elkhound, was like that. On the one hand, this lovable, fluffy dog—that lay at our front door to protect us and allowed the girls use him as a pillow—was a tremendous source of happiness. But there were other times that his presence would remind me of his connection to Jon and that he'd never see his master again. Other memories that used to bring a tear eventually brought a smile. But if I hadn't found the tools to help me work through my grief, triggers could have kept me trapped and isolated in a pit of despair.

Triggers cannot be avoided. And, sometimes, they shouldn't be. When you know they are coming, you can be prepared to deal with them. But when they take you by surprise, cut yourself some slack. There was so much that I had to process during those dark days, and triggers often led to other issues.

Faith

Being thrown down the stairs into sudden grief often caused me to face my struggles with faith. The box-checking religious life that I had lived before was over. There was no faking it now—no glossing over any of my doubts or faults. I was raw, real, and desperate. But it took time before I was ready to dig deep and find real answers to my hard questions.

In the first months after Jon's death, I didn't read the Bible much at all. I would open it at church, but it gathered dust otherwise. And yet, God found a way to still minister to my wounded soul. Christian music became a lifeline for me, and while I wasn't willing to meditate on Scripture, I was willing to listen to music. I rejoined my church's choir and played music at home, especially Michael English, Amy Grant, and Point of Grace. The songs filled with words of hope and encouragement gradually brought the light of God's love to my dark, bitter soul.

I spent time in prayer, but I wasn't listening for a response. Not yet. I would pour out my heart but, in my anger at God, I wasn't yet reaching out to Him. The one thing I did do was keep the promises that Jon and I made when we dedicated our daughters. We had promised to raise them in a Godly home, keep them connected to a church body, and encourage them to have their own relationship with God.

These were promises that I kept following, like a compass in the fog, like a plane flying by instruments in the clouds and in the dark. When you have spiritual vertigo, faith steps in to keep you on track when everything around you tells you the opposite. Even in my doubts, down deep inside I knew that God was real and in this dark season, He kept me out of the ditch as I limped along with Him supporting me.

Asking hard questions is important. God can handle every raw, angry, desperate question we throw His way. In the midst of the confusion and the sorrow, keep looking for His goodness. In time, you will see it.

Sprinkles of Sunshine

During the darkest days, God will give you sprinkles of sunshine to brighten your path, lighten your load, and remind you that He is there. He gave me plenty. One was when my neighbors landscaped my yard. Other sprinkles were the letters that I received from Presidents George H. W. Bush and Bill Clinton—I had them framed and hung them on my wall.

Some sprinkles were tied to specific dates. The check from Jon's life insurance policy arrived in the mail on the date of our wedding anniversary. It was like a warm embrace, reminding me of Jon's love. Everywhere we lived, Jon planted flowers, especially rosebushes. He loved growing things, and he took pleasure in seeing me cut flowers to display in vases in our home. One of the last honey-do's that he completed was planting several rosebushes on one side of our Seagrass Reach home. Seeing those rosebushes soon after his death would press a thorn of grief into my soul. But that pain was transformed on my first Mother's Day without my beloved Jon. That was the day when the very first rose bloomed on those bushes lovingly planted by Jon's hands. Don't tell me that was a mere coincidence.

A few friends hid 200 strips of paper with the words from Isaiah 43:2 everywhere in my house: in a box of pasta, in my deodorant, under my towels, in drawers, in the girls' rooms, etc. I even found one, years later, when we moved to another state. The constant—and sometimes humorous—reminder to not fear, that God was with me, and that He wouldn't let me be overcome by my tragedy gave me hope.

The Mission Friends class planted a beautiful dogwood tree and installed a plaque in Jon's honor at our church. The Disney trip that Jon and I had booked before he deployed went ahead as scheduled, except with another church family and my parents joining me and the girls. That first summer after Jon's death, Jordyn learned to swim and, in the fall, Taylor started walking. Many of these events were bittersweet, but they were sprinkles of sunshine just the same.

Sprinkles of sunshine will come, but you can miss them if you aren't looking. Expect them, remember them, and they'll give you the grace to get through.

Mind Games

When trying to find your footing, you go through mind games to help you cope. Most of mine were not healthy, long-term solutions. By far, denial was my most unhealthy coping mechanism. I still fantasized that Jon and the guys had been picked up by a boat and that they were on a little island somewhere, just waiting to be found. One minute I'd be mourning Jon's death, and the next minute I'd be asking God to quickly bring him home. Since Jon would have been at sea five more months after the time of his death, this denial was convenient to maintain.

I also denied the reality of how he died and what had happened to his plane. Knowing his plane rested in waters nearly a mile deep, I imagined that he was protected by his aircraft. Surely, no marine life would disturb his body at such depths. Surely, he and his Navy brothers were still buckled in their seats, peacefully at rest. As Jordyn began asking more questions about where her daddy was, I came up with a unique response. I told her that he was "down deep, deep, deep where the sharks don't go." This was true and also seemed to give Jordyn some peace.

Sometimes in prayer, I'd pretend that I could get messages to Jon. I'd cry out to Jesus and say, "Can you please tell Jon that I love him? Can you tell him that I miss him?" or "Can you wish Jon a happy birthday for me?"

Decisions

Making decisions in Jon's absence wasn't a new experience as a Navy wife but now that he was dead, every decision that I made had to be alone. My guiding principal, in decisions big or small, would be what would Jon do? What would make him proud? What would he want me to do?

I knew the old adage about not making any major decisions for the first year after losing your spouse, but there was still a myriad of decisions that couldn't wait. Once I'd worked through the initial financial and living issues, I was thankful for men in my Sunday School class who helped me sell our two vehicles and purchase one car that was more appropriate for a single mother with two daughters.

Some decisions were small, yet important. I bought a new comforter set for my bed to give me

> ... COME TO ME, ALL WHO LABOR AND ARE HEAVY LADEN, AND I WILL GIVE YOU REST. TAKE MY YOKE UPON YOU, AND LEARN FROM ME, FOR I AM GENTLE AND LOWLY IN HEART, AND YOU WILL FIND REST FOR YOUR SOULS. FOR MY YOKE IS EASY, AND MY BURDEN IS LIGHT. (MATTHEW 11:28-30 ESV)

a fresh start now that Jon would never share that intimate space with me again. Curtains were hung, which was one of the items that Jon and I hadn't finished on our new home. To honor his memory, I put a corner curio glass cabinet in our formal living room and filled it with his Navy medals, cover, white gloves, NFO wings, and more. A year and a half went by before I chose to re-enter the workforce and more than six months passed before I decided to move my wedding ring over to my right hand, when attending a college reunion.

That brings up the issue of dating, which is a touchy one for many widows. Men who have lost their wives start looking for companionship much sooner on average than women who have lost their husbands, and I was no different. As the months went by, several friends encouraged me to go out on blind dates—not for a committed relationship but to be treated like a woman for a change. In truth, I was terribly lonely, especially when I'd put my little girls to bed at 7:30 then sit around the house with nothing to do and no one to talk to.

I agreed to go on a few dates, but it was too soon for me, plus the men mostly complained about their awful ex-wives. My marriage had been beautiful—not a nightmare—and there was no way that I could subject my girls or me to a man with that kind of bitter baggage. Other men didn't want my widow baggage, especially when two little girls were attached to it. Eventually, I resolved not to resume dating until I was ready.

Putting off major decisions, if possible, is a wise thing to do. Don't let the Pound Cake People push you into something you're not ready for. Your True Blues will back you up and keep you from making major mistakes.

Firsts

There are so many "firsts" in that initial year of grieving. First anniversary, first birthdays (yours and your departed loved one's), first time to church alone, first Christmas, and on and on it goes. You can't avoid all the firsts and somehow you have to get through them. My church family and, particularly, my Sunday School class made sure that I wasn't alone on special days. The dogwood tree that the Mission Friends class planted became a living memorial for my girls and me, since we had no grave nearby to visit. We would decorate its branches on major holidays.

The first Father's Day was difficult, but I was determined to honor Jon and find a way for my girls to show love to their daddy. I decided to try an idea that a friend shared with me—attaching handwritten messages for a departed loved one onto helium balloons, then releasing them to float up to heaven. Jordyn drew a picture for Jon, and I wrote down what she wanted to say to her daddy. Taylor was almost one, so I wrote a note from her and one from me.

Since Daddy was buried in the ocean, my girls and I went down to the beach to launch our balloons. We said a simple Father's Day prayer: "Dear Jesus, please tell Daddy Happy Father's Day and we love him. And Jesus, please take care of him in heaven. Amen."

Tears filled my eyes as Jordyn jumped up and down, and we waved goodbye to our heaven-bound love notes. This was a very significant event for me and a very emotional one. I kept thinking: Does Jon see us? Does he know his little girls are sending him their love? Is he receiving our messages?

When Jordyn's fourth birthday rolled around, I didn't want her to remember Daddy's broken promise that he would be home by her birthday. I overcompensated in a big way by ordering multiple, large inflatables, booking a puppet show, and inviting every child that we knew. I succeeded in creating a grand extravaganza that the kids would never forget, but no amount of games or parties could ever erase our loss.

The first Christmas was tough because of our Rystrom tradition of Jon and me decorating our tree together. Friends from church came over and put the tree up for me, and I didn't mind, because I wanted Jordyn and Taylor to have a proper Christmas. But as soon as presents were opened Christmas morning, I took the tree down and put the decorations away. The sight of it all and the associated memories were too painful to bear.

As difficult as it was to get through that year of firsts, I found that the second year was even more difficult. When the second wedding anniversary or Christmas comes, you realize that it will be this way forever. Your loved one is not coming home. Many of those friends who helped pull you through the first year have returned to their own normal lives in the second year, and you are left to face the emptiness alone.

Although I missed Jon terribly, I'm glad I didn't stop celebrating and remembering life's precious moments. Jon would have wanted me to be happy, and my girls didn't need to miss out on the joy of special days. Make plans to not be alone and find ways to remember the sweet memories of the past, while making new ones for your future.

"Wids"

Thankfully, I wasn't alone on my grief journey. My sweet friends and sister widows from Bear Ace 603 grew into a much larger group of military widows living in our area. Years before Jon's mishap, the "Wids" began when several Navy widows formed a support group for one another. The group had become inactive over time, but after the tragedy of Bear Ace 603 hit the news, a lady from the original group contacted several of us and urged us to restart the Wids. She was certain that we weren't the only widows out there, and she was right.

That summer, as word spread, widows came out of the woodwork and soon there were almost 20 women interested. I was saddened to see so many other young widows with children, like myself. We'd meet together in someone's home, keeping our time together informal and laidback. We'd share our struggles and our questions. In this group, you could be raw and real and ugly. You could say: "I wonder if the fish have started eating my husband's body yet," or "Did my husband scream when he burned to death?"

We would discuss more practical things, like when and how to go through our husband's clothes or how to deal with the Navy bureaucracy. We understood each other in ways that no one else could, because we shared such similar stories. Eleven of the widows were there from Navy mishaps.

Lt. Cmdr. Fred Dillingham's wife came to one of our first meetings. When she said her husband's name, I gasped in shock. I remembered from Jon's letters that he had attended her husband's memorial service on USS Theodore Roosevelt just days before his own death.

We didn't limit our group to only Navy or military widows. When a news report shared the story of a local man lost at sea in a tragic boating accident, I invited his wife to come. When a commercial jet crashed in Pittsburgh and it was reported that a local man lost his wife (a stewardess on that flight) in the accident, he accepted the invitation to join our group. Regardless of how our spouses died, we helped each other on significant days and had a Santa party for our kids at Christmas.

Later, I contacted another Navy widow to come and talk to us. Her name was Jane Smith and her husband was Michael Smith, the pilot of the doomed space shuttle Challenger. I remembered hearing about the loss of Challenger and her crew years earlier when I worked at Port Folio, before Jon and I were engaged. I never dreamed that I would meet the wife of the pilot one day and certainly not under such difficult circumstances. Jane openly shared about her walk through grief. One day, our paths would cross again.

The Wids didn't just meet in homes and mourn together. Sometimes we went out and had fun. I remember one time when we all went to see the movie, "Sleepless in Seattle," in which Tom Hanks plays a widower who is struggling to open his heart to love again. We occupied an entire row and cried through the movie together. Over time, we attended each other's weddings and encouraged one another to continue living life.

At least a year after Jon died, the original "Wids" of Bear Ace 603 went to the Bahamas together to celebrate making it through our first year. We felt sorry for a newlywed bride that befriended us, because when she asked us how we knew one another, we didn't hesitate to tell her. She didn't talk to us again.

On that trip, I dusted off my scuba-diving skills and, leaving my non-diving widow friends behind, I enjoyed some time exploring underwater. The group dive that I chose was to a sunken ship, but unbeknownst to us, our boat was diverted to an alternate site. When we arrived and were ready to go, the dive master told us that we'd be seeing a downed plane instead.

My heart froze. I knew that my random dive buddy didn't want to hear my sob story, so I determined that I wouldn't have a meltdown 30 feet underwater. As we swam toward the small, private plane, I had an eerie picture of what it was like for Bear Ace 603. The magnitude of that moment was even more powerful than what I experienced at the Navy memorial service. Hundreds of people had viewed the missing-man formation that day; this moment was custom-designed for me alone.

When I returned from my dive, I shared with the other widows what I had seen, and I brought a small piece of carpet from the wreck for them to examine. Even on our vacation, we couldn't escape the triggers. I realized later how God had orchestrated this unique moment to help me heal and gain some much-needed closure.

I don't know how I would have made it without the support that the Wids provided. Today, there are many support groups for those grieving and wonderful counselors who provide effective therapy to work through your loss. Finding what fits your situation is worth the effort and will be a tremendous blessing on your road to healing.

Practical Things

When you get past all the triggers, Dead Books, Pound Cake People, loss, hard questions, and more, you still have to handle the everyday practical things of life and work through the nitty-gritty details of losing someone you love.

For me, what to do with Jon's clothes was one of those practical things. I didn't rush to clear his closet, and I often took comfort from his racks of clothing. But once I was past the denial and accepted that Jon was never returning, I was ready to part with his clothing. I put on my Navy widow hat, took the grief box off the shelf, and did what had to be done. I was on a mission. How could I distribute his items to bless others? I enlisted a trusted friend to walk beside me in the process.

Jon's khaki uniforms went to a Navy chief whose house had burned down in a fire. His casual clothes went to his nephews. Dress clothes and his hand-made silk suits from Hong Kong went to our Sunday School teacher, who was the same size as Jon. Through the sorting process, I was stoic and methodical. For once, I didn't break down.

What to do with Jon's bike was another consideration. As a cycling enthusiast, Jon loved his bicycle, but I knew that neither I nor his young daughters would ever ride it. I knew that Jon would have approved when I sold it and bought a bike that I could use to pull the girls around our neighborhood.

When facing practical issues, find a purpose in the task. Don't hesitate to ask a dear friend to help you through it.

Moving On

These topics cover many of my experiences as a new widow, but my grief journey was by no means over. Several significant events were still to occur before I could find the fulfillment of the promises that would bring me into lasting hope. My path was still foggy and filled with sorrow and pain and sometimes I felt that for every step forward, I took two steps back. But you rarely can see your true progress or discern the divine guidance that appears to be leading you nowhere. Like the poem, "Footprints in the Sand," in the moments that I felt abandoned and alone, the truth was that "someone" was carrying me on the road to healing. And some of what I had yet to endure would shake me to my core.

CHAPTER 28

Wreckage in My Hands

Love From the Bushes

My first summer as a widow arrived, but in my heart I was still in the winter of grief. For the first time since Jon had died, I wrote a letter. Letters had been an integral part of my life for so many years. I had met Jon through a letter, our relationship had been nurtured through letters, and letters contained the last words that we would ever say to each other on Earth. Months later, I was finally ready to turn the page and write letters again.

The letter I wrote was to President George H. W. Bush, who was known to be a letter writer. I wanted to let him know how much his kind words had meant to me so soon after Jon's death. Along with my handwritten letter to him, I included snapshots of our family. Perhaps it was silly, but there was a yearning inside of me to communicate to this leader how much I admired Jon for the honorable man that he was. I was thrilled when President Bush responded with this short, handwritten letter:

August 3, 1993
Dear Kris,

After reading your July 27 letter, written from the heart, I know that your abiding faith will carry you and those kids forward into a life of new happiness.
Jon must have been a great guy.

Love from the Bushes,

George Bush

When I sent my letter, I was not sure that he would respond, and I never dreamed that he'd write me a letter with his own hand. This sprinkle of sunshine soon joined the other framed letters proudly displayed in my home. But first, I took it to choir practice and showed it to my friends. They were happy for me, and everyone wanted to see the letter for themselves.

"One Woman's Story"

One of those friends thought this was the kind of story worthy of the local news and contacted WAVY-TV. Terry Zahn, a respected news anchor and journalist, reached out to me and asked if he could feature my story. I was very surprised, but I agreed. The news coverage at the time of Jon's death had featured my agonized reaction to the missing man formation. I was looking forward to showing the world a much calmer and dignified widow who had her act together. More importantly, it was an opportunity to honor Jon.

Terry Zahn and his crew taped footage of my girls and me eating ice cream, me singing in my church choir, my framed letters from the presidents, and a meeting of the Wids at my home. The piece was aired in late August, and Terry's lead-in was perfect:

Whenever there's a military air crash, we tell you about it. We tell you about who got killed. What we don't tell you about is the struggle for those left behind. How do they cope? How do they survive? Tonight, one woman's story of tragedy, healing, and hope.

Terry proceeded to tell the basic facts of Jon's death, and I didn't mind them using footage from my meltdown at the Navy memorial—not when the next scene showed me smiling and singing "I Must Tell Jesus" in the church choir. After featuring a few members of our Wids support group, I shared a final thought with a sweet smile on my peaceful face:

I just feel that I am going to see him again one day, and I want him to look at me and say, 'You did a good job, Kris. And I'm really proud of you,' because he was such a special guy.

Terry concluded the video with these chilling words: "Since June 1992, 23 naval aviators from Hampton Roads have died in the line of duty."

The report created a wave of positive response from the viewers, and I decided to send a copy of the video to President Bush as a thank-you for sending me his hand-written letter in the first place. I was pleased with the serene, peaceful persona that I presented, and it seemed to me to be an accurate reflection of my inner world. I still had sorrow, but I was making it. I was strong. I was stable. I was confident. I didn't need counseling like some grieving people did, because I was healing just fine on my own.

Nowhere to Hide

Hardly a week after the WAVY feature aired, USS Theodore Roosevelt was scheduled to come home. The squadron wives invited me and the other 603 widows to attend the celebratory Fly-In, but we weren't sure how to respond. These wives had helped establish a VAW scholarship fund for the children of downed Hawkeye and COD aviators and created cookbooks as a fundraiser for it. They proved their motto was true: "Once a Bear Ace, always a Bear Ace."

In the months after Jon's death, the guys from the squadron had been silent; they were focusing on their mission. Now that they were returning home, we didn't know if we should be there to greet them, or if our presence would be a major wet blanket on what should be a joyous celebration for them and their families. In the end, I decided not to attend. I knew the sounds and sights of the planes flying in would be more than I could stand, and I didn't want a meltdown from me to spoil their reunion.

> TRUST IN THE LORD WITH ALL YOUR HEART, AND DO NOT LEAN ON YOUR OWN UNDERSTANDING.
> IN ALL YOUR WAYS ACKNOWLEDGE HIM, AND HE WILL MAKE STRAIGHT YOUR PATHS.
> (PROVERBS 3:5-6 ESV)

Anytime a ship and an air wing came back to port after a cruise, the event received extensive coverage from the local media. I decided that, until it was all over, I would escape to somewhere peaceful to have fun with my girls. My chosen destination? A beachside hotel, where my girls could enjoy the ocean and play in the sand.

The day of the Fly-In for the Bear Ace Squadron arrived, and I was relieved to be away from Seagrass Reach and out of the daily flight path of military planes. We were settled in our hotel room suite, several stories high, with a gorgeous view of the ocean from the balcony. I was in a back room getting ready for the day when I heard a sound.

My heart seemed to stop beating as the sound grew louder. No. It couldn't be. That old familiar humming couldn't be confused for anything else but the unmistakable sound of an E-2C Hawkeye. This couldn't be happening.

I ran out of the room and onto the balcony. My nightmare was confirmed. Soaring over the ocean and toward land in perfect formation were four E-2C aircraft. Surely they would turn—surely they were headed somewhere else. I willed them away but it was no use.

Our hotel was in their direct flight path.

I stood frozen in panic, my hands gripping the balcony's railing, much as I had gripped the spindles of my stairway when the stripes were at my door. A tsunami of anguish, horror, and despair engulfed me. The deafening noise of the Hummers shut out the sound of my wailing as the Hawkeyes passed directly overhead. They were so close that I could see the black-and-red Bear Ace insignias painted on their sides—it seemed as if I could reach out and touch them. So close that I feared the aircrew could see me standing there howling on the balcony: Jon Rystrom's widow, distraught and alone, consumed with grief.

The Band-Aid of denial that I had carefully applied to my grieving heart was ripped off in a single moment. Any pretense I'd embraced that Jon was still at sea, that I was living the Navy-wife life, and that nothing had truly changed was shattered into a million tiny fragments. The strong, stable, confident widow with her calm, peaceful smile who had appeared on television a few days before was now reduced to a quivering and wounded wretch, lying in the fetal position on the balcony floor.

One reality reverberated in my soul: Jon is not coming home. For the first time, this reality hit me and it hit me hard. There could be no more playing make-believe, no more living in denial, no more sticking my head in the sand. The time had come to face the facts at last.

What was I thinking—trying to escape to the ocean at a beachfront hotel, nonetheless? I knew the ocean was a trigger for me. How could I have forgotten such pertinent information? But I knew this moment was arranged for me. God was telling me, "You have to face this. You can't run from reality anymore." As exceedingly painful as this moment was, it was also the turning point that exposed my wounds so that my grief could be expressed and my healing could begin.

My poor girls didn't know what to think of their sobbing mother, and after several gut-wrenching hours trying to regain control, I finally called a friend who lived nearby and arranged for us to come to her home so that I wouldn't be alone and my girls could be looked after.

In the days that followed, I found a qualified therapist and started regular counseling. Clearly, I was also in depression, a common condition for any widow. Any pride I'd had about not needing outside help had evaporated, and I willingly accepted a prescribed antidepressant.

When I hear people say that counseling is not necessary, that "Jesus can heal and you don't need that stuff," I like to ask them what they would do if they had a broken arm. Would they hesitate to go to a doctor and have it set? Why should a broken heart be any different? Yes, Jesus can heal you, but in the same way He often uses doctors to heal our bodies, He can use therapists and counselors to help heal our souls.

Mishap Mystery

With the squadron back from their cruise, the commanding officer of the Bear Ace Squadron invited the widows of 603, along with Mrs. Ardaiz, the mother of the only unmarried victim, to his home for a meeting. This was our first chance to hear a firsthand account of what happened on the evening of the mishap.

The CO was calm and understanding, but he didn't mince his words. He said that night was the blackest night he'd ever seen. There was no moon, a hazy cloud cover hung overhead, and there was no visible horizon. He told us the mission was a simple one, and even though 603's radar wasn't working, they were still a valuable player in the mission. His plane landed right before 603 approached the ship, and because he was exiting his aircraft, he didn't see them hit the water.

He had viewed the camera footage of the accident, and with the knowledge he had of what other pilots had experienced that evening, his best guess was that either the crew experienced vertigo, or there was some unknown distraction in the cockpit, or the plane had a mechanical failure. To him, every piece of evidence seemed to point to a normally functioning aircraft, and the cause of the mishap was a mystery to him.

That wasn't what we wanted to hear, but those were the facts. He went on to describe what the flight surgeon had told him. At the speed the plane was traveling when it impacted the surface of the water, it would be equivalent to a car hitting a brick wall at 180 miles per hour. The crew's necks would have snapped immediately, and they wouldn't have known what hit them.

Very little wreckage was recovered, but among the pieces salvaged were two flight helmets. The CO couldn't tell us who they belonged to, and since they were a part of the forensic investigation and would be studied to see how they withstood the impact, they would not be

returned. But he did have something that he could give us: small pieces of the shattered plane—two for each family.

My friends and I were crying throughout the entire meeting. After the shock of the Fly-In, the CO's unvarnished explanations were the death knell to any remaining illusions that I had regarding Jon's final demise. In some ways, I felt that as a military mishap, we had less rights than a civilian would expect. After the horrendous mishap, all that we got back from our deceased loved ones were a few tiny pieces of wreckage, which we could hold in one hand. I was thankful for the CO's efforts to give us what he could, but he wasn't even allowed to tell us to whom the flight helmets belonged.

My Husband's Coffin

Once we left the meeting, we discussed the situation among ourselves. Some of us were angry at the lack of information that we received, and we demanded answers. But if all we were to be given were a few pieces of jagged metal, at least they could let us sit in the seats where our loved ones had died. The CO was eager to help us gain the closure we needed and made arrangements for us to visit the Bear Ace hangar a few days later.

Our CACOs joined us for this grim tour, and my heart clenched in grief as we stepped out onto the tarmac to see a single E-2C Hawkeye awaiting us. The CO allowed us to enter the plane alone. We silently walked through the door on the port side, with Shelly and Paola walking up the narrow passage to the cockpit, while the rest of us scooted toward the rear, with me sitting in the middle seat between Mrs. Ardaiz and Katie.

The experience was painful—similar to returning to a crime scene or the scene of a fatal accident—like returning to Ground Zero for those who lost loved ones in the Twin Towers on 9/11. I was sitting inside my husband's coffin, my husband's final resting place.

I was struck by the tight confines of the space. Ejection was not an option, but even with the parachutes attached to the seats, I could not imagine Jon squeezing out of the narrow hatch at the back, especially in a time of crisis. Knowing what the flight surgeon had said, I realized that none of our guys ever had a chance to try.

I held the cold, heavy-duty buckles of the seats in my hand. Surely these would have held him in place when the plane hit the water. But there was no way to know for certain. At least I could remove the tormenting picture of Jon drowning as he struggled to escape the wrecked plane, and I decided to hang on to my image of him sitting in his flight suit, surrounded by the fuselage of his beloved Hawkeye, and resting in the company of his Navy brothers.

The seat I was sitting in represented the culmination of Jon's 15-year naval career. Jon loved being a CICO, playing the role of a quarterback in air missions, running the E-2C's advanced radar systems, and passing on his considerable expertise to the junior officers. Jon and I shared so many things, but much of his Navy life had been a mystery to me. Looking around at Jon's "office," I had a better understanding of the world he loved.

While I was proud of Jon and his sacrifice for his country, that day I was not proud—I was sad. Sad that Jon was gone, sad that this was how his life had ended, and sad that I couldn't give him a proper burial. The crew of Bear Ace 603 and those of us who loved them most were looked upon as victims, but I did not want that to be my story. The other ladies were crying as we sat together, and while the experience was cathartic for me, I was stoic more than passionate.

650 Pages ... for What?

I had a similar reaction when the Navy's final report from the JAG investigation was released a few weeks later. My CACO Rick helped me request my copy, and I was floored when more than 650 pages arrived. I didn't have the mental energy to dive into the endless pages of sworn statements, maintenance and safety records, radio transmission transcripts, pictures of some of the wreckage, ship's log, and so much more.

What little I did read made me angry. They mentioned that Jon hadn't flown in a few weeks, but how could he with all the bad weather they'd experienced? I wasn't sure that a few touch-and-go landings in advance would have made any difference on the night in question, not with Jon's years of experience and the fact that he wasn't flying the plane. The report also brought up "crew coordination": the idea that everyone onboard had the responsibility to keep an eye on the altimeter and speak up if something seemed amiss. I knew Jon took his role as the senior officer seriously, and Frenchy was perhaps the best pilot in the squadron. How could five guys have been asleep on the job at the same time? It just didn't make sense to me.

The official conclusion of the JAG investigation was similar to the CO's. "The exact cause of this mishap is not known," it said. The report pointed to the theory of vertigo as the most likely explanation. The JAG investigation did recommend several changes for the VAW community, which included crew coordination, refresher training, and altimeter alarms. The Navy was diligent in attempting to increase the safety level of the E-2C fleet and do everything within their power to ensure that this sort of mishap never happened again.

For me, once I received the JAG report, I dismissed it. I saw no purpose in its conclusions, for nothing anyone could say would ever bring back my beloved Jon. This brings up a key point that everyone who experiences loss shares: There will never be answers to all our questions. Somehow, we must come to the place that we can live with the tension of not knowing. Here I had more than 650 pages of evidence, but I still couldn't find answers to my most basic questions. Coming to peace with the unknowns would take time for me to achieve.

GEORGE BUSH

November 26, 1993

Dear Kris,

Your good letter and the videotape were waiting for me when I returned to the office today following two weeks abroad. I leave again Sunday for four days in London, but soon, when my schedule is less hectic, I will view the tape. I'm looking forward to seeing it and appreciate very much your sending it along.

I hope everything is going well for you and your beautiful family. Barbara and I send you our warm wishes for a joyous holiday season.

Sincerely,

G Bush

Mrs. Krista K. Rystrom
724 Seagrass Reach
Chesapeake, Virginia 23320

CHAPTER 29

Hello, Mr. President

"When God Doesn't Make Sense"

While I had to accept the fact that I would never have concrete answers to the circumstances surrounding Jon's death, there were deeper spiritual questions which I had to settle if I ever hoped to heal. My pastor, Dr. Reccord, was aware of my struggle and called me on the phone one day to see how I was doing. He told me that he'd recently read a new book entitled "When God Doesn't Make Sense." The author, Dr. James Dobson, a well-known Christian psychologist, had lost several close friends in a tragic plane crash, and the book explained how to hold onto faith during the difficult trials of life. Dr. Reccord thought it would be a significant book for me to read.

My stack of Dead Books looked like the Tower of Babel, but I trusted Dr. Reccord and I took his advice. Hesitantly, I went to our local Christian bookstore and picked up a copy, the first dreaded Dead Book that I had bought for myself. As I read through the pages, a light bulb went on inside. Though I had sat in church and Bible studies for years, I'd never had such a clear explanation of our fallen world and God's role in it.

Dr. Dobson explained that God did not cause the suffering in our world: the wars, disasters, crimes, accidents, diseases, and so on. He created the world without fault, but man fell when he gave in to Satan's temptation and sin came into the world as a result. The world is evil, not God. Man has a free will, and God does not stop people from sinning. And He doesn't stop every consequence of living in a fallen world.

> *She who is truly a widow, left all alone, has set her hope on God and continues in supplications and prayers night and day .... (I Timothy 5:5 ESV)*

He explained that "most of us seem to be protected for a time by an imaginary membrane that shields us from horror," most often when we are young and life is easy. But "without warning, the membrane tears and horror seeps into a person's life," creating a crisis of faith if the person isn't rescued. This results in "anger and a sense of abandonment" and, eventually, an estrangement from God for those who cut themselves off from Him.

Dobson went on to say, "Pain and suffering do not cause the greatest damage. Confusion is the factor that shreds one's faith." I was certainly confused by Jon's death, and I didn't know how to handle the life-shaking questions that it caused. Dobson wrote that while at times God does miracles for us, "when nothing makes sense, when what we are going through is 'not fair,' when we feel all alone in God's waiting room, He simply says, 'Trust Me!'" And often, "too much confidence is placed in what people feel and too little on the promises of God." I began to take Dr. Dobson's advice: "In your hour of crisis, don't demand explanation. Don't lean on your ability to understand. Don't turn loose of your faith. But do choose to trust Him ... The only other alternative is despair."

Choosing to trust is possible because of what God chose to do: He sent his perfect Son to die in our place so that we could live forever. God is able to make all things work together for our good. Not that He causes the hard things to happen to teach us a lesson, but He transforms our pain and sorrows if we turn to Him. Because of Jesus, death has no sting. He never leaves us or forsakes us. He is a father to the fatherless and a husband to the widow.

Another widow, Elizabeth Elliot, respected author and the well-known wife of martyred missionary, Jim Elliot, explained that when you've "put [your] heart and soul into something, prayed over it, worked at it with a good heart because you believed it to be what God wanted, and finally have seen it 'run aground,'" we need to remember that Earth is not our home. God does not want us to "settle for this world rather than the next." As humans, we must resist the temptation "to settle for visible things."

I had a choice. I could harden my heart to God and blame Him for Jon's death, or I could run to Him, hand Him my pain, and receive His comfort and healing. My heartache could be used for His glory. And as heartbreaking as my grief was, I knew that Dr. Dobson's observation was true: "... nothing is equal to the agony of a shattered faith." Opening up my heart to God was not easy to do, and it was a process that took time. Thanks in part to Dr. Dobson's book, my healing process turned a corner.

Holding Out Hope

Music continued to minister to my heart and one album in particular spoke to me deeply. I played Michael English's "Hope" CD over and over, and I found comfort in the lyrics to his song, "Holding Out Hope to You." Here's the chorus:

I'll be holding out hope to you
Even when this world breaks your heart in two
When your life is consumed by your fear and your doubts
I'll be holding out hope to you

As I listened to these words, I would cry and find myself praying. My prayers were often small and selfish, but faith was slowly awakening in my dark, bitter soul. On Sunday mornings, while singing in the choir, I would look up at a stained-glass-window image of Jesus holding His outstretched hands to the congregation below. In my heart, it was as if God were whispering to me, "I held out My arms to Jon and welcomed him home. Kris, he is here with Me, safe and loved for eternity."

The powerful messages from the hymns and praise songs that our choir rehearsed and sang each week were like a healing salve being gently massaged into my wounds of loss. Through the safe place of my church family and the sounds I surrounded myself with at home, God was restoring what Satan had intended to destroy. He was gently fanning the flames of His deep love for me through the gift of music, releasing a ray of sunlight into my bleak winter of grief.

God Nudge

The one-year mark of Jon's death was approaching, but one significant first remained: Valentine's Day. Being the day on which Jon proposed to me, the holiday was packed with triggers, so my therapist made sure to schedule an appointment for me on February 14. But when the girls woke up that morning, Jordyn had a fever. She couldn't go to the babysitter now. Of all the days to have to miss a therapy appointment, why today?

Later that morning, Taylor, who was now an active toddler, discovered a way to crawl up the steps, find a bottle of my red fingernail polish, and drop it from the upstairs to the tile floor below. The bottle shattered and red polish went everywhere, even onto the nearby carpet. I broke down—hysterical as I attempted to clean up the mess. Taylor was simply being a toddler, so I couldn't be angry with her. But my grief was always hiding under the surface, waiting to be triggered. That day was like a perfect storm and I was set off. Like the broken bottle of nail polish, my hope was shattered, and my dreams splattered in all directions.

I was still on my hands and knees trying to wipe up the remaining nail polish when the phone rang. A friend from choir and Sunday School was calling.

"Hey, Kris, I just dropped off my kids at school. Could I come by and make some Valentine's Day cupcakes with Jordyn and Taylor?"

Words cannot describe what a tremendous blessing it was to have my friend come to my rescue, without me even having to ask. This sprinkle of sunshine arrived at the perfect time, and I was able to see my therapist as planned on that difficult day. If a person in need comes to your thoughts, that may be a God nudge. Don't dismiss those nudges—someone needs a sprinkle of sunshine and that sprinkle could be you.

"Please Hold ..."

In early 1994, my parents retired and moved from Charleston, West Virginia, to be near the girls and me in Chesapeake. Having my parents experience life with us helped fill some of the holes created by Jon's absence. This was the first time, since leaving home at age 17 to attend Wake Forest, that my parents were a part of my daily life and their comforting presence was a blessing.

Mom read an article in the local newspaper that former President George H. W. Bush was giving a speech in Norfolk in a few weeks. Back in the fall when I'd sent him a copy of the WAVY-TV piece, he'd sent back a lovely note of thanks. Since we had established a sweet pen-pal relationship, I felt the urge to invite him to my home to meet me and the other military widows in our area. I knew that we widows held a valued place in the heart of this former president and naval aviator. And what did I have to lose?

I didn't receive a response, which was not a surprise, but I wanted to hear his speech and see him in person. For the occasion, I decided to wear a custom-made suit from my Hong Kong trip with Jon. I proudly displayed my "Gold Star" widow pin and Jon's gold Navy wings on the lapel. Not long before I left for the drive into Norfolk, the phone rang and a man's voice that I didn't recognize was on the other end.

"May I speak to Mrs. Rystrom, please?"

"This is she," I replied, having no clue what this was about.

"Please hold for President George Bush," he responded, and I was shocked beyond words. My mother was nearby, and she saw the surprised expression on my face. I whispered to her that President Bush was calling me, and we were both floored. My heart was racing when, only moments later, the president's familiar voice came over the phone.

"Kris, this is George Bush."

"Hello, Mr. President." I didn't know what else to say.

"I just wanted you to know that I got your sweet invitation, and if I had 15 more minutes in my schedule, I would be sitting in your kitchen having a cup of coffee with you."

"I understand completely. I'm looking forward to hearing you speak tonight." At least I had calmed down enough to carry on a conversation.

"You're coming?" he asked, sounding pleased.

"I wouldn't miss it." I paused and worked up the courage to ask him, "Would there be an opportunity tonight that I may get a chance to meet you?"

"Absolutely," he quickly replied. "Find a Secret Service man, tell him your information, and he'll direct you to where I am before I speak."

I expressed my thanks and we exchanged goodbyes. I hung up the phone and looked at my beaming mother and said, "I'm going to meet the president!"

Jon, Can You See This?

As I drove to Norfolk Chrysler Hall, I was excited and proud. Jon had given his life for the freedom of our country and was a hero in the eyes of President Bush, who cared enough for me to honor us both. I walked into the hall with my head held high. Few, if any, of the others in that building had offered the sacrifice that I had. In these days before cell phones, I decided against bringing a camera to the meeting, as I didn't want to cheapen the moment.

I followed the president's instructions and found a Secret Service agent in the auditorium. After telling him who I was and asking to see the president, he responded, "Does the president know you're coming?"

"Yes," I proudly answered. "He called me at home about an hour ago."

After verifying my information, the agent led me through a sea of people and behind the stage to the green room where the president was waiting before he faced the crowd. When I entered the room, he was standing there with his back to me, dressed in a tuxedo, along with a handful of other men. I was struck by how tall he was in person.

As I walked up to him, he turned to face me and I held out my hand.

"Mr. President, I'm Kris Rystrom," I explained, and instead of simply shaking my hand, he took it and pulled me into a warm hug. He kissed me lightly on the cheek and looked me in the eye with a gentle smile on his face.

"How are you and your girls doing?" he inquired, and I was touched by his genuine concern.

"We are doing well," I replied with a smile. "We are making it."

"I would like to introduce you to the people here," and he turned to the other dignitaries in the room, including former high-ranking officials from the Navy. Even at the highest levels, Navy guys were still brothers.

While we were all chatting, another lady walked into the room. I recognized her immediately. It was Jane Smith, the Challenger pilot's wife who had spoken at our Wids group.

"Hello, Jane," said President Bush warmly and greeted Jane with a hug.

"Hello, Kris," Jane said to me as we greeted one another.

"You two know each other?" the President asked with surprise.

"Yes, Mr. President," Jane responded with a smile. "We Navy families stick together."

I was so honored by the entire experience. Jane didn't say, "we Navy widows," but "we Navy families." Even though to the Navy bureaucracy I was officially a URW, an un-remarried widow, to this band of brothers and sisters, I still belonged in the Navy family. As I sat in the audience later and heard the president's powerful speech, I was starstruck. I thought to myself: Jon, can you see this? Can you believe whom I just met? Do you know that the president appreciates your sacrifice?

Not long after meeting President Bush, the girls and I traveled to Nebraska to visit Jon's family on the first-year anniversary of his death. As usual, Jordyn and Taylor loved playing with all their cousins, and I was thankful to have such wonderful in-laws in my life. But with my year of "firsts" behind me, I wasn't excited about facing my year of "seconds."

Kris with Jordyn and Taylor, Chesapeake Bay, Virginia.

CHAPTER 30

Balloons to Heaven

Spring was turning into summer and that meant our second Father's Day without Jon was approaching. I was so over it: all the grieving, the crying, and trying to keep special days special. But I knew the girls needed to continue the tradition of launching balloons to Daddy in heaven. Therapy and antidepressants were helping, but I was tired and drained and needed to keep things simple. There was no way that I would allow myself to be triggered by taking Jordyn and Taylor to the beach again that year. I decided to do the launch in our front yard instead.

When the girls and I went to buy our Father's Day balloons, we picked out three shiny, Mylar ones. One was round with "You're the Best" and the other two were heart-shaped: one with "Thinking of You" and another with flowers and butterflies that said, "You're So Special!" As the gal behind the counter filled the balloons with helium, she looked at my girls and grinned.

"Someone is going to be surprised," she said in a cheerful voice. I didn't want to ruin this kind lady's day by telling her where the balloons were really going. My unusual story seemed to suck the breath out of any innocent bystander who heard it. Jordyn looked up at me and I winked back. Even at age 4, Jordyn knew that not everyone wanted to hear about how her daddy was dead at the bottom of the ocean, so we both kept our mouths shut.

When we got home, pictures were drawn, love notes were written, and we attached them to the three balloons. I got out my camera, and we stepped out into the front yard. That Sunday was sunny with a bit of a breeze. We said our Father's Day prayer: "Dear Jesus, please tell Daddy 'Happy Father's Day' and we love him. And Jesus, please take care of him in heaven. Amen."

We released the balloons to float up to the sky. The girls were so busy jumping up and down and waving to heaven that they didn't notice when one of the balloons went off course and ducked out of sight behind the house. The other two soared higher and higher, getting smaller and smaller, until they disappeared completely from view. Where was the other balloon? I did a quick search and looked up to see the errant balloon caught way up high in the top of one of the pine trees in our back yard. I was frustrated, but as long as the girls didn't notice, it wouldn't matter. Otherwise, they'd be sad that Daddy didn't get all his messages of love. But I figured there was no need to worry. A helium balloon should work itself free and float away, especially if the breeze picked up.

On Monday, I got up early as usual, donned my old bathrobe and worn-out slippers, and prepared to start another exciting week in the life of a Navy widow. While I was brushing my teeth at my bathroom sink, something caught my eye out the large window over the Jacuzzi tub. I hadn't realized the day before that my Cry Room window perfectly framed the view of the trapped balloon, its silver Mylar surface reflecting the morning sun and the ribbon string with notes attached gently swaying in the breeze. I couldn't have positioned it better if I'd tried.

My heart sank. The balloon hadn't worked itself free as I'd hoped. What if the girls saw this? They would be so disappointed. Thankfully, they rarely came into my bathroom. The balloon was far enough away that I couldn't tell which of the three balloons it was. It was caught in branches so high—higher than our two-story house—that there was no way I could bring it down. The only choice I had was to hope the girls wouldn't spot it. But if they did, I'd have to come up with a creative explanation so that they wouldn't cry.

Tuesday came, and the balloon was still stuck. Wednesday came. Then Thursday. Friday. Saturday. Still stuck. Every time I looked out my bathroom window, it was there. Every time I backed out of our driveway, I could see it frowning at me from the top of the pine tree, barely visible over the peak of our roof. Another week went by. The balloon remained. Summer thunderstorms blew through our neighborhood, but the balloon hung on. A month went by and the shape looked more deflated, but the shiny surface glimmered in the sun just the same.

I had avoided doing the Father's Day launch at the beach to sidestep getting triggered by the ocean. Now I had a disturbing and daily reminder of Jon's death in the form of an entangled balloon residing outside my Cry Room window. My only consolation was that the girls couldn't see the misplaced balloon from their wooden playset in the yard below.

"So, Your Daddy Died?"

My girls loved to play, so I was thrilled when I was taking out the trash one morning through the side door in my garage and noticed a moving van down the street. Two pink bikes sat in the front yard, and the next day we walked over to welcome our new neighbors. The sweet woman who answered the door and invited us in had two little daughters of her own, and the girls went off together to play in another room.

I gave my friend an overview of our neighborhood, telling her about the retired couple that shared their pool and the pediatrician that lived down the street. She leaned in close to me, lowered her voice to a whisper, and said, "I heard that there is a young widow who lives here that lost her husband in a plane accident." Without missing a beat, I leaned in and whispered back, "Yes, that's me." A look of horror came across her face.

"Oh no! I'm so sorry!"

"It's OK," I laughed. "I'm used to it." I felt bad for her, but this little faux pas didn't keep us from becoming the best of friends. While I was finally acknowledging my widow identity, I didn't look the part to most people I met.

One day, I overheard Jordyn as she dealt with a more difficult comment. She had a new little friend over and the two of them were making cookies in our kitchen. While I was busy stirring the cookie dough at the counter, the girls were behind me, sitting at our kitchen island and sorting through our collection of sprinkles.

"So, your daddy died?" the friend asked innocently.

"Yes, he sure did," Jordyn replied without hesitation. This wasn't the kind of little-girl talk that I was used to hearing. I found myself stirring the dough a little faster, nervous about where this could be headed.

"Did he get eaten by a shark?"

My heart froze as my grip on the spoon tightened, and I vigorously stirred the dough in anger. What was this kid thinking? How dare she ask such a heartless question! How would Jordyn handle this? Should I step in to protect her? As much as I wanted to turn around and strangle that insensitive child, this was an opportunity to hear Jordyn's reaction.

"No," Jordyn said matter-of-factly, "'cause my daddy is down deep, deep, deep, where the sharks don't go."

I was proud of Jordyn's confident response, but it pained me to know that this was how my daughter would live out the rest of her life. Her little friend wasn't trying to be mean—she was asking an honest, child-like question. Friends at church were sensitive to Jordyn's situation, but she would have to face hard questions on her own as she got older.

Still Stuck

As the summer progressed, I was thankful that my parents were around to support and encourage us. But I knew that their heart was to retire to their beach house in North Carolina. As much as I valued their companionship, I didn't want them to feel obligated to delay their retirement indefinitely. I began to entertain the idea of selling our dream home and moving on.

In the meantime, I was trying to move on emotionally, but one thing made that difficult to do: that infernal balloon. For weeks now, it had hung there tangled in the pines. As I tried to go about my daily routine, the balloon peeked at me when I pulled out of the driveway and mocked me whenever I entered my bathroom. And while I was well into my second year of widowhood, my Cry Room was still a quiet place to release deep grief and offer desperate prayers. Jon's closet was mostly empty, but I still clung as stubbornly to his old brown bathrobe as that deflated balloon clung to the pine tree's branches.

August came and the balloon remained. September arrived. The balloon hung on. Jordyn and Taylor started preschool, but I struggled to return to regular life. On the surface, my normal appearance fooled most people around me, but inside I was aimless and drifting and lonely.

Remember Your Legacy

My church offered me a part-time position as communications director, and I jumped at the chance to get out of the house and earn some extra money. Working on the same days that my daughters were in preschool was the perfect arrangement. And because most of the staff knew my situation, this was a safe, small step into the outside world of employment for me. My coworkers were supportive and understanding, especially if I encountered an unexpected grief-slap across the face and had to excuse myself to deal with a possible torrent of tears. Our church had a large staff, but the halls of my church home were a place of comfort. My cubicle was close to the senior pastor's office. One day, Dr. Reccord asked me to come see him. I was honored that, with his busy schedule, he would take time to talk with me.

"How are you doing, Kris?" he asked, with a slight smile on his face.

"I'm doing OK," I nodded back. But we both knew that I wasn't and he hadn't called me in for a shallow, feel-good conversation. He was genuinely concerned about me.

"Kris, I want you to remember your legacy." He looked at me with kind eyes, but his words were firm and to the point. Perhaps my internal struggle was more obvious to others than I thought, at least to those with the wisdom to discern it.

His wise words reverberated in my heart. So many dreams had died when Jon's plane went down: plans for a career, to earn my Ph.D., to travel and experience the world, and so much more. I had always been a high achiever, and now my greatest accomplishment was taking out the trash on time. There was nothing wrong with being a mom to my daughters, but my life was stuck in a rut and heading nowhere fast. My greatest barrier was remaining shackled to my grief.

Picture Imperfect

When I picked up Jordyn from preschool soon after, my grief took the opportunity to kick me down the stairs and slap me in the face in front of all the other parents. In that day's class, the children had drawn pictures of their families, and the teacher was handing out the art work to the parents waiting in the hallway. I looked forward to seeing what Jordyn had drawn, but when the teacher handed me her picture, I felt like a knife stabbed my heart. She had drawn me, Taylor, herself, and Max. But not Jon.

Tears poured down my face and the teacher gave me a box of tissues while she finished handing out the rest of the pictures. Few of the other parents knew who I was and between my uncontrollable sobs, I attempted to explain the situation to them. How embarrassing. But it wasn't Jordyn's fault. What she drew was accurate and real. I was the one refusing to accept our new reality.

When we got home from school and I went upstairs, the sight of the deflated balloon did me in again. How much more could I take? I was trying to move on, but much like the spiraling branches that kept the balloon tangled in the tall pines, constant triggers that I continued to encounter kept me tangled in grief.

A chill filled the air as fall turned into winter. As leaves fell from the trees and color fled the landscape, the despised balloon stood out even more. Now, months after its capture in the pines, its Mylar material was wrinkled and shriveled, and the ribbon string with its notes of love was reduced to shreds. Storm after storm had blown through the tall trees, yet the balloon stuck like a leech.

I began battling with God every time that I saw the cursed reminder through my bathroom window. "God, I'm trying to move on. Why are You reminding me that I have a dead husband? You allowed this stupid balloon to get stuck in this tree. I get it. I'm not in control. But You are. What are You doing to me?"

There was no reply.

The Loneliest Season

The second winter after Jon's death was the loneliest season of my life. The Wids weren't calling each other like they once had—everyone was moving forward, moving on, or moving away. With my "firsts" behind me, I was facing the "seconds" alone, and I was joining my married friends and their families less often. As much as I loved Jordyn and Taylor, they couldn't fill the gaping holes in my heart. My depression deepened as the gray, dreary days grew shorter and the damp, frigid air grew nearer. Winter and grief came hand in hand and loomed over my house like a dark cloud.

Somehow, I managed to hang on through Thanksgiving and Christmas. And so did the balloon. New Years 1995 came. Something had to give. I couldn't face another year of grief in this house. My soul was empty and raw and the constant view of the horrid balloon was like pouring salt in the wound. I cried out to God, "You put this wretched balloon in the tree. Can't You take it away?"

One day soon after, I was backing out of the driveway with the girls to run some errands. I glanced up at our house and suddenly realized something: The balloon was gone. I put my foot on the brake and strained my eyes to make sure. But there was no mistaking it—the stubborn balloon had blown away.

For the first time in ages, a spark of joy entered my heart. I smiled as I backed up and turned onto Seagrass Reach. Finally, after nearly seven months of torture, the cursed balloon was out of my life, forever! My girls had no idea what I was thinking, and they couldn't hear my internal conversation with God.

"So, God, are You saying that I can move on now? You got rid of the dreadful balloon for me? It took You long enough, but thanks. I'm so glad the miserable thing is gone!"

I cheerfully turned the corner and continued making my way out of our neighborhood. After stopping at an intersection before heading onto the main highway, a glint of sunlight caught my eye. I instantly glanced up and my heart stood still: There was the cursed balloon stuck high up in yet another tree. I sat there for a moment in disbelief as resentment flooded my soul. I was glad Jordyn and Taylor couldn't hear my angry dialog with the Creator of the universe.

"Really?? Seriously?? You've got to be kidding me! Is this some kind of sick joke? What? Is the balloon going to start following me around now? Is there anywhere I can go and NOT be reminded that Jon is dead?"

For Sale

The tenacious claw of grief would not let go. All attempts to break free were useless. I couldn't escape its relentless grasp as long as I lived here.

The despised balloon had finally abandoned my Cry Room window, and on the next morning's commute, I discovered that overnight it had disappeared for good. Perhaps the balloon from hell had made it to heaven at last. I didn't care where it was as long as it was far away from me. I sighed with relief, but my mind was made up. I would put my house on the market, and my parents and I could move on to a new chapter in our lives.

Once the "For Sale" sign was displayed in the yard, the reality of what I was preparing to say goodbye to hit me like a ton of bricks. Over the next few weeks, as winter's grip persisted, the grip of grief was more than I could stand. So many losses: Jon, my lover, my best friend; being an officer's wife; my security; my girls losing their father; my dreams; and now, to top it all off, losing the precious home that Jon and I had built together.

No Response

One cold, rainy night, after I put the girls to bed, I entered my Cry Room, turned off the lights, and succumbed to overwhelming anguish and sorrow. Sobbing uncontrollably, I grabbed Jon's soft, brown bathrobe and his worn leather Bible and clung to them as I dropped to my knees in despair and bowed my head in mourning toward the cold bathroom floor. I had to stop the unrelenting pain—I couldn't take the torment any longer. The only imaginable way to remove my intense suffering would be the miraculous return of my beloved husband.

Heaving with bitter grief, I tearfully screamed out to God, "Bring him home! Bring him home! God, please! Let him come home!"

This was my darkest hour. Many hopeless hours had passed since Jon's sudden death, but this one was by far the worst—the rawest and the hardest. My heart had never ached for Jon as much as it did in that wretched moment.

I waited woefully for God's reply.

There was no response.

I wasn't delusional. I was desperate. Of course, Jon wasn't coming home. And I knew that even when the house was sold and the girls and I had moved away, the crippling grief that clung to me like a cancer would follow me into my new life. There was no easy escape. There was no reason to hope. Not if I had to face the dismal future alone. My Jon could not help me. But what about my God?

A great, deep sadness settled into my soul, and I cried out one last time in desperation, "Do You hear me? Do You know I'm here? Please, tell me that You hear me!"

In His Word, God repeatedly said He loved the widow, and He promised to be a faithful husband to the husbandless. Surely a loving God would swiftly answer my urgent cries. In the gloomy darkness, I anxiously waited on the cold, hard floor, expecting and yearning to hear the audible voice of God.

There was no response.

I don't remember how long I lingered there in the pitch blackness but, eventually, with a crushed spirit and an exhausted body, I stumbled to my empty bed, crawled under the chilly covers, and cried myself to sleep.

The morning sun streamed through my bedroom curtains and woke me from my fitful slumber. As my foggy mind gradually cleared, I remembered the agony of the hopeless night before. I sighed in deep disappointment as I realized that even my most desolate cries had brought no response from my Heavenly Father.

The last thing that I wanted to do was face another wearisome day, but I had two little girls that needed their mommy. Jon had told me that I was their security when he was away. I had to keep my promise. I slowly crept out of bed, threw on my old bathrobe, and shoved my feet into my worn house slippers. With my mommy hat in place, I deliberately put one foot in front of the other. I reluctantly went through the motions of walking the girls down the stairs, getting out their breakfast cereal, and turning on their favorite morning show, "Barney."

I noticed the calendar and groaned when it reminded me that today was trash day. Oh joy. Time to gather up the trash. I didn't possess the energy to consider all the other mommies in the neighborhood who had a husband to carry out this boring, weekly chore. I went into task mode and mindlessly collected all the trash in the house. I lethargically passed through the kitchen, lugging my large bag of refuse behind me, and wearily walked through the door leading to the garage. I shuffled past my vehicle and numbly unlocked and opened the side door as I had countless times before. I took one tiresome step outside into the crisp, morning air and, unthinkingly, looked down to see something odd lying at my feet.

It was the balloon.

Taylor and Jordyn, Father's Day 1994. Jon planted the rosebushes in the background.

CHAPTER 31

My Letter From Heaven

.

There it was lying before me—the old, wrinkled, dirty, withered, heart-shaped balloon—on the ground next to the garbage can, right side up—with its faded, yet clearly visible, printed message facing me:

"You're So Special!"

I couldn't breathe. Not for a few moments at least. I silently stood there in the early dawn, in the stillness of the damp morning—the trees dripping with rain from the night before—and I stared and stared at the tattered balloon resting at my feet.

"You're So Special!"

How could this be? My baffled mind was trying to process what my eyes were plainly seeing. Where did it come from? How did the balloon get inside the little privacy fence around my garbage can? And how did it land right side up, facing the side door, as if someone had precisely placed it there on purpose?

Wasn't this the same balloon that my girls and I had purchased more than seven months earlier? Wasn't this the same balloon that was released with two others but went in a completely different direction? Wasn't this the same balloon that got tangled in the pine trees outside my Cry Room window? The same balloon that mocked me for months on end, piercing my heart with the daily reminder that my Jon was dead?

Wasn't this the same balloon that blew a half mile away landing in another tall tree, subsequently disappeared for weeks, and then ... that morning it greeted me at my garbage can after a fierce night of wrestling with God, crying out in despair, and fervently asking Him, "Do You hear me? Do You know I'm here? Please, tell me that You hear me!"

He responded.

His answer was lying at my feet: "You're So Special!"

I dropped the bag filled with trash. I dropped my bag filled with grief. I instantly raised my hands toward the morning sky and lifted my head toward the heavens. Tears filled my eyes, but this time they were tears of joy. Light and peace and love saturated my broken heart as the oppressive weight of grief and my thick, gray cloak of despair dissolved in the glorious presence of my precious Savior.

"Thank you for hearing me, Jesus! Thank you for answering my cries!" I exclaimed as tears of rapture streamed down my beaming face.

He heard me! I was special!

What was meant to help two little girls show love to their daddy in heaven was used by God to show His infinite love to His cherished daughter on Seagrass Reach. He allowed the heart-shaped, Mylar balloon to be stuck in a pine tree outside my Cry Room window through June, July, August, September, October, November, and December. In January, He took the balloon on a journey, and where He had kept it during the weeks it vanished, only heaven knew. But one day, in His perfect timing, He did a reverse balloon launch and sent a life-changing message of love to me.

Stripes at my front door had ushered a torrent of grief into my life. But a Man with stripes on His back came to my side door and released a flood of hope into my grieving heart. He didn't meet me at a magnificent palace, on a majestic mountain top, or even in a soaring cathedral. He met me in a grimy, mundane, nitty-gritty moment of every-day life. Not when I looked my Sunday best with fine clothes, fresh make-up, and perfectly styled hair, but when I was shabby and exhausted, dressed in an ugly housecoat and worn-out slippers.

Just As I Am

I'm not the only one that Jesus met at such an unexpected and lowly place. In the Bible, Chapter 4 of the Gospel of John tells the story of Jesus meeting the woman at the well. Like so many of us, this wayward woman, who was hiding from the rest of the town because of her public sin, was searching for significance in all the wrong places. Jesus broke cultural tradition and didn't hesitate to refresh her soul with His living water and to renew her worth with His unconditional love.

Many of us are like that old balloon. We start off shiny and new, boldly proclaiming an uplifting message of promise, but inside we're just puffed up with air. All is well, until an unforeseen gust of wind blows us off course, and we find ourselves hopelessly tangled in the branches of our own bad choices, the hurtful actions of others, or the unavoidable suffering of life. We're stuck in our past, paralyzed in our present, and unable to move on. The air slowly leaks out of us, leaving us deflated and empty. We think we're set free, only to be entangled anew in another trap of our own making.

But one day, our Savior encounters us when we're tattered and wrinkled and worn, and He carries us gently in His nail-scarred hands. He lovingly transforms us into a new creation, freely breathes His eternal life into our spirits, and we rise again—victorious to live out our true God-given destiny, empowered by His measureless love.

For years, I searched for significance in what I could achieve in my own strength. My hunger for control resulted in an eating disorder that I battled for years. I hid my true needs from the people around me and even from myself. My relationship with God was all about following a religion and checking off the boxes, and while I believed in God to save me from my sin, I didn't know Him as a friend. In truth, Jesus had been with me all along, but in my brokenness I didn't recognize His presence. But after He met me at the garbage can, my eyes were opened and my relationship with Him grew into an intimate friendship that filled my life with a new sense of hope, joy, and peace.

> *YOU HAVE KEPT COUNT OF MY TOSSINGS; PUT MY TEARS IN YOUR BOTTLE. ... (PSALMS 56:8 ESV)*

Jesus doesn't expect us to have Pinterest-perfect lives. We don't have to exaggerate our accomplishments, pump up our abilities, or reach the highest rungs on our ladders of success. We don't have to cover up our faults or hide our weaknesses. Whether we are struggling with addictions, crippled by fear, incapacitated by grief, overcome with remorse, enslaved to sin, or mastered by insecurities, Jesus wants us to come to Him, just as we are—dirty, wrinkled, raw, and real. That's the only way He can begin to heal us.

That was the way He began to heal me. Like the story that the minister told Jon and me on our wedding day, I was the lady with the lost coin. Something precious was lost from my life, and I searched diligently until I found it again. And for a season, God was searching for me, desiring not only to regain but also to transform our relationship into one of tender intimacy, abiding love, and lasting joy.

Often in the midst of our suffering, we expect Jesus to come charging through the front door to rescue us from our crisis. And there are times that He will. But in other seasons, He will come in a way that we least expect, like quietly and gently slipping through the side door to meet us at the point of our greatest need.

My Savior met me at the garbage can. And I was forever changed.

Fingerprints of God

I would be a liar if I told you that my life was all rainbows and butterflies from that moment on. I still had to take out the trash. I still had to clean up after my girls. I still had to sleep in an empty bed and face the future without my beloved Jon. Some nights, I cried. Some days, I was triggered. And many of the questions that had troubled my heart were never fully answered. But now I had Him, and He had me. I could trust Him with the unknowns. I could trust Him with my future. And I could trust Him with my heart.

To make me whole, I didn't need another man to love me and take Jon's place. Jesus was the lover of my soul. I was finally complete. More complete than I was when Jon was alive. It was just me, the girls, and Jesus—all that I needed to make it through.

Looking back over my life with Jon, I can see the fingerprints of God from the beginning: how He guided our paths and brought us together, how He freed me from my eating disorder and healed Jon of his broken heart and restored his faith, how over time God transformed both of us, how He taught us about true significance, and how He blessed us with two amazing daughters. Jon's last letter to me demonstrated the depths of that transformation when he said:

I realize I need to eliminate "I" and put my faith and trust in God. It is hard sometimes, but God will take care of me ... I realize how insignificant making O-5 really is ... I just thank God for the great life He has given me.

What a contrast from the lonely, drifting man I met on a blind date in Virginia Beach!

Thinking of letters, I cherish the treasure contained in the letters that Jon and I wrote to each other. How thankful I am that I kept them all these years through multiple moves. Their powerful words still minister to me today. And by changing the words ever so slightly, the messages of love from Jon now reflect the relationship that I enjoy with my Savior. But more than that, these are Jesus' messages of love to us all. Can you imagine the Savior writing these words to you?

First off, I love you!

I never want to lose you.

My child, never forget how important you are to Me.

When you told Me how you felt, My heart wept when you did. I could feel the same emotions that you were feeling.

I am so glad you are finally getting My messages. As you can see I have been speaking every day. Oh, how I love you.

I have gained so much in our relationship through your prayers. I can feel your pain, your hurt, your joy, your intense desire to please Me. When I hear your prayers, I read between the lines and marvel at what an incredible person you are. My child, from before I made the world, I chose you as my beloved one and you are not a disappointment to Me in the least. My love for you cannot be measured and you care for Me more and more every day. I just love it!!!

You realize that the more you like yourself and believe in the person I've created you to be, the more of you that you can give Me.

Always remember, you never—I repeat never—will be without My love.

Now, can you imagine those same words of love from letters that I shared with Jon being shared with our Savior as though they were written to Him?

What I read in Your Word today are the warmest, most love-filled words that You have ever given to me. I will cherish them for the rest of my life. Thank you, Jesus, for loving me; that has made my life fulfilled because You have made my life complete! You are my world and I will do anything for You, always and forever.

I love you, Jesus, more than I could ever express. I think about You constantly. I give You the best that I could ever give. No conditions, no demands, no expectations ... Just me, with all of my faults and flaws, just the entire package ... And it is all Yours forever.

I thought of You all day today, knowing that because of You, we are able to celebrate freedom every day. Thank you for allowing me to have freedom, Jesus. You are so special and honorable to give so much for Your children ....

You changed my life and taught me how to live it. Thank you, Jesus. I will love You for eternity.

You are the only One in this universe that makes me feel alive, special, and loved. I want to go everywhere You go, do everything You do, be everything You are, and never, never be without Your love.

Of course, Jesus has written special words to each of us in His Word, the Bible. On my journey from grief to hope, I traded in Jon's letters from the sea for a beautiful letter penned thousands of years ago from our Heavenly Father for me. Needless attempts were being made in finding my intimacy with Christ through church activities and the endless pages from the Dead Books. But it was the Bible with its letters of truths and promises that began to heal my bleeding soul. It seems simple and obvious, and it is. God's divine Word is the healing salve for the hurting.

I had memorized Scripture when I was a child. I had opened the Word my whole life for Sunday School and church. But as I worked through my grief, I opened the pages for hope. Perhaps for the first time in my life, my Bible was my lifeline for redemption. There was nothing else. We can fill our lives with busyness and stuff, but for pure healing, the Great Physician has written His prescription within the pages of His Holy Word.

For some of you, this book is your balloon. Having this book in your hands is not a coincidence. He has been speaking to you through its pages, and He is reaching out His nail-scarred hands to inject life into your hopeless situation, to shine His light into your darkened spirit, and to release joy into your afflicted soul. You can stay stuck in the darkness or step out into the light. The choice is yours. I choose hope. What will you choose?

Kris Rystrom Emmert on USS Harry S. Truman on the 25th anniversary of Jon's mishap—the same stateroom he occupied on USS Theodore Roosevelt.

CHAPTER 32

H.O.P.E.

What is hope? As Andy Dufresne says in the "Shawshank Redemption," "... hope is a good thing. Maybe the best of things and no good thing ever dies." As I stumbled through my valley of grief, my one constant, nagging question was "How do I find hope again?" The Bible says that "hope anchors the soul." But how do we have an expectation of good happening in the future when our "anchor" is lost at the bottom of the sea?

I desperately wanted hope. Hope for joy again—for a life fulfilled. Hope for answers and for finding purpose. Hope for laughter again. For real laughter—the kind that makes your sides hurt and tears of joy come spilling out. Hope for a happy life for my girls—that this tragedy wouldn't define who they were and who they were to become. Hope that one day my grieving heart would heal. Hope was out there. At first, I didn't know where to find it. But the hope of finding hope gave me a reason to breathe again.

In the early days of grief, I couldn't understand what heaven would be like for a man and woman who had been married on this Earth. When I asked my mother if Jon would know me when I died, she reminded me of this Scripture: "... I shall know fully, even as I am fully known."

(1 Corinthians 3:12 ESV). I would cling to the simple promise that Jon and I would be together again. Despite my questions and anger toward God, I realized that my faith in a loving God was still there. That faith was like a tiny ember, but it was still present.

Faith is defined as "believing in things unseen." I always had faith that God would take care of Jon when he was flying. I had faith that our perfect life would continue on its predictable path. When that path took a shocking detour, faith suddenly became something different— much deeper. Faith was no longer about my checklist and what I wanted in life. Faith was now about eternity. Could faith be the vehicle to drive me to finding hope?

So where do you find hope again after you have experienced a crisis of belief? How do you put one foot in front of the other after tragedy? Perhaps you have not lost a husband in a plane crash, but loss is a way of life. We all lose. There is no way of avoiding it in this world. We live in a world that suffers loss—loss of a marriage, loss of a business, loss of a relationship, loss of health, loss of dreams, or even loss of hope. But you can win in the end—God wins in the end—and we can experience the victory He offers to us.

For many believers, they choose to run from God in anger and bitterness. Tears are shed, I imagine, in heaven when one of God's children turns his/her back on the One who loves them deeply with an everlasting love. No, we don't have answers, and perhaps we'll never know why we suffer in our fallen world. We have two choices and the choice is yours and only yours. No one can make it for you. Your choices are: Choose to live for yourself in bitterness and despair, or choose hope through the One who offers it freely. I chose hope.

Since Jon's mishap, I have found four simple truths that I have lived by which gave hope to my hurting soul. My prayer is that these truths will offer you hope as you wrestle with your questions and travel your own path in finding hope after heartache. Put together, these truths form the acronym H.O.P.E.

H . O . P . E .

H : HOLD ONTO GOD'S PROMISES

Promise: God loves you.

God loves every part of you. He knows your pain and you can rest in knowing that He gets down in the dark hole of grief and loss along with you. The natural question we all may have is "If God loves me, how could He allow such a tragedy to take place in my life?" This is a question that we may never know the answer to in this life. For me, I had to remember that God didn't create the Bosnian conflict, man did. God did not create wars, man did. God did not create heartache, man did. Death is a result of the fall of man, but God loves us and paid the price so that we can have victory over death. Satan cannot win this battle. And I was not going to let Satan win the battle that he had started in my life. I am loved by the King of Kings. I am a conqueror through Christ, and Satan was defeated at the cross.

"As the Father has loved me, so have I loved you. Abide in My love ... These things I have spoken to you, that My joy may be in you, and that your joy may be full." (John 15:9-11 ESV)

"... in all these things we are more than conquerors through Him who loved us. For I am sure that neither death nor life, nor angels nor rulers, nor things present nor things to come, nor powers, nor height nor depth, nor anything else in all creation, will be able to separate us from the love of God in Christ Jesus our Lord." (Romans 8:37-39 ESV)

"But God, being rich in mercy, because of the great love with which He loved us." (Ephesians 2:4 ESV)

Promise: God will never leave you or forsake you.

He wraps Himself around your hurts so that you can rest in His arms. Scripture tells us that He will never leave us or forsake us. Over and over, His Word tells us that we are to rest in Him. He will not turn His back on His children. Jeremiah 29:11 says, "He promises to give us a hope and a future." To know that we have our Comforter opening His arms to us gives us the rest we so desperately seek.

"It is the Lord who goes before you. He will be with you; He will not leave you or forsake you. Do not fear or be dismayed." (Deuteronomy 31:8 ESV)

"... Be strong and courageous. Do not be frightened, and do not be dismayed, for the Lord your God is with you wherever you go." (Joshua 1:9 ESV)

"Fear not, for I am with you; be not dismayed, for I am your God; I will strengthen you, I will help you, I will uphold you with my righteous right hand ... For I, the Lord your God, hold your right hand; it is I who say to you, 'Fear not, I am the One who helps you.'" (Isaiah 41:10-13 ESV)

In Jon's letters to me from his time at sea, he constantly told me to "be strong; you can do it." Now I was hearing those same words, except they were coming from my God. He was there for me and was promising to take care of me.

Promise: God is our Provider.

God is our Jehovah Jireh, our Provider. God cares about our every need. Worries and stress can overtake us. According to Philippians 4:19, "The Lord provides every need according to His riches in Glory." Scripture is filled with God providing for His children. In Genesis, Abraham was commanded to take Isaac to Mount Moriah and offer him as a sacrifice. God stopped him, however, and provided a ram caught in a thicket as the sacrifice. This is the first time in Scripture that Jehovah Jireh is written. Mount Moriah means "the Lord foresees" or "the Lord will see to it."

Just as God provided the ram for the sacrifice Abraham used for the redemption of his family, God offered His only Son as the ultimate sacrifice for the redemption of mankind so that we could know Him and have the provision of eternal life. Romans 8:28 tells us that God will see to it that in all things He works for the good of those who love Him, who have been called according to His purpose. We don't always see His provision. Sometimes we don't know that He has already taken care of our needs. We are unaware of His hand in our lives. God is our Master Weaver, and He is making a beautifully woven life in us. We can't see the threads interweaving or the design He is creating, but He is making something beautiful. We also know that in making a woven piece of art, there are knots, tears, and ugly spots on the back. While we traverse our own knots and tears in life, we must trust His hand as He sees the big picture and creates His masterpiece in us.

Promise: God is the Father to the fatherless and the Husband to the husbandless.

As I dug into His word searching for answers, I continued to see a recurring theme: He takes care of the widows and orphans.

"Father of the fatherless and protector of widows is God in His holy habitation." (Psalms 68:5 ESV)

He treats us differently. He treats us with a gentle care more than any other person in the Bible. For those of you who have not lost a husband to a physical death but to a marital death, I believe this promise is for you as well. Many of our children are left fatherless, especially in today's world. Find comfort, my friend, in knowing that your Heavenly Father is there to be the father to your precious children.

"But You do see, for You note mischief and vexation, that You may take it into Your hands; to You the helpless commits himself; You have been the helper of the fatherless." (Psalms 10:14 ESV)

Psalms 56:8 tells us that He collects our tears in a bottle. When you weep, God sees every tear that you shed. He weeps with us. I often cried out in my anger, "How could You, the Almighty, possibly know how this feels or understand this pain?" But suddenly I was reminded that He does know how this feels. He gave up His Son for mankind. He watched His only Son be murdered on a cross. Yes, my Lord does understand your pain. He grieves with you as He holds your weeping soul in His comforting hands.

This world is not our home. We are here on this Earth for only a moment compared to our eternal home.

Promise: God carries you through your storm.

In the first days after the crash, my Sunday School teacher and his wife hid strips of paper with the Scripture reference Isaiah 43:2 all over my house. I had never read that passage. Curiously, I opened my Bible to see why this Scripture was so important that this couple felt it necessary to cover my house with it. What I read has carried me every day for the past 25 years. This has become my life verse:

"When you pass through the waters, I will be with you, and when you pass through the rivers, they shall not overwhelm you; when you walk through the fire, you shall not be burned; and the flame shall not consume you." (Isaiah 43:2 ESV)

Promise: God draws near to those who draw near to Him.

One final promise that needs to be emphasized is the subject of prayer.

"Draw near to God, and He will draw near to you. ..." (James 4:8 ESV)

God wants to have a relationship with you and we do this by praying. Yes, praying. I realize that you may not want to have anything to do with prayer, which is simply having a conversation with God. He can handle your frustrations, your pain, and your needs. He is God and He made you. Remember, He loves you deeply and wants to show His love to His child.

Praying became part of my everyday conversations. I prayed out loud. I prayed in the car. I prayed everywhere I went. These were not eloquent, fancy words. I talked, yelled, cried, and whispered my every thought. If I was going to be friends with Jesus, then we were going to talk—and talk a lot. The more I prayed, the closer I came to knowing the "the peace of God, which surpasses all understanding." There was no way to explain it other than God and I were becoming best friends.

O: OPEN YOUR HEART TO OTHERS

We need to get to the place where we understand that life hurts and it is filled with hurting people. Grief pushes us down into a hole and covers us in loneliness. The temptation is that we keep our head in the hole while life passes us by. Your motto could be, "Let others live their lives; mine is ruined," but you will find yourself falling further into the pit of self-pity and despair.

Let people into your world; others want to help you in your time of need. Of course, the Pound Cake People will be around for a season, but the True Blue friends will walk with you every step of the way. They want to help you find wholeness and wellness again, and God will use their love to throw you a lifeline. Even when you least expect it, your cries will be replaced with smiles.

> *AND WE KNOW THAT FOR THOSE WHO LOVE GOD ALL THINGS WORK TOGETHER FOR GOOD, FOR THOSE WHO ARE CALLED ACCORDING TO HIS PURPOSE. (ROMANS 8:28 ESV)*

The Bible tells us in 2 Corinthians that we are to help others as we have been helped.

"Blessed be the God and Father of our Lord Jesus Christ, the Father of mercies and God of all comfort, who comforts us in all our affliction, so that we may be able to comfort those who are in any affliction, with the comfort with which we ourselves are comforted by God." (2 Corinthians 1:3-4 ESV)

This is one of the reasons for this book: to help others and, perhaps, it was written to help you. There is healing for your soul when you minister to others. To listen, to cry with them, to sit beside them while they cry—these are all steps to making you stronger. You are a much different person than you were before your loss.

For me, I found that I had empathy for anyone who was suffering. While most people feel uncomfortable when talking with a friend or family member who has experienced loss, I now have courage to sit in a room with a friend as her husband breathes his last breath. I call my new widowed friends my "soul sisters." We are the body of Christ and when there is a hurting part, we are to join together to help heal the part that needs it.

As the "Wids" helped each other through the valleys, I ask that you look for someone who is hurting and offer help in their storm. By doing this, God gently brings blue skies to your cloudy days, as He uses you to be the ray of sunshine in someone's life.

P: POSITION YOURSELF FOR OBEDIENCE

By far, this was one of the hardest areas for me. Obedience. What does that mean for any of us when we are seeking help and answers? It seems to be such an obscure word, but its meaning could have a profound impact on anyone who heeds its command. Positioning yourself for obedience is following biblical obedience, which is defined as "to hear God's Word and act accordingly." So, biblical obedience to God means to hear, trust, submit, and surrender to God and His Word.

For me, personally, obedience was honoring the promises that Jon and I had made to each other and to our daughters. Jon and I chose to honor the Lord in our home. At Jordyn's and Taylor's baby dedication services, Jon and I made a covenant with God to raise them under His authority and under the authority of the Bible. After Jon's death, I didn't get a pass just because he was no longer around to hold me accountable to this covenant. My covenant was a promise to God. I would continue to submit to His authority whether I felt like it or not.

Some days out of anger toward God, I had no desire to step foot in church, read the Bible, or sing any song of worship. But just the act of worshipping with other believers and being in fellowship with God's people was a step of obedience.

Obedience doesn't always feel good. It isn't about feelings. It is about promises and commitment. There were some Sundays that I wanted to keep my sweet, little, grieving family at home, sleep in, make a big breakfast, go to the beach, watch cartoons all day, and forget that we needed to go to church. That was the easy way out.

For a single mother of two small children, going to church on a Sunday morning or a Wednesday night was no easy task, especially during cold, rainy, winter mornings. It took planning and work. I had a baby. Anyone who has a baby knows that it is much easier to keep the baby at home. Diapers, bottles, snacks ... more diapers, bottles .... It was at times an overwhelming task; nonetheless, it was one I had promised to carry out while Jon was gone.

Now that he was gone forever, would I continue to follow the path of obedience? The choice was mine and I chose to position myself to obey and to submit to my higher Authority. What relief to know that I didn't call the shots. I could rest in knowing that as long as I submitted to the authority of Jesus, He would lead our family down the path that He chose. I was frail and fragile, but my Savior was strong and able.

"By this we know that we love the children of God, when we love God and obey his commandments. For this is the love of God, that we keep his commandments. And his commandments are not burdensome." (1 John 5:2-3 ESV)

"And this is love, that we walk according to his commandments; this is the commandment, just as you have heard from the beginning, so that you should walk in it." (2 John 1:6 ESV)

I also was obedient to the role of being a mother that God gave me. Naturally, our days were filled with coloring books, Play-Doh, and walks around our neighborhood. Wouldn't parenting be an easy road if that was all we were expected to do? Being a responsible mother, however, meant being obedient to the nurturing of and provision for our daughters. Keeping the girls healthy and cared for meant carrying out even the most boring and mundane tasks. Bills, doctor appointments, car maintenance, and even taking out the trash were just some of the ways I was obedient. As we walk in submission to our God through our everyday jobs—no matter how insignificant they may seem—He finds joy in blessing us because we are His children.

E: EMBRACE THE PAST AND FACE THE FUTURE

While embracing the life that you once had, understand that there is a future in front of you. I have always loved the quote from the movie "Shawshank Redemption" when "Red" Redding states, "Get busy living or get busy dying." I didn't die in that plane and neither did my girls. What a wasted sacrifice Jon would have made if, when he died providing freedom for us, I had chosen to throw his sacrifice back in his face by giving up on life.

No, I chose to live life to the fullest and to search for joy in the living. A golden sunrise, a blooming flower, Max's soft fur, a sappy movie, and the giggles from my girls were freely given to me. Life is good and God is good. Finding the good is easy through a grateful heart and I, like Jon, was grateful for the great life that God had given me.

We all have this choice to make: What do we do with the bad stuff of life we've been handed? Maybe you have carried around in your bag the stuff of neglect, abuse, addiction, or abandonment, even from a young age. Or perhaps your bag of stuff isn't filled with situations of loss but with words and/or actions of hurtful people.

God tells us in Jeremiah 29:11 that He "has plans to give [us] hope and a future." Striving to find hope in your world of grief does not make you forget the person you have lost. It doesn't mean you have stopped loving that person. I have told my girls that I will always love their daddy, and he will always be my husband. But there is a season for everything—there is a time for mourning and, conversely, there is a time for love and life.

Throughout years in ministry, I have met many people who stay stuck in their grief and never move past it. They let it define who they are and who they will be for the rest of their lives. There is a beautiful life in front of each of us. God has so many people and places for you to discover.

Joy is a fruit of the spirit and though it may seem hard to believe, you will experience joy again. You must be ready to take those first steps into a new future. Start with trying something new. Take a class, join a gym, or attend a book club. Consider making small changes. Buying a new comforter set for our bedroom was a small change to make, but it was a huge accomplishment for me at the time. As I began making little changes to my surroundings, they became personal to me. These were not decisions that Jon and I had made together; these were decisions that I made on my own. And it felt good. Making individual decisions on my own created a sense of accomplishment and independence. I was doing it. I was living without him and doing it well. Yes, friend, life is good and God is good.

A Lasting Hope

If you have read through the book to this point, congratulations! I know that my journey through grief was difficult to experience, and perhaps you shed a few tears as you turned through these pages. Many tears were shed by all involved throughout the process of writing this book, but reliving those moments and conveying those emotions were vital, if we were to provide promise to you, the reader.

And that is the goal: to provide promise to you. Hope—lasting hope—is available to everyone. I'm not telling you that if you get on your knees tonight and cry out to God for a balloon that you'll find one on your doorstep tomorrow, but I can promise you this: God answers the cry of every seeking heart. You will encounter Him in an extraordinary way that is unique to you. He will meet you where you are, perhaps when you least expect it. God knows how you are knit together, and He knows exactly what you need and when you need it.

But He will come.

H . O . P . E .

Isabella, Jon's granddaughter, honors Daddy Jon on the 25th anniversary of his death, Norfolk Naval Base.

CHAPTER 33

Providing Promise

"So Life Does Go On"

On the 25th anniversary of the loss of Bear Ace 603, former squadron mates of Jon, Frenchy, Billy Ray, Aardvark, and Bob gathered from across the country to join the widows, survivors, and their families and friends for a memorial remembrance weekend in Norfolk, Virginia. This was the first time since the tragedy that we had come together to honor and remember the fallen crew.

In the midst of tours of aircraft carriers, a visit to the Bear Ace hangar, and a remembrance dinner, a special memorial service was held at the David Adams Memorial Chapel at Norfolk Naval Base, the same chapel where the Navy honored Bear Ace 603 a quarter-century earlier.

As a representative of the widows, I was asked to share a few words on the solemn occasion. Standing before the assembled crowd, on the same spot where my Jon was honored so long ago, the significance of this full-circle moment was not lost on me. I could see the aisle that my daughters and I had walked down together and the front row where there hadn't been a seat. And I was standing on the same stage where my church choir had previously gathered, behind the table that had once displayed the photographs and Navy covers of the lost Bear Ace 603 crew. Just outside the chapel door was where I had been slammed with grief when the Hawkeye missing man formation flew overhead. This resulted in the local paper publishing a front-page photograph of me as a grief-stricken widow.

But crippling grief did not rear its head that day. For though my heart still ached over the loss of my beloved Jon, I was a far different person at that moment than the mournful widow I was back then. As I stepped behind the podium, I looked over the congregation and smiled. These were my friends, my sister Wids, my Navy family, and my personal family. I was so honored to be in that sacred place and share words of encouragement for all of us.

Twenty-five years ago, there were five families who sat in these rows right here in this chapel and they received a folded flag. To most Americans, a folded flag stands for honor, service, and sacrifice. To the five families from Bear Ace 603, our folded flags represented love lost, families ripped apart, and dreams and futures completely shattered. My family was one of those families.

So what do you do when your whole life completely crumbles before you? What do you do with your faith? What do you do with your "whys?" Why us? Why our guys? Why our families? And certainly, why our children?

Anytime you go through any type of devastation, loss, or grief, you can't help but ask those "why" questions, especially if you believe in a God that loves and cares for you. You go through a crisis of belief beyond anything you've ever experienced before.

On Thursday night, March 25, my girls and I began our nightly ritual: Jordyn, Taylor, and I went into the playroom, and we cut the link from our paper chain that we used to count down the days until Daddy got home. And like we did every night that Jon was deployed, my daughter Jordyn prayed. And she said, 'Dear God, please protect my Daddy as he flies in his airplane.'

So how do you tell a 3-year-old the next day that God didn't protect her daddy on the airplane, and she is never going to see her father again? How do you then explain to her that God loves her? God loves me? So how do you explain that to anyone who has gone through crisis, devastation, and loss? Where are those explanations?

For most people, when they go through this crisis of belief, what happens is that they make the choice out of anger and despair and desperation to turn their backs on God. But then there are those who decide to change and face their God for comfort, love, and hope. Because if you turn your back on a God who says He loves us, you have no hope. Hope is gone.

For me and for the four other families that are in this room, we chose hope. We chose to face our God. We didn't have any answers. We still to this day don't have any answers. But we chose to go to our Lord for comfort.

So where are our answers? Our answers are in what I found—in four very simple letters that spell "HOPE."

> TAYLOR'S VERSE:
> KNOW, THEREFORE, THAT THE LORD YOUR GOD IS GOD, THE FAITHFUL GOD WHO KEEPS COVENANT AND STEADFAST LOVE WITH THOSE WHO LOVE HIM AND KEEP HIS COMMANDMENTS TO A THOUSAND GENERATIONS .... (DEUTERONOMY 7:9 ESV)

I went on to share my acronym of "HOPE": Hold on to God's promises, Open your heart to others, Position yourself for obedience, and Embrace the past and face the future. I concluded my comments by reading Jon's last precious letter to me, ending with his phrase, "So life does go on."

And life did go on, I continued. And I did find a new future as did the other widows of 603. And we took one day at a time, and we continued to heal. And I embraced my Jesus as I walked through those valleys.

I don't know what kind of flag has been handed to you today; I don't know what kind of grief you may be dealing with. But I ask you, as a widow of 603, to embrace your faith and let Jesus cover your folded flag.

As I stepped down from the podium, I was thankful for that weekend so lovingly arranged by the Bear Ace family to help provide healing to the widows and surviving families of 603. But I'd like to think that we helped to provide promise to the former squadron mates of our husbands and brothers. We have healed. The process took time, but we have found joy, hope, life, peace, and purpose again. And that's something that all of us need to find.

After I returned to my seat, I glanced around at my family and my sister Wids. We had come a long way in the 25 years since that mournful day when the Navy first honored the crew of Bear Ace 603.

Where Are They Now?

Frenchy's widow, Shelly Messier Hill, now lives in Marietta, Georgia, with her husband, State Senator Judson Hill. They have been married for 22 years and have three children. At age 25, Shelly was the youngest member of the Wids.

Billy Ray's widow, Paola Dyer McNeil, has been married for 21 years to her husband Matt, a successful businessman from Midlothian, Virginia. Paola and Matt have three children, including Billy Ray's son Christopher. Christopher Dyer graduated from Davidson College, thanks to the VAW-VRC scholarship fund, where he also played for Davidson's baseball team. He lives in Charlotte, North Carolina, and works as a financial services recruiter at Aerotek. Christopher also coaches 9-year-olds in AAU baseball.

Katie Forwalder Riley, Bob's widow, is married to her husband of 22 years, Captain Greg Riley, a retired U.S. Navy F-18 pilot, who now flies for American Airlines. Residing in Woodbridge, Virginia, Katie and Greg have four children, including Bob's son Sean, who was born soon after the mishap. Sean Forwalder graduated from the Naval Academy in 2015 and was also a recipient of the VAW-VRC scholarship fund. LT. j.g. Forwalder has been assigned to the helicopter Squadron HSC-9, the Tridents, assigned to the aircraft carrier USS George H.W. Bush out of Norfolk, Virginia. Sean is married to Kathleen Hawkins Forwalder.

Mrs. Ardaiz, the mother of Patrick "Aardvark" Ardaiz, is well up in years but her family has a remarkable, positive outlook on Patrick's short life, and they actively honor his memory still today.

Shelly Messier Hill, Kris Rystrom Emmert, Katie Forwalder Riley, and Paola Dyer McNeil in the cockpit of an E-2C Hawkeye during remembrance weekend.

As for me, I married my amazing husband, Joe Emmert, in 1996 at the same church where, three years earlier, Jon's memorial service was held. Dr. Bob Reccord performed our ceremony. Joe adopted Jordyn and Taylor, and we had two children, Cole and Makenzie. We reside in

Knoxville, Tennessee, where Joe is the senior pastor of North Knoxville Baptist Church.

My oldest daughter, Jordyn Rystrom Emmert, graduated with honors from Eastern University in Pennsylvania, thanks to the VAW-VRC Memorial Scholarship Fund. Jordyn received her juris doctorate from Thurgood Marshall School of Law, where she graduated with honors. She is a practicing attorney in Houston, Texas, and is raising

Jon Rystrom's girls today on the tarmac at the VAW-124 hangar during the Bear Ace 603 remembrance weekend.
L to R: Isabella, Jordyn, Kris, and Taylor

her daughter and our granddaughter, sweet Isabella—a bright, outgoing second-grader.

Taylor Rystrom Emmert lives in East Tennessee. Thanks to the VAW-VRC Memorial Scholarship Fund, she graduated summa cum laude from Carson-Newman University in Tennessee in 2014, where she was awarded outstanding graduate as well as the presidential scholar award. She works as a systems coordinator for Atrio and is marrying Will Ford, Citadel graduate, in fall 2018.

My father, Chuck Windham, passed away several years ago, but my mother Doris is still going strong and joined us for the remembrance weekend. She still resides at her beach home on coastal North Carolina.

Kris Rystrom Emmert's family today. Back row: Joe, Cole, Makenzie, Jordyn, and Taylor
Front row: Kris and Isabella

The Rest of the Story ...

Over the Bear Ace Remembrance weekend, my sweet little granddaughter Isabella stole the show during our naval tours. We began with a ship that represents the future of the Navy: USS Gerald R. Ford, the Navy's most technologically advanced aircraft carrier.

My granddaughter's inquisitive nature, high-energy personality, and Rystrom sense of humor continued to garner smiles the next day when we toured the Bear Ace hangar and a working E-2C Hawkeye plane.

But her high point had to be the final and most significant tour. Twenty-five years to the day when Bear Ace 603 was lost, on March 26, 2018, our family and my coauthor and her husband toured USS Harry S. Truman, a Nimitz class carrier, the same class shared by both USS Carl Vinson and USS Theodore Roosevelt. The gracious captain invited us to his spacious cabin to warmly welcome us aboard on that memorable day. Our custom tour included many of the places touched by Jon's story: the hangar bay, officer's mess, hospital ward, and ready room, including the location of Jon's TR stateroom.

Isabella enjoyed climbing above the flight deck and up into the island and the bridge. While proudly sitting in the captain's chair, Isabella examined a map of the Ionian Sea, provided by our gracious tour guides who pointed out where Daddy Jon's plane went down on that fateful night. As always, Isabella was full of questions.

"Do these phones work?" Isabella inquired, looking up at the communications equipment surrounding the captain's chair. One of our tour guides eagerly demonstrated how they operated—in a way a second-grader could understand. "Can you order some cookies on this thing?" she wondered, and the crew on the bridge laughed. Isabella shared Jon's sweet tooth, and she remembered fondly the plates of chocolate chip cookies that the staff of USS Gerald R. Ford had given us two days before. Isabella was always on the lookout for a yummy treat!

Our time on the flight deck was brief, in part because it was being resurfaced in preparation for their upcoming deployment and also because of the gusty, bitter winds sweeping across the ship. The frigid, gray harbor was similar in temperature to the chilly waters of the Ionian Sea that swallowed Bear Ace 603 so long ago. Isabella's small hands were like ice before we retreated to the warm comfort found inside the ship.

Place of Honor

26 MAR 2018
12:52 Eastern Daylight Time UTC-4
Arlington National Cemetery
Arlington, Virginia, USA
MH 657
38.87.83 N, 77.07.50 W

On the hallowed grounds where a grateful nation lays to rest those who have died in service to their country—the ones whose bodies were never recovered also have a place of honor. Down the hill from the Tomb of the Unknown Soldier lies a distinguished memorial section for those who never came home. These somber markers are placed near a wooded area, as these stones will not disturb the hidden roots, unlike traditional graves.

The warm, afternoon sun was filtering through the towering oak, hickory, and pine trees near grave marker MH 657. Located near a newly-planted dogwood tree, this white marble stone, one of many arranged in neat, orderly rows, was found directly in front of another bearing the same date. Two Navy brothers united in life and united in death.

The solemn markers are a lasting testament to lives well lived and costly sacrifices made. The sight of so many markers and the horrific losses they represent is sobering. But nothing is buried on this tranquil hillside. No coffins rest in repose under the surface. The bodies of those honored there lie concealed in foreign lands, were destroyed in unspeakable calamities, or were grimly lost at sea.

While it is a tragedy that these noble soldiers cannot be properly entombed, the greater tragedy still is when the living bury what should never be abandoned. But when the Son appears, some things once buried will rise again. Faith. Hope. Love. And the children of God.

That is a promise.

Jon A Rystrom

CDR

US Navy

Jan 21 1955

Mar 26 1993

VAW-124

OPERATION

PROVIDE PROMISE

Glossary of Acronyms and Select Terms

ACO (pronounced "ay-koh") — Air Control Officer — in the E-2, the naval flight officer who has the responsibility for supporting the mission commander by controlling aircraft and handling other specific mission tasking, providing command and control of aircraft and other platforms in the performance of their missions, and maximizing the situational awareness of the platforms under their control.

AOCS — Aviation Officer Candidate School — where pilots and naval flight officers get their initial officer and aviation training.

CACO (pronounced "kay-coh") — Casualty Assistance Calls Officer — the official representative of the Secretary of the U.S. Navy whose responsibility is to assist families when a service member suffers a casualty, ensuring they receive the benefits and entitlements due.

CAPT — Captain — a senior officer rank with the pay grade of O–6. It ranks above commander and below rear admiral (lower half). It is equivalent to the rank of colonel in the other uniformed services.

CDR — Commander — the commissioned officer rank in the U.S. Navy above lieutenant commander and below captain and is equivalent to the rank of lieutenant colonel in the other Armed Services.

CICO (pronounced "see-koh") — Combat Information Center Officer — the mission commander on the E-2 aircraft who oversees the combat information center on the aircraft and the other two naval flight officers in the crew, the stationing or positioning of the plane, and the execution of the mission.

CO — Commanding Officer.

COD (pronounced "cod") — Carrier On–Board Delivery — the primary mission of the C-2 Greyhound to ferry personnel, mail, supplies, and high- priority cargo such as replacement parts from shore bases to an aircraft carrier at sea. The C-2 is often referred as the "COD."

COMOPTEVFOR — Commander Operational Test and Evaluation Force — the U.S. Navy's sole independent agency responsible for test and evaluation.

CONUS (pronounced "konus") — Continental United States.

Crossing the Line Ceremony — When a ship initially crosses equator, this is the ceremony that recognizes a mariner's transformation from slimy pollywog, a seaman who hasn't crossed the equator before, to trusty shellback, also called a Son or Daughter of Neptune.

CSG — Carrier Strike Group — an operational force of the U.S. Navy. It is composed of roughly 7,500 personnel, an aircraft carrier, one or more cruisers, a destroyer squadron of at least two destroyers or frigates, and a carrier air wing of 65 to 70 aircraft. Previously called "Carrier Battle Group."

CVW — carrier air wing — an operational naval aviation organization composed of aircraft squadrons and detachments of various types of fixed–wing and rotary–wing aircraft. All aircraft assigned to an aircraft carrier are part of an air wing.

D–Gar — Diego Garcia — an atoll just south of the equator in the central Indian Ocean owned by the British that houses a military base.

DI — Drill Instructor — a non–commissioned officer, usually a Marine sergeant at AOCS, who is assigned the duty of training new recruits entering the military.

ENS — Ensign — a commissioned officer of the lowest rank in the U.S. Navy and Coast Guard, ranking above chief warrant officer and below lieutenant junior grade.

Fly–In — in this book, when a flight squadron returns to home base after a cruise at sea.

FOD (pronounced "fod") — Foreign Objects Damage — an organized walk down the flight deck from bow to stern to pick up any loose items or material that could be sucked into and damage an aircraft engine or be blown into aircraft or personnel.

helo — slang form of the word "helicopter."

Hummer — nickname for the E-2C Hawkeye. Comes from the sound that the aircraft's engines make when operating.

IFF — Identification Friend or Foe — a system that enables identification of civilian and military aircraft as friendly or enemy (foe) and determines their bearing and range.

island — on an aircraft carrier, the multistoried structure on the starboard side of the ship that houses the ship's bridge, primary flight control, flight deck control, and other spaces and the mounting point for the ship's mast, radar and communications antennae, and other sensors.

knot — a unit of speed equal to one nautical mile per hour, exactly 1.852 km/h (approximately 1.15078 mph).

LCDR or Lt. Cmdr.— Lieutenant Commander — a commissioned officer rank in the U.S. Navy. The rank is superior to a lieutenant and subordinate to a commander.

LSO — Landing Signal Officer — a naval pilot specially trained to provide guidance for pilots making their final approaches to the carrier.

LT. j.g. — Lieutenant junior grade — commissioned officer rank in the U.S. Navy senior to ensign and subordinate to lieutenant.

marshal stack — holding pattern from a designated marshal point or fix where aircraft hold until sequenced to start their approach to the carrier during nighttime and adverse weather conditions.

NAS — Naval Air Station — a U.S. Navy air base, a permanent land-based installation that is the home port for aircraft when they are not deployed on an aircraft carrier or other air stations.

NATOPS (pronounced "nay-tops") — Naval Air Training and Operating Procedures Standardization — a program/manual that prescribes general flight and operating instructions and procedures for the safe and standardized operation of all U.S. naval aircraft and related activities.

NEACP (pronounced "kneecap") — National Emergency Airborne Command Post — aka the "Flying White House" or "Doomsday Plane" from which all military operations would be controlled if ground-based military command centers were destroyed during a nuclear attack.

NFO — Naval Flight Officer — a commissioned officer in the U.S. Navy or U.S. Marine Corps who specializes in airborne weapons and sensor systems and the execution of the mission of their specific aircraft. Pilots fly the aircraft, and NFOs assist with navigation, communication, and situational awareness while handling the aircraft's assigned mission.

nugget — a first-tour aviator.

PIM (pronounced "pim") — Plan of Intended Movement.

Primary Flight Control — Pri–Fly — looks out over the flight deck from the ship's island, with the primary focus of ensuring that planes launch and land safely. All air operations within 5 NM of the ship are controlled from Pri-Fly.

rack — bed.

RAG (pronounced "rag") — Replacement Air Group — squadron that provides initial and refresher training for aviators pilots and NFOs in a specific aircraft type before going to their fleet squadrons. While still used, RAG is an old term and the training squadron is now often referred to as the "Fleet Replacement Squadron" or "FRS."

ready room — the squadron's headquarters aboard ship where they conduct business, hold meetings, and brief for missions.

RIO (pronounced "ree-oh") — Radar Intercept Officer — sits behind the pilot in certain jets and manages the battlefield and mission execution.

RO — Radar Operator — In the E-2C Hawkeye, the NFO in the combat information center who supports the mission commander with assigned mission tasks and takes care of the turn-on, set-up, and maintenance of the weapon system.

ROE — Rules of Engagement — a directive issued by a military authority controlling the use and degree of force, especially specifying circumstances and limitations for engaging in combat.

rotodome — on the E-2 Hawkeye, a rotating radome which is a domelike shell transparent to radio–frequency radiation, used to house a radar and IFF antenna.

RVAW–120 — Carrier Airborne Early Warning Training Squadron 120. It is the RAG, or FRS, for the E-2 Hawkeye and C-2 Greyhound.

SAR (pronounced "sar") — Search and Rescue — the combined use of various aircraft and surface vessels to search for and recover survivors of aircraft downed at sea as well as Sailors and passengers of sea vessels in distress.

sea duty — duty in the U.S. Navy performed with a deployable unit (such as a ship or aircraft squadron).

shore duty — naval service at land bases.

SIOP (pronounced "sy-op") — Single Integrated Operational Plan — the United States' general plan for nuclear war from 1961 to 2003.

SSGT — staff sergeant — the first of the staff non–commissioned officer ranks in the U.S. Marine Corps.

USS Carl Vinson — aka "Chucky V," the U.S. Navy's third Nimitz–class supercarrier and named for Carl Vinson, a Congressman from Georgia, in recognition of his contributions to the U.S. Navy.

USS Independence — aka "Indy" — an aircraft carrier of the U.S. Navy. She was the fourth and final member of the Forrestal class of conventionally powered supercarriers.

USS Texas — aka "CGN-39" — a Virginia-class, nuclear- guided missile carrier.

USS Theodore Roosevelt — aka "TR" — the fourth Nimitz–class aircraft carrier. Also known as the "Big Stick," her radio call sign is "Rough

Rider," the nickname of President Theodore Roosevelt's volunteer cavalry unit during the Spanish–American War.

VAW squadron — Carrier Airborne Early Warning squadrons that fly the E-2 Hawkeye.

wave-off — on an aircraft carrier, the signal to an aircraft making its final landing approach that it is not to land but is to climb to an assigned altitude and set up to make another approach.

Wings of Gold — naval aviator or naval flight officer breast insignia.

XO — Executive Officer — The XO is typically responsible for managing day-to-day activities, such as maintenance and logistics. The XO supports the commanding officer (CO). In aviation squadrons, the XO becomes the CO at the end of the CO's tour.

A portion of the proceeds from Providing Promise will be donated to the ...

VAW-VRC Memorial Scholarship Fund

After the mishap of Bear Ace 603, Captain Ed Caffrey, who was commodore of the East Coast Wing, and a group of aviators' wives established the VAW Officers' Wives' Association and the VAW Memorial Scholarship Fund on July 3, 1993. The purpose of the fund was to honor those men and any other member of the VAW community who died while in a duty status, to let the spouses and children know how deeply that sacrifice was appreciated, and to help provide for the children's higher education as their parent would have wanted.

Our family is grateful for the dedication and support of this association. Because of this foundation, my daughters, Jordyn and Taylor, were able to use this scholarship to attend and graduate from the colleges of their choice.

Mission Statement

The mission of the VAW/VRC Memorial Scholarship Fund is to provide for the Navy family in the education of its children, and in particular, those of active duty or reserve service members in the VAW and VRC communities who are lost as a result of a combat aircraft loss or as a result of a military aviation-related mishap, or U.S. Navy enlisted personnel who are lost as a result of a combat aircraft loss or as a result of a military aviation-related mishap while assigned to a VAW or VRC Squadron. The VAW/VRC Memorial Scholarship Fund is managed by the VAW/VRC Officers' Spouses' Association (VVOSA), a non-profit social organization.

For more information, please go to http://vaw-vrc-memorialfund. org/.

Works Cited

Chapman, Nancy. "Meeting Through the Personals." *Port Folio*. Vol. 5, No. 1. 06 May–12 May 1995. Print.

Department of the Navy. "Investigation Into the Circumstances of E-2C Aircraft BUNO 161549 and Crew in the Ionian Sea on 26 March 1993." *JAG Investigation*, 603 Mishap, BUNO 161549.19 Apr. 1993. Norfolk, Virginia.

Dobson, Dr. James C. *When God Doesn't Make Sense*. Tyndale, 1993, ch. 1.

English, Michael. Lyrics to "Holding Out Hope." *Hope*, Curb Records, 1993, track 3.

Shawshank Redemption. Dir. Frank Darabont. Perf. Tim Robbins, Morgan Freeman. Castle Rock, 2007. Film.

Woolley, John and Gerhard Peters. "The President's News Conference With Chancellor Helmut Kohl of Germany." *The American Presidency Project*, 26 Mar. 1993, presidency.ucsb.edu//ws/index.php?pid=46377.

Woolley, John and Gerhard Peters. "Remarks to the Crew of the USS Theodore Roosevelt." *The American Presidency Project*, 12 Mar. 1993, presidency.ucsb.edu//ws/index.php?pid=46330.

Kris Rystrom Emmert

Kris Rystrom Emmert impacts readers and audiences with her powerful message of enduring unspeakable tragedy and discovering unshakeable hope. With a contagious zest for life, Kris weaves her story of loss into a life-changing encounter that inspires others to experience their own healing and to uncover their God-given destiny.

Kris has a Bachelor of Arts in Communications from Wake Forest University and a Masters in Communication from Regent University. Kris is a highly skilled public speaker combining her extensive education, real-life media experience, talents as a senior leader in Premier Designs, Inc., years of being a professor at various higher-education institutions, and her multiple motivational presentations before thousands of people.

As a first-time author, pastor's wife, mom to four children, and grandmother, Kris is ultimately a down-to-earth woman who loves her family and lives life to the fullest in East Tennessee.

You may contact Kris by email: kris@providingpromise.com or visit her site, www.providingpromise.com.

Follow Kris on Twitter: @KristaEmmert.

Like Kris on Facebook: Facebook.com/Kris Rystrom Emmert.

Julie Voudrie

Julie Voudrie is a versatile storyteller. Whether through books, cakes—Julie was a contestant on the TLC network's internationally-aired baking competition, "Next Great Baker"—children's audio and radio dramas, years of televised cooking demonstrations, or singing and songwriting, Julie communicates compelling truths that capture hearts and minds.

As a mother of seven, grandmother, home educator, former missionary, public speaker, and entrepreneur, Julie has a passion for inspiring others to reach their potentials and fulfill their God-given destinies. Her life verse is Isaiah 55:1-2.

Julie and her husband of more than 30 years, Jeff, live in the beautiful Appalachian Mountains of Northeast Tennessee. To contact Julie, look for Baking with Julie on social media, see her website at BakingwithJulie.com, or email her at Julie@bakingwithjulie.com.